This journey showed me through personal experience that there is no better moment to experience than the present moment and that there is no greater realization than to know that the universe supports me unconditionally.

JEEVAN GOUNDEN, ENTREPRENEUR, JOHANNESBURG, SOUTH AFRICA

*

I have not yet finished *The Presence Process* experientially, but I have already experienced some profound changes in the quality of my life and experiences. Michael has empowered me with the tools and confidence to uncover many suppressed feelings and beliefs from my past—most of which I did not even realize were there. Something powerful and wonderful was waiting there and seems to be emerging in their place.

ROBERT FLICHEL, PERSONAL TRAINER & YOGA INSTRUCTOR, VANCOUVER, CANADA

*

The Presence Process caused me to wake up and take an honest look at my drama.

ULRIKE SCHMIDT, CHILDREN'S WORKSHOP FACILITATOR, GERMANY

*

I was an alcoholic and addicted to sleeping tablets and painkillers. This Process returned me to life and my life to me.

INGRID ERIKSON, YOGA INSTRUCTOR, JOHANNESBURG, SOUTH AFRICA

*

The Presence Process is not just another self-help book, but rather a practical tool to help us take charge of our life and our purpose in a respectful and compassionate way.

BARBARA MOWAT, PRESIDENT, INSTITUTE FOR GLOBAL LINKAGES & IMPACT COMMUNICATIONS, ABBOTSFORD, CANADA

*

This Process assisted me to face my fears and to literally sweat out my past. It is for those willing to "get real".

TERRY BETTY, WRITER, JOHANNESBURG, SOUTH AFRICA

*

Understanding the Seven Year Cycle has shown me how to anticipate events in my life that are caused by the same reoccurring unintegrated emotions. I am no longer ambushed by these emotional upheavals.

ANMOL CHAWLA, PROJECT MANAGER, PUNE, INDIA

Since completing this journey I am at ease with myself, and consequently I am at peace with others.

SHEHNAZ CHAWLA, JOURNALIST/HOMEMAKER, PUNE, INDIA

*

Could it be that some unconscious program within us is really in charge? The Presence Process invites us to access the answers to this question experientially.

PETE PIETRIE, HORTICULTURIST, DHAHRAN, KINGDOM OF SAUDI ARABIA

*

The Presence Process is a fresh, original, and extraordinary book that just in reading shifted me into a heightened state of consciousness. Through Michael Brown's lullaby-like language, his powerful and insightful teachings and the quality of his own Presence, he shows us how to step out of the time-based paradigm into the joy and aliveness of the secret of enlightenment itself: present moment awareness.

VICTORIA RITCHIE, BOOK EDITOR/SPIRITUAL TEACHER, MILL VALLEY, CALIFORNIA, USA

*

I came to realize how many emotions I had unconsciously bottled up. I experienced a definite shift of energy and a real change in the direction of my life.

KARIMA D. ADATIA, SALES & MARKETING MANAGER, DALLAS, TEXAS, USA

*

You have to be brave to do this. You must want to look deep into yourself, to face all your demons and baggage and to sincerely want resolution.

DOT JOHNSON, PERSONAL ASSISTANT, JOHANNESBURG, SOUTH AFRICA

*

I liken this Process to that of a soiled pane of glass. This pane of glass has the imprint of our past, maybe the imprint from the hand of a stern father, maybe the teardrop stain of not being heard. One could go on. Through this Process, these imprints and smudges can be removed from this 'pain of glass' and the clarity that was already always there can be revealed. Just by reading this book, I felt this process had already begun.

VIM ROLAFF, ENTREPRENEUR/PHOTOGRAPHER, VANCOUVER ISLAND, BRITISH COLUMBIA, CANADA

I can truly say that I am to a large extent now free from life-long rage, regret, grief, guilt, blame, fear and depression.

SHARON BOTHA, COFFEE-SHOP OWNER, PRETORIA, SOUTH AFRICA

*

This is an experience for those of us truly seeking the truth about who and what we are and why we are here on this planet.

NIKOLAS JANKOVICH, FINANCIAL ADVISOR, DURBAN, SOUTH AFRICA

*

It has shown me how to respond to the external world instead of reacting to it.

DIMITRI ANASTASIOU, RESTAURANTEUR, JOHANNESBURG, SOUTH AFRICA

*

I was able to resolve emotional issues that both affected my personal relationships and my professional experiences.

AMITHA HUGHES, TV & RADIO NEWS JOURNALIST, JOHANNESBURG, SOUTH AFRICA

*

I now feel a deep understanding for what has been, a gratitude for what is, and an acceptance for what is to come.

JOAN TINKER, JOHANNESBURG, SOUTH AFRICA

*

Being more present has slowed me down so that I can focus more on what I am busy with now and not just on the outcome.

WEPENER BOTHA, FREELANCER, PRETORIA, SOUTH AFRICA

*

The Presence Process gave me immediate and sustainable outcomes that significantly enhanced my inner peace, personal relationships and ability to give and receive love.

JEREMY HARRIS, GEOLOGIST/IT CONSULTANT, GAUTENG, SOUTH AFRICA

*

It opened me up to greatness. The little things that used to upset me do not get me down anymore.

TAMSIN LODGE, ACCOUNT EXECUTIVE, GAUTENG, SOUTH AFRICA

I would like to see these techniques taught in schools.

*

It gave me the understanding that my perception of everyone is a reflection of my inner condition.

*

The Presence Process restored my integrity and showed me the importance of being responsible for the consequences of my choices.

*

Also see < www.namastepublishing.com >

THE
PRESENCE
PROCESS™

THE
PRESENCE
PROCESS™

A healing journey into
Present Moment Awareness

———∞∞∞———

MICHAEL
BROWN

Namaste Publishing
Vancouver, Canada

Beauford Books
New York, NY

LIBRARY OF CONGRESS CATALOGING-IN-PUBLICATION DATA

Brown, Michael, 1962–
The presence process : a healing journey into present
moment awareness / Michael Brown.

ISBN-13: 978-0-8253-0537-5
ISBN-10: 0-8253-0537-3

1. Awareness. 2. Spiritual life. 3. Alternative medicine.
4. Brown, Michael, 1962– —Health. I. Title.
BF311.B755 2005
204'.4 —DC22   2005019805

Co-published by

NAMASTE PUBLISHING   BEAUFORT BOOKS
P.O. Box 62084   1102 - 27 West 20th Street
Vancouver, BC, Canada v6J 4A3   New York, NY 10011
www.namastepublishing.com   www.beaufortbooks.com
namaste@telus.net   service@beaufortbooks.com

Distributed in North America by
MIDPOINT TRADE

Designed by Val Speidel
Front cover photograph by Scott Morgan

Printed and bound in Canada by
FRIESENS PRINTING

TO MY FAMILY

Joan Tinker

Anthony Brown

Fiona Austin

Amanda Tinker

Sharon Pellegrini

Alan Austin

Franco Pellegrini

Mathilda Engelbrecht

Derek Brown

& Jessica Austin

Thank you for your unconditional love and support.

TO EVERYONE WHO READS THIS BOOK

Thank you for entering our flourishing
garden of present moment awareness.

CONTENTS

ACKNOWLEDGEMENTS

CHRIS CHAPMAN—for teaching me how to use my head to write what I feel in my heart. Dr. Robert Prall—for assisting me to make the initial leap. Sarah Darden Prall—for taking my hand and gently leading me into all of this. William Rebold—for being such a humble example of how to be an effective teacher. Indio Maldonado—for providing the opportunity for me to awaken naturally to present moment awareness. Jo Dunning—for introducing me to the power and possibilities of emotional cleansing and the fun of the phonetic language. Eliav Medina—for staying with me through the storm. Leonardo Mercardo—for "the medicine", the drum, the circle, and the songs. Raven Mercado—for the friendship and for "the Raven food". Moses Mercado—for reminding me how to play. The late Nelson Fernandez—for alerting me to the necessity of discipline. Kevin Costello—for the laughter and for reminding me how to breathe. The late Jonathon Bailey—for always being 100% present with me. Pete Pietrie—for holding the picture that a book such as this was possible and for walking with me all the way to this moment. The late Colin Kingfisher—for teaching me how to pay attention. David and Chen Eagleheart—for allowing me to take care of the fire. Graywolf and Devaki—for giving me a place to be when I didn't know what to do. Charles Ganzon—for saving my life and for showing me what the word "unconditional" really means. Marybeth James—for watching over me while I was healing. Erika Cardenas Arroyo—for showing me the way home and for preparing me to make the journey. Dot Johnson—for sup-

porting this vision with your body, mind, and heart. Connie Kellough—
for your unshakable faith, your impeccable guidance, your "gentle" and
wise contributions, and for saturating each word on these pages with the
Presence of your loving attention. To all who have come to me for personal facilitation through The Presence Process—thank you for leading
by example.

THANK YOU, ONE AND ALL.

INTRODUCTION

REDISCOVERING PRESENT MOMENT AWARENESS

IT GIVES ME GREAT JOY and satisfaction to know that *The Presence Process* is now available to you. This experience has been designed to accommodate anyone who has realized the importance of choosing to reconnect with the power of his or her Inner Presence. The Presence Process is a guided journey that contains all the practical techniques, perceptual tools, and knowledge required to consciously extract our attention from the illusions and trappings of time in order that we may reenter the present moment of life. It is a safe and gentle experience that is simple to follow. The benefits are real and therefore lasting.

The Presence Process is the outcome of a quest that consciously began in the Arizona desert in 1996. It was there that I had my first three real experiences of what I now call present moment awareness. Before these encounters, I had for almost 10 years been preoccupied with the task of attempting to cope with and heal myself from an acutely painful condition called Horton's Syndrome. This condition began in 1987 and manifested as daily bouts of indescribable agony. I do not wish to go into any detail about the symptomatic nature of this condition other than to say that I was told by one of South Africa's top neurosurgeons that my ailment had no known cause or cure. He also warned me that, because of the intensity of my condition, I was a potential candidate for heroin or morphine addiction and for suicide.

In an attempt to find relief, I literally tried everything from visiting a South African Xhosa Sangoma and having cortisone injected into my face, to having my wisdom teeth removed and a variety of spiritual healers lay their hands and crystals upon me. I followed every recommended allopathic course of prescription medication, and in pure desperation, I also tried every suggested alternative whim. Nothing brought relief or release.

In 1994, about one year after moving from South Africa to San Francisco, I came to terms with the realization that nothing and nobody "out there" could assist me, so I embarked on a quest to heal myself. I began by studying Swedish massage and then qualified as a Reiki Master. As a consequence of experimenting on myself with different physical, mental, and emotional procedures, I discovered that if I maintained what I then called "a high personal energy frequency", I could substantially lessen the levels and occurrences of the pain that I was experiencing. This discovery was the first whispering of what I now know to be my level of present moment awareness.

My first real introduction to a powerful experience of present moment awareness was initiated in 1996 in a Native American Sweat Lodge in Tucson, Arizona, through the guidance of a Yaqui Indian Medicine Man. It is unlikely that I will ever forget the resonance of those first few moments when I stepped out of the sweat lodge after my first two-hour journey through heat, steam, drumming, singing, and praying. For the first time in my life, I truly felt as if every aspect of my being was vibrating with life. I felt as if I had been reborn. In fact, I felt as if I had only *just* been born. That particular moment was my first taste of what it meant to "show up in my life". I realized that up until that instant I had not been living my life; instead, my life had been living me. Back then, I did not understand the full significance of that experience. All I knew was that for the first time in my life I could feel the blood flowing through my veins, my breath massaging my lungs, the rhythm of my own heart beating, and the presence of my own Inner Being dancing with spontaneous joy and gratitude.

My second introduction to a profound present moment awareness experience was facilitated a few months later by ingesting a tea made from the peyote cactus. Peyote is considered to be one of the most alkaline substances occurring naturally on the planet. Native Americans who use this plant as a sacrament in their Native American Church ceremonies also refer to it as "the medicine". My initial experience of ingesting this "medicine" was that after one hour of increasing inner discomfort and nausea, I appeared to awaken as if from a deep and dark dream into what I now accept to have been a momentary experience of 100% present moment awareness. I felt complete. I felt whole. I felt physically present, mentally clear, emotionally balanced, and spiritually connected. Being able to feel and commune with my own Inner Presence during the course of that experience was akin to being introduced to the most precious part of my Being that had until that very moment been obscured by the endless distractions of my outer life.

During that experience, I was metaphorically able to step through a veil. On the other side, I witnessed how all life is connected by the same intimate, intelligent Presence. I saw how the true luminous beauty of the natural world of this planet remains hidden from us because of our preoccupation with time. In that moment, I also became aware that my own painful condition was a result of my body doing everything in its power to call me back from where I had unconsciously scattered and attached my attention to the illusory web of time. In that state of consciousness, the pain did not reveal itself to me as my enemy but as my friend and facilitator, obediently calling me to return to the Now of my life experience.

Consequently, I accepted that the greatest journey that I could undertake was to find a way to navigate my experience towards achieving an ongoing state of 100% present moment awareness in my own life. It was clear to me that unless I could discover a way to begin accomplishing this for myself, I could be of no real use to others. It was also clear to me that the mechanisms of this journey had to be natural. It had to be a pathway that anyone upon the planet could follow no matter what his or her life circumstance. Therefore, it had to be an accomplishment that was based on inner work and not outer conditions, medicines, tools, ceremonies, rites, and rituals.

The first clue of how to begin accomplishing this task was revealed to me in that same year when I was introduced to the obvious but somehow completely overlooked procedure of consciously connected breathing. This is the practice of breathing consciously without pausing. It may sound simple, but practicing consciously connected breathing is as phys-ically challenging as the profound mental and emotional effects it initi-ates. Following the sweat lodge and the peyote experiences, consciously connected breathing was my third introduction to the experience of present moment awareness. After my first few facilitated breathing ses-sions, I realized that the outcome of these intense experiences was also a drastically increased sense of present moment awareness and that this automatically led to decreased physical pain.

These breathing sessions also initiated explosive insights. One of these was the realization that my intention to attempt *to heal myself* was completely misguided. This was why I had never succeeded despite my sincere efforts to do this. By enabling me to have real moments of detachment from my outer life experience, this natural breathing tech-nique enabled me to integrate that there was a distinct difference between my Self and my experience. I had not been able to see this before. I had always been so enmeshed in my outer experiences that they had mistakenly become the beginning and ending of who and what I thought I was. As a consequence of this breathing technique, I could clearly see that it was my life experience that had become acutely unbal-anced and in urgent need of adjusting—not *me*.

By using consciously connected breathing to become increasingly present in my life, I discovered that I automatically began making choices that restored my sense of inner emotional well-being. Conse-quently, ever-increasing comfort and harmony automatically manifested in my outer experiences, and my painful condition gradually began sub-siding. After years of having suffered greatly from pain and the conse-quent frustration, anxiety, anger, grief, and depression that ensued, it began dawning on me that there was no greater healing tool at my dis-posal than the power of my Inner Presence. What was equally profound was the realization that my own breath was the key to opening the door to the experience of this Inner Presence. By 1997, I began facilitating others with this breathing technique and closely observing the conse-quences of their encounters with it.

These powerful moments in which I was introduced to my first three doses of present moment awareness became a yardstick by which I measured all my subsequent explorations into the healing arts. If anything I explored led to an increase of personal present moment awareness, I embraced it as a real experience. If it did not, I wasted no more time on it. The experience of present moment awareness was my trusted barometer, and it assisted me to brush aside all the impotent rituals and ceremonies that often window-dress and falsely glamorize the healing arts.

In addition to exploring consciously connected breathing, I also began investigating the shamanic paradigm. Over a period of four years, I was trained as a Fire Chief in the Native American Peyote Church. I also crossed the Arizona border into Mexico to attend and participate in the ceremonies with the living ancestors of "the peyote way", the Huichol Indians. Whenever I had the opportunity, I used my body, mind, and heart as the laboratory for my experiments into activation of present moment awareness and my subsequent life experience as the arena to observe the consequences. I worked with and learned from a wide variety of teachers and tested every so-called "healing" technique that I could attempt on myself.

As the years unfolded, I began to develop an increasingly powerful personal relationship with what I now call my Inner Presence. I became aware that present moment awareness is not only a *state* of Being; it *is a Being*. Present moment awareness is, indeed, "a Presence". The Being and the state of Being have revealed themselves to me to be One and the same. By entering It, one becomes It. Present moment awareness is, therefore, a state of becoming. It is awareness embracing its fullest potential.

In reflection, my personal odyssey may appear romantic. However, it was seldom easy and often unclear. Initially, I had no point of reference for what a present moment awareness experience was. I did not have a vocabulary to explain to others what I was seeking to accomplish. I was placing one step in front of the other, following a trail that only appeared to make sense to me. There were numerous occasions when I became very confused and disheartened. There were moments when I doubted my own sanity. Fortunately, I always had a way to reconnect with my quest: I connected my breathing and re-entered the encouraging confirmation of my Inner Presence. By doing so, I would remember that the quest I was on was a simple one. I could not verbalize it outwardly back then, but I can now:

"How can I become increasingly present in such a way as to leave a trail for others who also want to show up in their life experience?"

I did not realize back then that by embarking on such a quest I was ultimately searching for a specific procedure. However, I can now clearly see that as a consequence of my intention, my subsequent life experience consciously and unconsciously unearthed the practical techniques, perceptual tools, and knowledge that have today evolved into The Presence Process. In essence, I dragged the concept of achieving present moment awareness out of the mental realm and rooted it upon this earth as a practical, methodical procedure.

In 2002, after nine years away, I returned home to South Africa knowing that I had accomplished the first step of my quest; I had accumulated the raw materials for a powerful procedure that would enable others to activate, maintain, and continue to accumulate present moment awareness. Later that year, 15 years after I had crumpled to the side of a dirt road in the Transkei during my first attack of Horton's Syndrome, I began consciously living my purpose by sharing The Presence Process with others.

Now, with The Presence Process available to you in this book, another significant step in this journey has been taken.

No matter how many individuals I personally facilitate through The Presence Process, I remain in deep awe as to what this procedure accomplishes for everyone who is willing to step into his or her own emotional abyss. The Presence Process is a rare jewel. It is an inner doorway that offers us all a methodical procedure to overcome the outer obstacles that distract us from experiencing that which we all share: our Inner Presence. It is an invitation to step upon a path that automatically begins liberating us from the invisible prison of an unconsciously distracted mind. I have witnessed how everyone who makes a commitment to enter and complete this journey is literally reborn into his or her life. I have seen how they become available as ambassadors of life itself and how they begin walking among their families and communities as peacemakers.

By facilitating this Process myself and freely sharing all the knowledge I have about the art of facilitating it, it became clear that training others to facilitate The Presence Process is not an approach I am willing to take. It is my opinion that such an approach to the development of this work would lead to it becoming diluted, misinterpreted, and turned into a specialized means of income for facilitators, instead of an accessible tool of awakening for everyone. I have seen through my own experience that only life itself can prepare us to have the integrity to facilitate another and that life accomplishes this by inviting us to have the integrity to first facilitate our own self. All the information in the world cannot replace real life experience. Therefore, instead of transforming The Presence Process into a modality to be shared through the medium of trained facilitators, I have instead chosen to make it directly available to you in this book. This way you will always have it in its purest form. *The Presence Process* is, therefore, deliberately written and presented in a manner that enables *you* to become the facilitator of *your* journey into present moment awareness. Now, everyone who seeks to consciously awaken from the unconscious sleep of time has access to this work for the price of a book and not the fee of a facilitator. I do, however, encourage you to be companions to each other and to support each other in whatever way you find appropriate as you embark on this magnificent journey.

I am eternally grateful to all the teachers who laid their life experiences before me so that I could successfully uncover this profound procedure. It is now my personal opinion that The Presence Process makes it possible for anyone to experience the power of his or her Inner Presence without having to take the long and challenging path that I did.

It is also clear to me now that even though plant medicines and ceremonies can activate an experience or the memory of present moment awareness, these outer tools can only point to the journey. They are the signposts, not the road itself. Throughout my life, I have embraced all these outer tools, ceremonies, medicines, and their dedicated caretakers as powerful allies. I know that they were deliberately placed on my path to assist me to remember what is possible and what has been forgotten through time. However, I do not believe that they are *the way* to get there because the way is within each of us. Although these outer rituals and ingested substances do initiate a present moment awareness experience, after a short period, their effects decay almost completely. Those who use them to enter this state of Being, therefore, use them repetitively, and this creates a reliance on an outer substance. These substances definitely provide powerful insight, but not the accompanying life experience required for permanently holding the insight in our awareness. Thus, they are potentially as useful as they are misleading. It is my opinion that a real and lasting present moment awareness experience has to be accomplished naturally and inwardly through the conscious and sober accessing, accumulating, and applying of personal inner will and discipline to be maintained. Achieving present moment awareness is a way of life, not a one-time quick fix. It is a journey, not a destination.

The beauty of The Presence Process is that it paves the way for us to begin returning to our authentic state of spontaneous joy and creativity in a manner that requires no artificial instruments or outer activities, no ceremonies, rituals, dogmas, or belief systems. It requires only a conscious and disciplined use of our attention and intention. Experiencing this Process automatically activates the inner tools that we all have in common, enabling us to accumulate what I consider to be the most precious and rare commodity on this planet right now: present moment awareness. Through this book, this experience can now be accomplished safely within the structure of our day-to-day life, no matter where or how we are placed in this fast-paced paradigm. It does not on any level require a departure from where our destiny has placed us.

The Presence Process also introduces us to a concept that is very foreign to the outer world of changing conditions: that the power of our Inner Presence knows *no order of difficulty*. I have personally witnessed this Process successfully resolve conditions of depression, cancer, phobias, drug and alcohol addiction, grief, anger, fear, allergies, lack, and many other outer indicators of inner imbalance. It also accelerates the recovery from physical injuries, enhances sporting and creative abilities, and enlivens spiritual activities from yoga to meditation. This Process has repeatedly demonstrated to me that it is our deeply suppressed emotional issues that unconsciously distract us from the present moment of our life experience, and that the mental states of mind caused by this distraction lead to the physical manifestations of imbalance that become symptoms of disease. In essence, The Presence Process is a pathway that empowers us to release and integrate these emotional blockages. Therefore, it is a journey into our own emotional growth. It is literally a way to consciously "grow up".

Accumulating present moment awareness is a real and intensely rewarding journey that appears to have no limits. It activates a way of Being that empowers us to respond to life as opposed to reacting to it. It automatically leads us towards what we share rather than to what causes separation. Yet until our personal present moment awareness is consciously initiated, it is a reality that remains hidden by the mundane demands and distractions of our outer world. Awareness of our Inner Presence is the rarest of treasures in a world that is consciously and unconsciously enslaved by the illusionary mental paradigm we call "time". In the world we occupy today, present moment awareness is the unknown frontier as much as it is the ever-open doorway to personal liberation. Like you, I am a curious explorer of this unknown inner continent.

Activating present moment awareness in our life experience is not only the greatest gift we can give ourselves, it is also the most responsible contribution we can make to our humanity. By entering it, we become it.

The Presence Process is an invitation to consciously activate the power of our Divine Presence. This opportunity is not a means to an end; it is a gift that empowers us to transform our entire perception of what life is. We must, therefore, not hurry into or through it. We must not treat this experience as a task that we have to get done to arrive somewhere else. Everything that we have been looking for has already found us. It is already waiting within us. The Presence Process is an opportunity for us to experience personal confirmation of this truth.

And yes, I have successfully resolved the unconscious emotional condition that manifested as my painful ailment. I accomplished this by entering an intimate relationship with my Inner Presence. This very same omnipotent Presence is also within you, waiting patiently to bless the quality of your entire life experience.

Thank you for giving yourself this wonderful gift.

Kindest regards,
Michael

What Is Present Moment Awareness?

PRESENT MOMENT AWARENESS is a state of Being as opposed to something we do; therefore, it is easier to say what it is not than what it is. A reliable indicator that we have entered present moment awareness is that our life experience, no matter how it may appear outwardly in any given moment, is infused inwardly with the resonance of deep gratitude. This gratitude is not founded on comparison. This is not a gratitude that only blossoms because our life is unfolding exactly how we want it to or because everything in our experience is easy. It is a gratitude for the invitation, the journey, and the gift of life itself. It is gratitude that requires no reason. Gratitude is the one single marker that we can depend on as an indicator of how present we are in our life experience. If we have no gratitude for being alive, it is because we have strayed from the present moment into an illusory mental place called "time".

Very few of us are able to be present in our life experiences because we are all born into a culture that exists in a world of time. This is the curse of what we call "civilization". We have thirsted for progress, but in most cases, progress has led to the structuring of life in such a way that we do not have to be present when it is happening. The more automated our life experience becomes, the less involved we are in the art of living.

In the world of time, it is challenging to be grateful because nothing appears to be unfolding the way we think it should. The past holds regrets and the future holds the promise of improvement, while the present moment appears to us as an event that requires adjustment. We therefore spend all our moments reflecting on what did not work for us in the past and mentally planning the adjustments we must accomplish to eventually attain the state of peace and fulfillment we seek. Because these adjustments are continually directing our attention into some "great tomorrow", we have forgotten how to allow ourselves an opportunity to arrive at any meaningful juncture today. Subsequently, the world we live in now and everything in it is a means to an end. Living like this appears normal to us. It appears normal because we do not have access to another world experience that is qualitatively different to the one we are having right now. We do not have another experience to which we can compare our current one.

By living this way, we consistently leapfrog over the present moment. Even though the past is gone and cannot be altered and the future has not yet come into being, we still choose to mentally occupy these illusory places rather than to fully enter and experience the one moment we are always in. By habitually dwelling in the mental state that enables us to reflect and project our attention into these illusory places, we are missing out on the very real physical and emotional experiences happening to us *right now*. We are almost completely oblivious to the only moment that contains the vibrancy and the fullness of what life is. We think that we are living but are not; we are existing. We think we are moving, but we are spinning in circles. We have become completely mental about everything and have consequently sacrificed the experiences of being physically present and emotionally balanced. Subsequently, our mental state, as advanced as we may believe it to be, is riddled with confusion.

We are so accustomed to this state of "not-being", that it appears perfectly natural to us. We aspire to it. Yet it is not natural because it knows no balance or harmony. We know this because somewhere in the midst our mental leapfrogging, we all feel that something is amiss. The lack of peace that we feel within is reflected as the ongoing chaos we experience in our outer life experiences. Our lack of inner peace is also reflected in the way we shy away from any experience of stillness or silence. The theme of this age is: "Let there be noise; let there be movement."

We do not know what it is that we are missing because we cannot remember what it is that we have lost. We cannot find it because we seek it in the pictures of the past and in our scanning of the future. Our insatiable needy and wanting behavior is testimony to the emptiness that our current approach to life cannot fill. We are turning every piece of this planet over in our desperate search for peace. Yet nothing we do brings peace to our state of Being because we have long since forgotten that peace is not "a doing". It cannot be enforced nor mechanically installed. Our state of internal unrest manifests as external physical, mental, and emotional symptoms of discomfort and disease. No matter what we take for it, no matter where we run in our attempts to escape it, no matter how we distract ourselves from it with our endless doings, real relief consistently appears just moments out of reach. Just like a sleep-deprived human inevitably enters a physical, mental, and emotional breakdown, our neglect of the oasis of present moment awareness is also fast leading us into an experience of planetary societal disintegration.

This mental condition of "living in time", of relentlessly running from yesterday and of frantically chasing tomorrow without rest or peace, is the predicament that The Presence Process addresses and soothes. By assisting us to understand how we individually arrived in this predicament, it simultaneously gives us the methodical procedure and perceptual tools that empower us to begin finding our way out of this illusion. It throws a rope of awareness to us and empowers us to pull ourselves out of the pit of our distractions with the past and the future so that we may return to the only ground that is solid, safe, and peaceful: the present moment. The Presence Process accomplishes this by bringing awareness to the authentic Presence that we really are in a way that encourages us to consciously begin dismantling the inauthentic pretence that we made to shield ourselves from our fear, anger, and grief. It demonstrates that the only way we can authentically change our world experience is by liberating ourselves from the perceptual virus of time and that liberating ourselves from this mental disease is therefore the greatest act of service we can perform *right now*.

We are not the experiences that we manufactured to feel safe and accepted in this world. And no matter what the future may promise, the only moment that can be real for us has nothing to do with yesterday or what may happen tomorrow. While we continue to react unconsciously to the events of our life, we are not even seeing what is right in front of us; we are in a mentally-driven nightmare, recoiling from ghosts of the past and projected phantoms from the future. This is no way to live. This is not life. What life really is cannot enter time. This time-based experience is a perceptual hell guarded by the bars of our unresolved fear, anger, and grief. It does not take us anywhere; it never did, and it never will. In time, nothing happens; we only *think* it does.

The good news is that although this may be the only quality of life experience that we are currently aware of, it is definitely not the only experience that is available to us. There is another paradigm running parallel to the world of time. We call it "the present moment". We know it exists because we all seek it even if we do not consciously realize that this is what we thirst for. We all know it exists because Zen Masters and Spiritual

Teachers from all castes and creeds, as well as many ordinary human beings from all walks of life, have re-entered it and are living it right now. Right now there is a growing community upon this planet that is living from present moment awareness.

This experience of present moment awareness is accessible to us wherever we are. We do not have to go anywhere or enter any outer "doings" to activate it. However, we cannot consciously enter it while we unconsciously cling to an illusory past and future.

Our journey through The Presence Process automatically activates our ability to begin consciously making the perceptual transition from the time-based world we are in now to the state of Being we have sought in all our endless doings. It facilitates us in gently stepping onto the wondrous path that leads to ever-increasing present moment awareness. It assists us in refocusing our attention and intention so that we consciously begin to steer our awareness towards the awaiting radiance of our Inner Presence. It invites us to consciously enter the present moment of our life and therefore to embrace a state of Being in which we become open to the joy, health, and abundance that is inherent in each moment of life.

A joyful, abundant, and healthy life is pouring itself
upon us in each moment.
When we "live in time", the vessel that we are
is turned upside down.
We therefore spend our life experience getting
instead of receiving.

Present moment awareness is not a concept; it is an *experience*. It is an effortless way of Being that is the birthright of every human in this world. Entering it now is an inevitable consequence of our accelerating evolution. Its invitation is here, now, for all willing to receive its blessings. It calls to every one of us in a silent voice that says, "Stop! There is nowhere to go and nothing to do, but there is everything to be." This is the invitation, this is the journey, and this is the gift which The Presence Process makes possible.

So what is present moment awareness? It is a state of Being in which we effortlessly integrate the authentic and Divine Presence that we are with each God-given moment that we are in so that we are able to respond consciously to every experience we are having. By accomplishing this, our response is always the same: gratitude—a flow of gratitude that washes us of all our illusions. Entering such a state may sound hard and complicated when we are living in time. It is, however, effortless and completely natural because present moment awareness is our birthright. It is the kingdom of awareness through whose gates the prodigal children return. The hard part has been attempting to find what we did not know we had lost. The best part is realizing that we have been looking for something that has already found us.

PART I

ATTUNING TO THE PROCESS

THIS ENTIRE BOOK is a structure that has been designed to support the experience called "The Presence Process". By reading this book, we are led gently into it, we are then invited to experience it, and finally, we are led gently out of it and into a life experience transformed by it. *The Presence Process* is, therefore, all about consciously activating present moment awareness through the experience of a deliberately guided process. When we have completed this journey, we will have been trained to be facilitators of our ongoing journey into present moment awareness. We will also have been reconnected with an aspect of our Being that will always be available to guide us. Therefore, we will be freed of having to seek this guidance from outside sources. In this light, *The Presence Process* is a tool of liberation.

The Presence Process is a journey that we are deliberately choosing to take *into* ourselves. It is a journey that will take us through forgotten memories into emotional territories that are unfamiliar to us and that we therefore may initially perceive as uncomfortable. It is a journey that is designed to successfully equip us with the means to move beyond the suppressed fear, anger, and grief that seep into our life experience. This inner terrain that we are about to enter may at first appear alien to us, yet it is this forgotten landscape that we must pass through to be successfully reunited with our innocence, our spontaneous joy, and our inherent creativity. The Presence Process is a pathway that successfully initiates a journey that will lead us beyond the inner debris of the past so that we can begin returning to the heart of our Inner Presence.

Even though it may appear that we are making this journey alone, we are not—and we cannot. Part I of this book is deliberately designed to prepare us to realize this; it is written to intentionally awaken our relationship with our Inner Facilitator. Although we may not know where we are going right now or how we are going to get there, there is an aspect of our Being that does know. There is an aspect of our Being that knows everything. It is the One that brought us to the entrance of this particular pathway into ourselves. This authentic aspect of our Being, which we shall call our Inner Presence, knows what we are *really* looking for and what it is going to take to assist us to consciously make this rediscovery. It is our best friend, our closest companion, our champion, and our guard of honor. It carries our flag and our supplies. It sends us off enthusiastically, and it will be waiting to greet us joyfully in the moment we achieve completion.

Part I of The Presence Process automatically empowers us to become receptive to the communications coming from our Inner Presence. It teaches us to understand "the language of authenticity" in which this Process is written. There is no difficulty in this procedure because we automatically learn all that we are required to know about communication with our Inner Facilitator simply by reading. All that is required is that we do not hurry, that we carefully read the information, and that we allow it to sink in gently. It is not necessary to take notes or to consciously memorize any part of this written material. However, it is beneficial to attend to our reading in quiet moments when we are feeling relaxed and receptive. If at any point we feel overwhelmed, it is a sign that we must put this book down in order that we may integrate what we have read. "Integration" in this context means giving ourselves the time and space to emotionally, mentally, and physically digest the information that we have read or the experiences this reading material is setting into motion so that we may gain the required wisdom from it. The subject of integration and how it is incorporated into the approach of The Presence Process will be discussed in detail in The Integrative Approach in Part II of this book.

To be accessible to everyone, The Presence Process has two levels of entry open to us: Introductory and Experiential. Part I of this book plays a very important role in assisting us to make an informed choice as to which level will be most suitable for us. At the same time as providing us with an opportunity to make an informed choice, Part I also begins aligning us with the overall intentions of The Presence Process.

It sets our intention.
It places our attention.
It introduces us to our Inner Guide.
It opens the door and points the way.
It makes us ready and guarantees our success.

THE HEARTBEAT OF REINFORCEMENT

THE PRESENCE PROCESS is more than a book: it is "an experience of present moment awareness" being delivered to us in the form of a book. For this reason, it is written and structured in a manner to which we may not be accustomed. Although it employs our thinking mind as a tool to assist us in activating present moment awareness, it is not written for our thinking mind. The thinking mind can never experience present moment awareness because it can only operate in a time-based paradigm. When we truly enter present moment awareness, one of the indicators that this has occurred will be the absence of thought. However, because we have become servants to our thinking mind, as opposed to having it serve us, achieving this inner silence and stillness requires a very deliberate procedure of "undoing". This is what The Presence Process is—a procedure of "undoing". For this reason, the rhythm of the text may appear quite unorthodox.

The thinking mind and the ego it supports may at times struggle with the tempo of the text. It may say to us, "This is very repetitive. This has already been written and explained in detail, so why are we going through this again? Does the author think we lack intelligence?" It may react to the text this way because the thinking mind is all about "understanding". When it already believes that it understands something, it becomes offended or bored when the same subject matter is repeated—especially if it is repeated in exactly the same way. The thinking mind can see no purpose for information beyond its role as a tool of understanding or analysis. Yet the information contained in this book has deeper dimensions of purpose than merely assisting us to "understand". One of these dimensions is that the information on these pages also enables us to gently move *in formation* with the flow of this very intricate procedure.

When the thinking mind encounters a book, it automatically assumes the book has been written for it. It therefore wants every sentence to be new and exciting. It wants every chapter to end with a cliffhanger. It is hungry for and addicted to constant change. It wants to be entertained. It cannot stand the silence and stillness that is inherent in all cyclic experiences—especially the depth of the silence and stillness out of which this book arises and into which it invites us. To the thinking mind, "cycles" are meaningless repetition. That is why the thinking mind cannot sit on a beach and quietly watch the endless waves. Nor can it savor the silence of a sunset. Nor can it enjoy the stillness inherent in the company of a tree. Once the thinking mind has seen one wave, one sunset, one tree, it believes it has seen them all. Repetition annoys it and causes it to moan, saying: "What is the point of repeating this?" It will react this way despite the fact that most of the thoughts it entertains *are* meaningless cycles of repetition. The thinking mind wants noise, movement, excitement, constant change, and what it perceives as "newness". Yet life in its truest essence is not "new". Life is always what it has been and will never change from its essential truth. In this light, life in this world is an endless stillness and silence that flows in and out of form upon a tide of ongoing cycles. These cycles are not repetition; they are reinforcement. In this world of phenomenon, they are the very heartbeat of Beingness.

This is the quality of awareness that we are invited to hold as we read The Presence Process. What appears to our thinking mind as "repetition" in the text of this book is actually "reinforcement". It is the gradual awakening of the heartbeat of present moment awareness. This text is not written to entertain our thinking mind. The only task for our thinking mind here is to assist us to read it and to enable us to mentally contain the information so that we can assimilate it into the fabric of our physical and emotional experiences.

Why the text flows as it does and why certain information cyclically reenters the pages we are reading will make greater sense to us in hindsight. However, it is helpful for us to understand some of the structural intentions behind the text before we enter it fully. This will calm our thinking mind and shield us from its propensity towards boredom or annoyance.

As already stated, the text of The Presence Process is designed to activate a procedure that will enable us to undo the false perceptions that are masking our Inner Presence from our conscious awareness. This procedure, once activated, causes perceptual shifts and therefore adjustments to the quality of our life experience. It causes what was once unconscious to us to begin surfacing into our awareness. As this unconsciousness surfaces we must have certain information repeatedly reinforced so that we remain aware that what is happening to us is supposed to happen. The text will also gently activate our awareness of our child self—an aspect of our Beingness that we automatically abandoned when we departed our childhood. As this aspect of ourselves surfaces into our awareness for healing, certain information must be repeatedly reinforced so that our child self knows that it is safe to join us in "the Now" of our present life experience. The text is therefore not only speaking to the part of us that is consciously turning these pages. It is simultaneously speaking to our childlike self, as well as other aspects of our awareness that are still unconscious to us. Children require this reinforcement, as does the unconsciousness we still carry as adults.

The structure of the text also takes into account that The Presence Process offers us two levels upon which to approach the experience of present moment awareness. The first level is entered simply by reading the text. The second level of entry involves an experiential procedure that gradually unfolds over a period of 11 weeks, or longer. What therefore may appear as repetition to us when we are simply reading the text all the way through, will definitely not appear so when we are taking 77 days or longer to complete the Process. Under these circumstances, repetition again serves the purpose of reinforcement. It is the heartbeat of our heightening awareness.

This book is a river of experience-activating information that carries us into the eternal ocean of present moment awareness. Sometimes it flows slowly, sometimes the currents quicken, and sometimes it feels as if we are moving through the same terrain again. Yet, it is all deliberately written to carry us safely and gently beyond our thinking mind and into the embrace of the sacred silence and stillness out of which all life flows.

We are therefore encouraged to read this book with an open mind and to patiently embrace the manner in which it is written. It will not serve us at all to jump around from section to section. It will not serve us to skip sentences or paragraphs because our thinking mind perceives them as meaningless repetition. The information being presented to us throughout this book is deliberately delivered in layers and in a specific order of importance. It is written in a format that is designed to prepare us to make powerful changes to the quality of our life experience without the assistance of an outside facilitator. We are therefore encouraged to approach it maturely and responsibly. By following the simple instructions, by taking it page by page, step by step, day by day, and moment by moment, we will gently clean our perceptions and permanently anchor present moment awareness into every aspect of our life experience.

⌘

ALIGNING OUR INTENTION

ACTIVATING PRESENT MOMENT AWARENESS and the unlimited power and possibilities of our Inner Presence is the overall intent of The Presence Process. Our Inner Presence literally knows no order of difficulty, and so activating this state of Being empowers us to consciously process the nature of any unintegrated life experience. However, the realities of Inner Presence and present moment awareness cannot be found in or validated by concepts. They cannot be explained to us by anybody else. We have to experience them firsthand before we can begin to grasp what the word "Presence" really means. Everything written in this book is therefore an invitation to an experience. It is an invitation to us to open the doorway and walk into this state of Being ourselves so that we may know through our own experience what the gift of present moment awareness really is.

It does not matter whether the information contained in this book is true or not. What matters is whether the experience activated by reading and applying it begins navigating our attention from a time-based experience into present moment awareness. The words a mother uses to sing a lullaby to a newborn child are irrelevant because the child cannot understand them anyway. The effectiveness of a lullaby can only be judged by whether its emotional content soothes the child to sleep when it is troubled. In the same light, the writings throughout this book can only be judged by whether they successfully activate the experiences that awaken us to present moment awareness.

By entering The Presence Process, we are simultaneously making a commitment to ourselves to finish this journey. This commitment must be made unconditionally because we will not know what the experience of The Presence Process is really about until we reach a point of completion. Part I of this book is carefully designed to give the encouragement and information necessary for us to make this commitment.

The greater part of this journey is designed to take us into and through places within ourselves with which we may as yet not be familiar. Therefore, it is inevitable that we will have experiences in which it feels as if we do not know where we are going or in which we do not understand what is happening to us. This is normal and is supposed to happen. During The Presence Process, our most accelerated personal growth will occur during these moments of "not knowing". Even when this journey is over, it may still be challenging for us to explain to another what has occurred. This is also normal because much of the journey is emotional and not mental. However, upon completion, we will have no doubt that this experience will have been one of the most precious and loving gifts we have ever given to ourselves.

In life, we automatically grow physically through putting the correct or appropriate nutrition into our body. Our mental growth is also spoken for when we enter and attend the basic schooling experience. Yet our emotional growth, which usually begins to slow drastically at about seven years of age, receives no real attention as we move into and through adulthood. In this world, we humans have proved ourselves to be remarkably physically adaptable. In the last hundred years, we have also become mental giants, but sadly, we have also become increasingly emotionally dwarfed. The turbulent state of the world we live in today is a testimony to the fact that it is the playground of the emotionally immature. The journey that we embark on throughout The Presence Process is therefore essentially a journey of achieving emotional growth through reactivating physical presence and mental clarity.

Physical presence is an experience that occurs as we learn how to anchor our awareness in our physical body. Most of us believe that we occupy this body, yet we do not. To think about the past or the future means that we have to enter the mental realm. The mental realm is not confined to the location of our physical brain. It extends as far as we can think. If we are thinking about a friend in another country or are revisiting a memory of the last encounter we had with them, we may assume that we are still in our physical body, but we are not. We are where our point of attention has been cast. We are definitely not physically present. Something may be unfolding right in front of our eyes, yet we may find ourselves completely oblivious to it while lost in our own thoughts. Physical presence only occurs when we consciously enter present moment awareness. The physical body, although it symptomatically reflects our past experiences and future projections, is 100% present. It is 100% present in its functioning; the heart only beats in the Now. When we experience physical presence, we can feel our own heart beating. Often the closest we come to experiencing this is by default: when we almost have an accident or when we suddenly receive a fright. In the few moments that follow such an experience, our awareness enters our body fully, and we can feel our blood pumping through our veins and our heart beating in our chest. However, when we spend our life experience in the mental realm that we call "time" we are not even aware that we have a heart, let alone are we able to hear or feel it. Therefore, The Presence Process starts off by assisting us to achieve physical presence—or the ability to begin anchoring our awareness in our physical body. Then the next steps are to achieve mental clarity and emotional balance. Achieving emotional balance, through firstly gaining physical presence and then mental clarity, is the pathway that effectively initiates emotional growth. Later in this book, we will examine in detail why the intent to initiate emotional growth is the only natural way to begin resolving our symptoms of physical and mental imbalance.

Emotional growth may be one of the most challenging accomplishments in this world because the necessity for it will seldom be supported, let alone understood, by those around us. Although the instructions given to us throughout this journey are intended to make this challenging experience gentler for us, the journey itself is not intended to be easy or to initially make us feel good. Feeling "good", "nice", "fine", "okay", and "alright" are words used by us when we have become emotionally numb. For the duration of this experience, we are encouraged not to judge our progress by how "good" we feel.

The Presence Process is about remembering how to feel "real". Feeling real may initially include experiencing suppressed emotional states such as fear, anger, and grief. The Presence Process specializes in assisting us to gently access our suppressed emotions—emotions that we would ordinarily not want to acknowledge. During this Process, we deliberately allow this to occur because these suppressed emotions are the unconscious causes of the behaviors and the experiences that do not serve us right now. By accessing and releasing the negative charge of these suppressed emotions, we automatically begin returning balance to the quality of all our life experiences.

This Process will convey to us experientially why we must commit to the task of emotional growth above and beyond our ability to understand why this is necessary. As we will discover, mental comprehension is seldom part of emotional integration. Like any journey into the unknown, we will only see where we have been and why certain circumstances have unfolded as they did when we reach some point of completion and can reflect.

Throughout The Presence Process, the word "emotion" is an abbreviation for "energy in motion". Emotional growth requires that we first free our suppressed and blocked emotions and then relearn how to channel this energy responsibly so that it enhances the quality of all our life experiences. To accomplish this, we will be learning some simple but profound perceptual tools that will serve us for the rest of our life as a means to navigate towards a joyful and authentic experience—no matter what.

The Presence Process is not about changing who or what we are. This is impossible. Instead, it is about releasing our attachment to our manufactured identity so that we may gently return to an awareness of our authentic Presence. It is about moving from pretence to Presence. It is about consciously connecting with that aspect of our Being that always remains constant. It is about honoring that aspect of our Being that is always present. It is not about becoming something or somebody else. It is about remembering and experiencing who and what we really are and have always been.

The Presence Process is not about changing the nature of what the stars have marked on our forehead, hands, and feet. It is about waking into the fullest potential of each moment that is already destined. It is about responding to our life as it is unfolding right now and not reacting to it as if something else was supposed to be happening. The Presence Process intends to reveal to us that our mistaken desire to change what is happening to us in any given moment is usually born out of an inability to show up and fully enjoy the wonder of our life experience as it is *right now*.

The Presence Process awakens within us the awareness that it is in the nature of our interaction with what is happening to us *right now* that we sow the seeds for what is to come beyond the borders of this life experience. It assists us to see that the quality of the seeds that we sow in any given moment is very different depending on whether we choose to react or to respond to our experiences. Reacting to our experience means that we are making our decisions based on what we think happened to us yesterday and what we think may happen to us tomorrow. We are only responding to our experience when we make choices based on what is happening to us right here, right now. It is only possible to respond to our experiences when we unlearn the behaviors and belief systems that lead us into reaction. This "unlearning" is what The Presence Process assists us to accomplish.

There are no failures in The Presence Process, as it is an individual journey driven by commitment, curiosity, and intention. It cannot be experienced for someone else or because of someone else. Activating present moment awareness is an individual responsibility. It is therefore an experience that is by nature immune to comparison or judgment.

The Presence Process is not an end to anything; it is the continuation of a lifelong journey that we have already been making into the heart of our own present moment awareness. As we begin this leg of our life's journey, let us commit to consciously attending to our emotional growth for the rest of our life experience—no matter what. Let us begin this part of the journey by being clear about what our intention is in entering The

Presence Process. It is beneficial for us to take a moment to be still and to carefully consider the following question before reading further:

What is my intention in entering The Presence Process?

THE MECHANICS OF THE PROCESS

THE PRESENCE PROCESS is an experiential journey in which we are trained in the art of activating present moment awareness through the practice of conscious breathing, the application of the Presence Activating Statements, and the learning and applying of perceptual tools.

The Presence Process is not a process of "doings". It is about embracing not-doing in order to effortlessly undo what stands between us and an experience of pure Being. We are already breathing; this Process empowers us to now breathe consciously. We are already thinking; this Process empowers us to now use our thought processes in a manner that serves us. We are already feeling; this Process empowers us to now begin feeling present. We are already reading; this Process empowers us with reading that enables us to now use reading as a tool to mentally activate present moment awareness. We are already automatically wielding our tools of perception; this process empowers us to consciously begin perceiving the world as it is unfolding *right now* instead of as we unconsciously perceive it through interpretations and belief systems based on the experiences of the past. The Presence Process is structured in a series of Sessions that are spaced seven days apart. These seven-day periods between Sessions enable us to gather the required experience necessary to integrate the information we receive through the Process materials.

Information, when combined with experience, becomes knowledge. When this knowledge becomes the frequency upon which we base our thoughts, words, and deeds, then we are entering the resonance called wisdom.

From the commencement of the first Session, we are instructed in a consciously connected breathing technique that is both natural and safe. We are required to breathe as instructed for 15 minutes at the beginning and the end of each day during the entire duration of this journey. This breathing exercise is the backbone to this Process, as it enables us to consciously accumulate present moment awareness daily. This daily breathing practice requires a mature level of commitment and personal discipline.

Throughout The Presence Process, we are working with the two most prominent tools that we have as conscious beings: our attention and our intention. Our attention is the tool of our mental body and is the "'what" of our focus. Our intention is the tool of our emotional body and is the "why" of our focus. We all use our attention and intention to automatically navigate towards, through, and out of all our life experiences. For the most part, we do this unconsciously. The Presence Process is designed to bring increasing consciousness to this procedure because the quality of our life experience is determined by how consciously we wield our attention and intention.

With each Session, in addition to our daily breathing, we are given a statement to activate Presence. We call these "Presence Activating Statements". We are required to apply the Session Presence Activating Statements not as wishful or positive thinking but as responses to the experiences stimulated in our daily life by this Process. We are also given reading materials that contain perceptual tools as well as insights that automatically awaken us from our unconscious behavior.

The Presence Process is not about being fixed by anybody or anything: it is about learning how to consciously take responsibility for the task of accessing the power of our Inner Presence. It teaches us how to increasingly withdraw our conscious and unconscious attention from our past and projected future to become available to the present moment of our life.

The Presence Process, by teaching us how to detach from and observe our experiences, enables us to see that there is nothing wrong with us; we are not broken. Instead, it enables us to integrate that it is the quality of the experiences that we are having in "time" that must be brought into balance. In this way, The Presence Process assists us to see clearly that there is a difference between who and what we are and the experiences that we are having.

There is no magic or mystery about how and why The Presence Process accomplishes its intent. It is purely a procedure of what may be called Higher Science. It aligns itself with The Law of Cause and Effect. Through experience, we will see that all the procedures and the knowledge contained within the experience are quite natural and often very obvious.

What distinguishes The Presence Process from many other introspective procedures is that it has no outer rituals, ceremonies, or dogmas. There are no toys or "power objects" for us to cling to. This Process involves no belief systems, no religious concepts, or philosophies. Everything that we accomplish during this Process is done through disciplining our own will to consciously wield our attention and intention. This Process is about departing the illusory mental corridors of our mind and becoming real with our experiences and ourselves. For this reason, we are given an opportunity to experience each part of the Process as real events in our daily life experience. By applying ourselves to this experience, and then witnessing the results, we realize through personal experience that nothing (no thing) outside of us can have a more powerful and lasting impact on how we feel within than developing an authentic relationship with our Inner Presence.

This is not an experience we can enter for someone else or to prove something to someone else. Entering under such a pretext will make it exceedingly challenging to reach completion. The will to complete this journey must to some extent come from within us and not only be sourced as a reaction to external circumstances. Before entering it, we must be ready and willing to let go of our victim mentality because we are going to be asked to take full responsibility for the quality of all our life experiences.

Through experience, The Presence Process enables us to integrate that real growth always comes from *what we do not know*. This truth cannot be overstated. It also cannot be understood by the ego because an attribute of the ego is that it assumes it already knows everything worth knowing. As we enter this journey, we must be open to the possibility that we do not know who we are, where we are heading, what we really seek and therefore how to achieve it. We must be open to the possibility that we may have been wrong about everything. If we think we know exactly what is going on in every aspect of our life experience, it will be challenging for us to surrender to this Process because *we can only grow when we admit we do not know*.

Though it is definitely not essential, it is strongly recommended that individuals choosing to enter The Presence Process do so in pairs. Not that this Process is actually accomplished together. As it is an "inside job", it is an individual journey. However, companionship along the way is highly beneficial. The reasons for this recommendation are:

1 **To give each other support.** During this journey, our intention is not to attempt to feel good, but rather to feel real. Our authentic or real state of Being is spontaneously joyful and creative, but to re-awaken to our authentic state, we must journey through the present condition of our emotional body. This is a journey that takes us through our suppressed fear, anger, and grief. In this world, these states of emotional imbalance are automatically suppressed because we are taught by example to believe that when they occur something is "wrong". Our ongoing intention to try and feel good all the time stems from our continual desire to suppress the predicament that what we are really feeling is afraid, angry, and full of grief. When we enter The Presence Process, we deliberately intend that these suppressed feelings surface. That is why we are simultaneously taught the perceptual tools to assist us to gently balance and integrate these uncomfortable states. It is natural and expected that the world around us will become concerned and instinctively attempt to make us feel better when these suppressed emotions begin surfacing. In other words, the world will encourage us to *re-cover* (to cover up our suppressed emotions again). When we make this journey with a friend, we will have someone by our side who will instead support us in our intent *not* to re-cover, but to discover.

2 **Submerging in water.** During Sessions Seven, Eight, and Nine of The Presence Process, we are given the option of submerging our body in a bathtub of warm water. The how and why of this specific procedure is explained in great detail in the Process materials. Although it is completely safe to experience this alone, it may be challenging for

some of us who have medical problems or who are elderly. Under these circumstances, it is advisable for us to have someone to sit with us as we go through this part of our experience. There is nothing for a companion to do but to be present without judgment or concern for what we may go through and to assist us in and out of the bathtub if this is necessary.

3 **Confirmation.** Like any journey into a new terrain, we will go through places within our Being that are unfamiliar. If we are in contact with someone who is taking a similar journey into themselves, we will see that what we are going through is supposed to be happening. We will recognize the commonality of the experiences we are going through. Therefore, one of the main benefits of being in close proximity to someone who is also making this journey is that their presence serves as confirmation.

It is not essential to have someone to share this experience with, as the bottom line is that The Presence Process is a journey that one can only take within oneself, for oneself, and by oneself. However, company along the way is facilitating, supportive, and encouraging.

Bringing consciousness to our breathing is an integral part of The Presence Process because our breath is the most efficient and accessible tool that we have with which to anchor our attention in the present moment. Initially, we may assume that the breathing technique used throughout this Process is Breath Work or Rebirthing. Though similarities will always be present, the intent behind this particular application of consciously connected breathing is unique to The Presence Process, and it should not be assumed to be aligned with or have the same agendas or practical approaches as Breath Work or Rebirthing. The primary intention for placing our attention on our breathing in this Process is to activate and accumulate the experience of present moment awareness and to simultaneously bring our conscious attention to any unconscious obstacles in the way of realizing this experience.

How and why does consciously connected breathing activate present moment awareness? Most of us spend our waking hours either thinking about circumstances of the past or events yet to occur. Unconsciously, our mind is almost exclusively engaged in this activity. This is a mental addiction and affliction that has imprisoned humanity in an inner world of illusion that is reflected outwardly as our ongoing planetary imbalance. For the purpose of The Presence Process, we shall call this illusionary and unbalanced state "living in time". It is a condition that lacks the experience of present moment awareness and thus the conscience of consequence. We cannot consciously and responsibly navigate the quality of our life experience, be truly available to support others around us, or experience our intimate connected-ness with all life unless we have attained a certain level of present moment awareness. Without present moment awareness, it is impossible to see the connection between cause and effect. A being who is present cannot knowingly cause harm to other life forms, as the intimately connected nature of present moment awareness enables one to *feel* the consequences of one's behavior. The insensitive behavior that dominates on our planet is a testimony to a distinct lack of present moment awareness.

Yet we are not completely lost within the illusions of this time-based paradigm because a lifeline to the paradigm of the present moment lies within us all: our breath. Our breath is a lifeline because there is no breathing in the past, and there is no breathing in the future. By becoming conscious of our breathing, we activate a powerful and reliable inner tool that enables us to consciously extract our attention from the past and the future. Consequently, we automatically accumulate present moment awareness.

By focusing our attention and intention on our breathing, we are forcing an aspect of our awareness to remain consciously anchored in the present moment. This simple procedure has profound consequences. One of them is that it automatically and effectively activates a process that starts revealing to us where we are consciously and unconsciously attached to the past or a projected future. It does this by making us aware of our suppressed and unintegrated memories. The Presence Process is therefore designed to empower us to deliberately facilitate this unfolding experience consciously and responsibly. That is why great emphasis is placed on following the instructions carefully and on gradually moving through this experience as a process and not on entering it as a quick fix.

One of the intentions of The Presence Process is to bring our unintegrated and suppressed memories to the surface as gently as possible and to simultaneously empower us to safely integrate them, to gain wisdom from them, and to neutralize their destructive impact on the quality of our present life experience. By accomplishing this, The Presence Process assists us to answer the two questions that we have been asking ourselves unconsciously since childhood: "What happened?" and "How can I stop this from happening again?" These are the two unconscious questions that have been deflecting our attention out of the present moment and into the corridors of the past and the projected future since we departed our childhood. These two questions are the voice of all our anxiety. The Presence Process automatically calms and brings this voice to rest.

Though it is the backbone of this Process, consciously connected breathing is but one of the array of tools that make up the mechanism of it. This Process must therefore not be assumed to be associated with Pranayama Yoga or any other technique that deliberately magnifies our awareness of our breathing in an attempt to activate or access spiritual experiences. This Process does not concern itself with breath-control but rather with releasing unconscious control over the breath to establish a normal and healthy breathing pattern. The Presence Process is definitely not intended to be a spiritual process, although it undoubtedly has what may be thought of as spiritual consequences. The Presence Process is best viewed as a physical, mental, and emotional procedure that has a profound impact on our overall level of personal present moment awareness in *this* world. It is about showing up in and learning how to consciously navigate through our present life experience. It is about being here, now.

THE CONSCIOUSNESS OF QUESTIONS

WHENEVER WE ARE ASKED a question about our life experience, we will notice that our thought process automatically examines our memory for the answer. As a consequence of this searching process, there will be some things that we automatically know and can therefore answer immediately without thinking about them. Then there will be other things that we appear not to know or to remember so must apply a thinking process to attain the answer. However, even after much thought, we will discover there are some things that we appear not to know at all and that we cannot consciously remember no matter how much we think about them. We can therefore divide our ability to answer a question about our experience into three outcomes:

1   **Some answers we know.** For example, if we are asked what our name is, we answer without thinking because it is something that we know.

2   **Some answers we uncover through the process of thinking.** For example, if we are asked what the first song was on the radio that we loved, we might have to think a bit about it to recall the title and performer.

3   **Some answers we apparently do not appear to know or seemingly cannot remember and no amount of thinking appears to assist us.** For example, if we are asked what happened to us at 10:35 PM on the morning of our 3rd birthday, we will most likely not remember no matter how much we think about it. Consequently, we may conclude that it is something we do not know.

When we observe the nature of our own mental process a little closer, we will notice that whenever we are asked a question about our life experience, our mind-field automatically searches itself to see whether we can access the answer or not. We will notice that it keeps searching until the moment we say something like "I do not know" or "I cannot remember". The moment we say something like this, our mind-field will then bring closure to its investigation, and we will usually mark this moment consciously or unconsciously by labeling ourselves with a limiting self-judgment. For example, once we realize that we cannot recall the answer to a particular question about our life experience, we may say something like:

"I cannot remember that because my long-term memory
is not that good."
"I cannot remember that because it is not really important to me."
"I cannot remember that because it was probably too painful."
"I cannot remember that because it happened too long ago."

The reason we punctuate our inability to answer a question and the closure of our attempt to do so with a limiting self-judgment is because there is an aspect of our experience that cannot cope with the possibility that it does not know everything. Instead of embracing the unknown, what this aspect of our experience automatically does is seek to blame a condition or circumstance for the apparent lack of ability to access the information. During The Presence Process, we shall call this aspect of our experience "the ego".

The ego is an inauthentic identity that we manufactured from early childhood to safely enter the seemingly treacherous adult experience. As opposed to Presence, this inauthentic persona functions from a point of *pretence*. Instead of being spontaneous, it is calculated. We will explore the nature and structure of the ego in more detail during the course of this journey. For now, we will define it as that aspect of our experience that we manufactured to be acceptable amongst adults. For now, let us think of it as that which stands between us and the experience of present moment awareness.

The ego always covers up its limitations by making excuses and casting blame. The limiting self-judgment that we automatically and quite often unconsciously lay upon ourselves when we bring closure to the mind's search for an answer is the ego's way of hiding the fact that there are certain memories that are beyond its thinking ability. In other words, the ego does not want to let on that there is a real limit to the process of *thinking*, that we had a life *before* thinking, and that there is an experience of life *beyond* thinking. The ego is in love with the mind and therefore with *thinking* and *understanding*. Its identity is founded on the false belief that the mind is God. The ego is a devoted and unshakable disciple of mind.

An honest way to explain our inability to access an answer to a question about our life experience would be to say:

"I am presently unable to recall that information with my mind because there are some things that cannot be known or remembered using the thinking process."

The ego cannot cope with such a statement because it actually thinks the mind knows and understands everything and that everything worth knowing can be accessed through the thinking process. The ego is mental.

The ego wants us to mistakenly live our life experience believing that if we cannot know something through the thinking process, then what we are attempting to know is either not true, did not really happen, or does not really matter and is therefore of no real importance to us. Or, that we are dysfunctional or stupid. By punctuating the end of our conscious search for an answer with a limiting self-judgment (an excuse), the ego establishes a self-fulfilling prophecy. By telling ourselves that "we cannot remember something because…", we automatically close the door to that knowledge being delivered to us and so activate a scenario that confirms our limiting self-judgment.

Yet we have all had experiences of not bringing conscious closure to our mental search for something and then consequently having the answer *given* to us when we least expected it. This usually happens when we are attempting to access an answer that we feel is "on the tip of our tongue". Because the answer feels just out of reach, we do not consciously terminate our mental search for it but instead say something like this to ourselves:

> "I know I know that."
> "It will come to me."
> "It's on the tip of my tongue."

The consequence is that it does come. Later on when our attention is completely taken up by something else, the answer mysteriously pops into focus as if it was always there. These types of experiences show us that all the information that we seek about our life experience is available to us if we apply the correct access method. This method does not always necessarily involve thinking. It involves *being open to receiving the answer from the aspect of our Being that knows everything*.

The idea that we can access information without the use of the conscious thinking process is foreign to us because of the mind-dominated nature of our educational system. However, many inventors will testify to the fact that the crucial piece of information that made their inventions possible came to them when they had taken their attention off the task at hand and were doing something else, like indulging in a relaxing nap. The *thought* of applying such a technique to gain information is threatening to our ego because it reveals that contrary to the assumption of our ego, our conscious mind is not the beginning and end of everything. It is merely a tool and therefore has limitations.

Throughout The Presence Process, we are encouraged to ask many questions about our life experience. In order not to lessen the power and potential of this aspect of our journey, we are asked right from the outset not to approach these questions in a self-limiting manner. If we automatically apply the above self-limiting antics of the ego, we will deprive ourselves of many profound insights. We will also close the door to the wonderful experiences of intuition and inspiration. We are therefore encouraged to approach every question that we are asked during The Presence Process as follows:

Throughout this journey, the process of finding the answers to the questions that we are asked is not as important as asking the questions sincerely with an open mind.

We must not even be slightly concerned if we do not immediately receive the answer to a question that we ask ourselves. Our task is complete once we have sincerely asked the question. If the answer is not immediately apparent, we must choose to keep an open mind on the matter and thus allow it to be given to us in a moment when we least expect it.

There is no point in thinking intensely about the answers to questions we are asked and then becoming frustrated because we cannot consciously access them. This approach will cause us to react to our frustration by bringing closure to our search with a limiting self-judgment. During The Presence Process, no one is going to mark our answers *because there are no right answers*. Our answers cannot and will not be graded by comparison because our journey will be uniquely tailored to fit our individual requirements. There will be no answers that we are *supposed* to arrive at either. We must ask the questions and keep our mind open, thus *allowing the answers to be given to us*. By not automatically bringing closure to our search for the answers with limiting self-judgments, we will protect our thought processes from being shut down by the insecurities of the ego.

The law of the universe is that for every cause there will be an effect. This can also be translated as "Seek and we will find", "Ask and we will receive", and "Knock and the door will be opened". In other words, when

37

we ask a question and do not terminate the process of attempting to access the answer, the answer must inevitably be delivered into our awareness in some form or another. The question is the cause and the answer is the effect. The one guarantees the other. This is the approach that we are asked to take with all the questions that are placed before us during The Presence Process. Whenever we ask ourselves a question, we must be patient and allow the answer to be given to us in a manner that is most beneficial to our journey through this Process.

Our present predicament is that we, as we presently know ourselves, do not know everything. In fact, we, as we presently know ourselves, know very little. Yet there is an aspect of our Being that we may as yet be unaware of that *does* know everything. It knows everything without having to "think" about it. It knows. This is our Inner Presence. It has been the silent witness of every experience that we have ever had, and it remembers everything in every moment of these experiences as if they are still happening to us right now. To it, all the experiences we have ever had are happening right now because present moment awareness knows no time. One can say that the difference between the ego and our eternal Inner Presence is that the ego has to think to attempt and understand, while our Inner Presence *knows*. Our Inner Presence knows because it is a constant witness to all our life experiences; whereas, the ego's focus is attached to and determined by our outer world and what others are doing in it.

When we approach a question with the assumption that we can only access the answer by thinking, we are enlisting the ego as an accomplice and simultaneously limiting ourselves to the thinking mind as the only mechanism available to accomplishing the task. Thus, we are shutting out our present moment awareness. This shutting-out process occurs automatically because our Inner Presence abides by the law of non-interference. It remains still and silent if we insist on attempting to gain information only through the process of thinking and understanding. Yet the moment that we are prepared to accept and act on the notion that what we have "'made" of ourselves (the ego) is unreliable, and that the mind as a tool has its limitations, then we automatically invite our all-knowing present moment awareness to give us the answer. In this manner, we automatically open ourselves to effortlessly accessing inner knowledge. In this world, the mind will always be the means whereby knowledge is conveyed to us, but it is not necessarily the only means to access knowledge.

Asking all our life questions from this point of awareness allows the energy of insight, intuition, inspiration, and revelation to awaken into our everyday life experience. It allows us to enter the place of knowing without having to know why. It is essential that we allow ourselves to enter the experience of knowing without knowing why, because during The Presence Process we are going to be accessing experiences that we had before we learnt language. These experiences occurred before we could attach mental concepts to them. Many of these experiences are purely feelings, vibrations, or sensations. They are "knowings". They are energies in motion. These are the emotional experiences that happened before we had a grasp of mental language. These are vibrational experiences that happened in the womb and shortly after we were birthed into this world. If we insist on always having to know why to accept what we know is true and real for us, then we will not allow our awareness to enter and thus activate these early vibrational memories in order that their negative impact on our present life experience be neutralized.

The questions that we choose to ask throughout our life experience are extremely important. Because of the Law of Cause and Effect, if we keep our mind open, the answers to all our questions will always manifest in some form or another. Keeping this in mind, we may want to consider the possibility that our life experience in any given moment is an unfolding answer to questions that we have been asking. The reason that this may not be apparent to us yet is because most of the questions that we have been asking have been asked unconsciously. The Presence Process assists us to rectify this predicament by teaching us how to begin eliminating this unconscious behavior and to simultaneously begin consciously asking questions that serve us. By understanding and accepting that all our questions will inevitably be answered, we can then place our full attention on the process of asking useful questions and remove it from the process of attempting to "think" the answers. We are being asked to keep our mind open. We are being invited to explore the experience of allowing ourselves to receive. We can initiate this experience right now by asking the following question:

What are the most beneficial questions we can ask
before entering The Presence Process?

———— ◯◯◯◯◯ ————

THE PATHWAY OF AWARENESS & THE SEVEN-YEAR CYCLE

TWO OF THE REVELATIONS that gave rise to the intentions behind and the mechanics of The Presence Process are what we shall refer to as The Pathway of Awareness and The Seven-Year Cycle.

The Pathway Of Awareness

Acknowledging and operating in line with a Pathway of Awareness that is automatic and completely natural to all human beings is what makes The Presence Process so immensely powerful and yet simultaneously effortless. Everything in our experience comes into being by a mostly unconscious application of our attention and intention along this pathway. It is, therefore, second nature to us all. Yet surprisingly, it remains well hidden until brought to our conscious attention. Understanding the simple dynamics of this Pathway of Awareness helps us to integrate why it is necessary to access and adjust the emotional core of our experiences to affect real change in the mental and physical aspects of our life. Once we consciously recognize The Pathway of Awareness and The Seven-Year Cycle in our own life experience, we will be able to better integrate the causes of many of the uncomfortable experiences we are having, or at least know where to begin looking for the causes.

This Pathway of Awareness is very easy to identify by watching the normal development of a newborn child. Even though our emotional, mental, and physical bodies are already evident and developing simultaneously alongside each other from the moment of our birth, there is a specific pathway that our individual awareness uses to move consciously into them. First a child cries (emotional); then, it learns to talk (mental), and only then does it learn to walk (physical). The Pathway of Awareness therefore is:

From emotional to mental to physical.

When we exit the womb, we are primarily emotional beings. All that we are able to do is emote. We do not have a verbal language and its associated concepts to identify or effectively communicate with our experiences. Nor do we have the motor skills to physically participate in anything. Our experience of the world is that it is purely *energy in motion*, or emotion. We remain in this purely emotional state until we recognize something. So our awareness begins in the emotional realm.

Our entry into the next step along The Pathway of Awareness, the mental realm, takes place when we learn to deliberately use our emotions to achieve a particular outcome. When this occurs, our emotions are no longer a reactive reflex to our circumstances. They now become a means to respond to and hence to direct the outcome of our experiences. In other words, the moment we use crying or smiling as a tool of deliberate communication to consciously manipulate our life experience, then we are no longer purely emoting; we are now also mentally participating in our experience. This entry into the mental realm is made concrete when we learn our first word. Our first word is our act of naming something. It is automatic that we name that which we recognize *because* we recognize it.

Being able to name aspects of our experience that we recognize shows that the doorway is now opening into the next step along The Pathway of Awareness: the physical realm. Once we begin recognizing and naming aspects of our experience, it is because these specific aspects no longer appear to us as *energy in motion*. The moment we name anything, it is because its appearance of being energy in motion has subsided and begun to appear as solid matter. We name something because it "matters" to us. Recognition and the subsequent act of naming something is the consequence of acknowledging that what was once flowing energy has transformed miraculously into what appears to be solid, dense, and stationary matter. Part of our process of entering this world experience is that we have somehow become addicted to "making everything matter". This addiction is what enables us to perceptually enter into and have a seemingly solid physical experience of a paradigm that is actually purely light and sound, or luminous, vibrational waves of energy in motion. To enter a physical experience, we literally have to create an illusion of "stopping the world".

As children, once our perception has literally stopped the world and we have started naming it, we then crawl curiously towards what we have named to have a personal encounter with it. This outward movement of our attention and intention, triggered by our curiosity, is what leads us out of a purely emotional and mental experience and into the third step along The Pathway of Awareness; the physical realm. Curiosity is necessary for us to literally make the effort to take our first baby steps into a world that matters to us.

This Pathway of Awareness from the emotional to the mental and then into the physical that we all move along to enter our experience of this world is acknowledged unconsciously by the outer behavior of the world. Recognizing how the world acknowledges it, reveals what is known as our Seven-Year Cycle.

The Seven-Year Cycle

The purely emotional experience that begins for us the moment we leave the womb begins tapering off and in many cases ceases its development when we reach the age of seven. At seven, our childhood is officially over. We then become young boys and girls. This is why we start our schooling around the age of seven, because this time in our life marks the point at which we exit our emotional body development, our childhood, to place a greater focus on our mental body development.

From seven to fourteen years old, we then learn to mentally grasp and develop the basics of the trinity of our communication skills: speaking, reading, and writing. We also learn how to behave in a manner that is deemed acceptable and appropriate to the society into which we have been born. These seven years of intense focus on the foundations of our mental skills then begin to refocus around what we call puberty. From about fourteen years old, our mental development then starts to become focused upon what others anticipate is required for us to know in order to take up a meaningful physical role in society. This adjustment of our focus is simultaneously marked by an increase in our physical awareness of our environment and the relationship we have with it.

The hormonal changes that take place in the body around fourteen years old mark our departure from our seven-year mental socialization and acclimatization cycle and signal our entry into our third Seven-Year Cycle. This third Seven-Year Cycle intensifies the development of our relationship with the outer physical world. We are then declared "teenagers". During this third Seven-Year Cycle, we become very aware of our physical body and our physical place in the world. It is also during this period that we become attracted to or repelled by other human beings. It is here that we choose our group. It is also during this cycle that emphasis is placed on figuring out how we are going to take up our roles as physically responsible and capable humans. The closing of this third Seven-Year Cycle is often acknowledged by the celebrating of our 21st birthday. At the close of this cycle, we are declared to be young adults.

The Presence Process will demonstrate to us through personal experience that because of the nature of this natural Pathway of Awareness and the three initial Seven-Year Cycles that unfold accordingly, the seeds of our present physical experiences cannot be found in our present outer physical circumstances. Nor can they be found in our present mental thought processes. By first teaching us how to become physically present, then mentally clear, this Process will reveal to us that the seeds of all our unbalanced experiences of today are to be found in the realm in which we planted them: the unintegrated emotional experiences of our childhood.

In other words, this Process will show us that the first emotionally-driven Seven-Year Cycle of our childhood is the *causal* point of all our present uncomfortable experiences. It will show us that all the emotional seeds that were planted then that were not consciously integrated into our experience have sprouted the negative mental belief systems that in turn have manifested as the unbalanced physical conditions or circumstances we are experiencing *right now*. In The Presence Process, we call the mechanics of this seed-planting procedure "emotional imprinting". We will be exploring it in greater depth during our actual journey through the Process writings.

One of the most profound revelations that The Presence Process makes possible for us is that emotionally, *nothing new has happened for most of us since we exited our first Seven-Year Cycle*. It will show us that even though we may appear to be continuously going through new physical circumstances and experiences, on an emotional level nothing really changes. Emotionally, every seven years, we are repeating the same cycle that was imprinted into our emotional body during the first seven years of our life experience. When we teach ourselves how to identify the emotional undercurrent that permeates through all our mental and physical experiences, we will clearly see that it only *appears* that we are growing up and having varied and different experiences.

By the time we are fourteen years old, our attention and intention are habitually and literally *trans*fixed on the physical circumstances of our life. As adults, we only see the solid surface of things. Because the physical world by nature always appears to be changing and therefore appears to be making itself anew in each moment, this creates an illusion of constant change. This is a trick of the physical world. This is the great illusion. In the East they call this Maya.

By teaching us how to see beneath the physical surface of things, The Presence Process will reveal to us the true nature of the physical world's illusionary sleight of hand. This will be accomplished by using our mental capabilities to look beyond the physical and to "see" the emotional content of our life. This seeing is accomplished by allowing ourselves to feel aspects of our experience that we have for so long suppressed. When we accomplish this seeing, we will realize that we are all diligently and quite unconsciously repeating a pattern that was imprinted into our emotional body during our childhood. Repeating this emotional pattern unconsciously gives rise to the experience that we call "living in time".

Being able to see the world energetically as a tapestry of energies in motion, as an emotional current, is what enables us to see that we are indeed living in the past and writing a future that obediently replicates the emotional content of this past. It reveals to us that most of us died an emotional death when we turned seven years old. This is the real death from which we are being asked to awaken. This repetitive emotional pattern is the dream that, on the surface of things, appears to be real. When we learn how to see beneath the surface of our world of pretence, we will discover something quite startling:

Adults are dead children.

The child within us had to die so that we could become acceptable as an adult. Now it is up to us to break through our self-created perceptual

44

prison bars of adulthood to free our child self from the dungeon of pretence. By gaining the experience necessary to rescue our innocence, we enable ourselves to enter a whole new paradigm—one in which innocence and experience come to rest upon the balanced scales of wisdom. It will only be by making a conscious journey into the dynamics of our emotional undercurrents that we will understand why we have heard ourselves and others repeatedly say:

"I do not know why this keeps happening to me."

Or

"Why does this keep happening over and over again?"

Our journey through The Presence Process will help us realize that when we make statements or ask questions such as these, we are not actually talking about a physical event, but about our feelings towards or in reaction to the re-occurring emotional cycles in our life. It is the unintegrated emotional content of our life experience that constantly repeats and causes us to manifest mental and physical imbalance. Once we realize that we are unconsciously recreating the emotional resonance of our childhood, we have taken the first step to awakening ourselves from this dream. We will then also realize that it is pointless meddling with the physical circumstances of our outer life to effect real change to the quality of our experiences. The uncomfortable physical circumstances of our life right now are the physical manifestation of the emotional ghosts of the past. We can chase them all we want, yet we already know that such activity, such motion and commotion, such drama, accomplishes nothing.

The main reason why the emotional experiences of the first seven years of our life experience remain undigested is because this world that we enter is not solely an emotional experience; it also has powerful mental and physical components to it. To fully integrate our experiences here, we must be able to embrace them emotionally, mentally, and physically. During the first Seven-Year Cycle, we have powerful emotional capacities, yet our mental and physical capacities are not yet fully developed. This is why the world unconsciously steps in and ends our intense emotional development around seven years of age, because unless it does we

45

will not begin to focus on developing our mental and later our physical capacities to enable us to become fully integrated beings.

At this point in our discussion, it is relevant to bring to our attention that we have another seven-based cycle that pre-'seeds' the emotional cycle that commences at our moment of birth. This is our seven month vibrational cycle. This cycle commences the moment our awareness enters our womb-experience, roughly two months after conception. The Seven-Year emotional cycle that commences when we are birthed into this world is a repetition of the pattern imprinted into us vibrationally during these seven months in the womb. However, in The Presence Process, we do not attempt to integrate the vibrational experiences that we had during this womb-phase of our development because we are not exposed to our vibrational paradigm during our journey through this world and hence we do not attain a vocabulary to communicate it to each other. To access and integrate this vibrational cycle requires us to make our own journey into inner silence and stillness through the practice of meditation. This is the authentic purpose of meditation.

What many call "a spiritual experience" is actually "a vibrational experience". The journey to consciously integrate our vibrational body (our spiritual body) can only be undertaken when under the guidance of a teacher who has him/herself integrated their vibrational body. Because integrating the vibrational body enables us to activate inner perfection despite the perfect imperfection of the outer world experience, we call these teachers Perfect Living Masters. Their science is the highest science that can be encountered or comprehended in this world. We only enter this phase of integration and come into contact with such a teacher when it becomes our Soul intent to move beyond the physical, mental, and emotional experience completely.

The Presence Process is equipped with all the tools and knowledge to assist us to fully integrate our physical, mental, and emotional experiences, thereby enabling us to initiate the intention of becoming a perfect Being "in this world". It gives us the knowledge that enables us to deliver ourselves to the very brink of the vibrational journey that makes the realization of this perfection possible. Historically, the pathway of vibrational integration is called Mysticism.

The Presence Process concerns itself with teaching us to fully embrace this life experience, rather than moving beyond it. It teaches us to show up here and now. It accomplishes this by teaching us how to hear the messages of the emotional ghosts of our past and how to use our attention and intention to return to the place where our emotional growth ended abruptly and transformed our present moment awareness into deathly pretence. By accomplishing this, we realize firsthand why we must journey beneath our physical illusions and through our mental confusions to reactivate and revitalize the energies that are responsible for real movement in our life experience. In other words, why we must consciously journey seemingly backwards along The Pathway of Awareness we used to enter the physical world and deactivate the negative affects of The Seven-Year Cycle on our present experiences. Only by accomplishing this will the veil of the past and the projected future be torn so that the joy and beauty inherent in the present moment be truly apparent to us. This is no small task, but when we really undertake it, we will quickly begin to integrate that it is one of the most important quests that we can set upon during our lifetime.

Journeying "backwards" is not really an apt description of this procedure; it makes sense because we are living in time and therefore perceive ourselves to be constantly moving forward. Yet if the truth be told, until we integrate our past, we are actually spinning in circles like a puppy attempting to catch its tail. A more appropriate way to describe the journey activated by The Presence Process is that we are commencing a movement "inwards" and that our journey of life thus far has been one in which we have been moving "'outward" into the physical experience. The most outer aspect of our experience is physical. It will remain physical while it "matters" to us. As we learn how to take steps inwards, we will first enter the mental. As we take another step into our Being, we will again consciously re-enter the emotional. The emotional, as we have just discussed, is one step away from the vibrational, or what we may think of as an authentic spiritual experience.

This return journey that we must take into ourselves along The Pathway of Awareness to achieve wholeness in this life experience is not something unfamiliar to us. We do it already in many ways. Whenever we wish to return to or make contact with our Source, we make this journey automatically. To see it clearly in action, we can watch a child praying. First they kneel down and put their hands together (the physical). Then they speak to God (the mental). Then their words of innocence touch our hearts and activate our feelings (the emotional). So the return journey along The Pathway of Awareness is:

From physical to mental to emotional.

This is exactly opposite to the outward pathway our awareness embarks on from the moment we enter the physical world. As already mentioned, the practice of meditation is also designed to activate this pathway of return into ourselves; first we adopt a physical posture, then we repeat a mental mantra, and only then do we evoke an emotional experience of inner love and devotion. This emotional experience then fuels our ability to penetrate the vibrational realm. Meditation in its purest form is a tool intended to draw us out of this physical world experience along a mental pathway into our hearts. When we are in our hearts, we are one step away from our Divine Presence. It is our Divine Presence which then oversees our entry into the vibrational realm.

The Presence Process pays homage to the pathway of return that is required to begin reactivating a conscious awareness and relationship with our Inner Presence. It does this by making us conscious of the pathway we all took in departing from our childlike emotional innocence as we moved outward into the adult world. By teaching us how to metaphorically return to the first Seven-Year Cycle that made up our childhood with an intention of bringing balance by integrating experiences that were first imprinted into our emotional body, this Process enables us to understand what is meant by the expression:

"Unless we become as children again, we cannot enter
the Kingdom of Heaven." (Matthew 18:2–4)

Another way of communicating the same teaching is:

Unless we return along The Pathway of Awareness
and bring peace to our emotional child self, we will not
be able to neutralize the negative impacts of the unintegrated

experiences of our first Seven-Year Cycle. Until this is accomplished, we cannot activate real movement in our life or restore balance to our mental and physical experiences in this world. And until we accomplish balance, we are unable to move beyond the confines of this world and return to our Source.

This is the pathway The Presence Process invites us to step upon. This is what making contact with our Inner Presence makes possible. At this point in our discussion, it is important to take note that The Seven-Year Cycle, as we have described it in this discussion, is adjusting itself in line with the present acceleration of our evolution. The children of today have cycles that may now have been shortened to six or even five-year cycles because the transition from emotional body development to mental body development that takes place when we enter schooling is occurring at an earlier age. However, for the purpose of The Presence Process, we will refer to this emotional cycle as our Seven-Year Cycle and simultaneously be open to exceptions to this rule.

By putting ourselves through this Process, we are consciously initiating a change in our experience of this Seven-Year Cycle. We are gradually neutralizing the negative impact it has on the quality of our present life experience. Repeating this Process more than once begins dismantling the cycle altogether because it removes the energetic barrier caused within us by the emotional death we experienced when we entered adulthood. Once this cycle is sufficiently dismantled, we will then find ourselves standing at the edge of our personal void: the place we have for so long *avoided*. This is where our awareness of having a past and projected future fades into an eternal moment of being present Now. This is where the energetic experience of polarities begins to dissolve and merge into the vibrational experience of Oneness.

We must not be concerned if we cannot yet discern the evidence of the Seven-Year Cycle in our own life experience. Perceiving the footprints of our Seven-Year Cycle requires that we begin detaching our attention from the surface events in our life and become increasingly conscious of the emotional undercurrent that runs through it. This ability takes an accumulation of present moment awareness. The Presence Process empowers us to accomplish this.

MOVEMENT BEYOND MOTION

ONE OF THE WAYS that we are being prepared to enter The Presence Process is that we are being invited to change our perception about certain aspects of our life experience. For example, we have been asked not to judge our experience of this Process by how good we feel as we move through it. We have also been asked not to expect this journey to be easy. Instead, we have been asked to intend an experience for ourselves that is "real", even if this experience may initially be what we perceive as uncomfortable. We have also been asked to embrace the possibility that the key to restoring balance to the quality of our life experience is through personal emotional growth. We have been asked to consider that this personal emotional growth only comes from surrendering ourselves to an experience of "not knowing". To assist us to begin activating this process of surrender, we have been asked to consider changing our relationship with the question and answer procedure. We have been invited to do this by placing our focus on the procedure of asking the question and not on the procedure of attempting to find the answer. In this way, we allow the answer to be given to us unexpectedly, and this automatically opens our experience to "receiving". Now we are being asked to adjust our perception of what we think "movement" is.

Generally, in the outer physical world experience, when we speak of movement we are referring to a physical event, as in our movement from one physical location to another. Or at least the involvement of some physical activity, like the spinning of a wheel or the movement of our limbs. As far as the outer physical world is concerned, there is no possibility of a journey without this outer movement. Yet the consequences of entering and completing The Presence Process are that we are going to be experiencing very real movement that is not initiated by outer physical activity. The movement that we will be experiencing is therefore not that which we may automatically associate with the *concept* of movement. For the purpose of The Presence Process, outer physical activity is not considered *real*

movement. A better word for this outer activ.
going to experience as a consequence of entei
real movement, movement that is not generate

What do we mean by "movement that
motion"? This can be best illustrated by the fo
dissatisfied with the quality of our life expe
attempt and change our life circumstances by
city, or country. This will require a large amour.
may discover that after all this outer motion, tl
our new location, despite our altered outer circu
experience of dissatisfaction returns. This is b
motion, we have made no *real* movement *within* o
this experience in one form or another. There is
tures this predicament:

> **"Wherever we go, there we are."**

This behavior of running around and getting
movement that is strongly endorsed by the outer wo
tify any dissatisfaction that we have with the quality
In The Presence Process, we regard this type of point
as commotion. A better word for commotion is "dra
word we will use throughout these writings to descrik
less activity. Drama does not only pertain to point
motion, but also to all pointless mental and emotiona.
experience.

One of the intentions of The Presence Process is to
drama by simultaneously assisting us to activate *real* mo
experience. Our Catch-22 nature is such that until w
movement in our life, we will always resort to drama,
resorting to drama, we will not attempt to activate any
our life experience. The Presence Process helps us in brea
scious approach to life. It helps us in accomplishing th
inner movement by gently and consciously freeing u
emotions. By accomplishing this inner task, we will autom;
real outer movement in our life experience without havi

pointles
drop ou
enterin
ourselv

per
Th
wo
ac
"u

or
er
u

P

s outer commotion or drama. Only then will we be prepared to
r drama because its pointlessness will become self-evident. By
g The Presence Process, the real movement we intend to initiate for
es is from:

> *Doing to Being.*
> *Looking to seeing.*
> *Hearing to listening.*
> *Pretence to Presence.*
> *Imbalance to balance.*
> *Separation to Oneness.*
> *Reacting to responding.*
> *Inauthentic to authenticity.*
> *Fragmentation to integration.*
> *Seeking happiness to allowing joy.*
> *Revenge and blame to forgiveness.*
> *Incorrect perception to correct perception.*
> *Complaint and competition to compassion.*
> *Behaving unconsciously to behaving consciously.*
> *"Living in time" to experiencing present moment awareness.*

All of the above movements are varying descriptions of the exact same
ceptual shift, a perceptual shift that does not require outer motion.
s shift cannot be achieved by rearranging the conditions of our outer
rld experience. It cannot be accomplished by trying. It cannot be
omplished by drama. It can only be accomplished by "not doing" and
doing". It can only be accomplished by inner work.

By understanding the nature of the real movement we are embarking
throughout The Presence Process, we will save ourselves the wasted
ergy of attempting to complement this experience by embarking on any
nnecessary outer activity. What do we mean by this?

Often when we embark on the type of experience we are about to in The
resence Process, we do so because we are seeking to change ourselves. Yet
hat we are about to discover is that we cannot "change ourselves"; we can
nly change the quality of our experience. Not realizing this powerful
ruth is what leads us into endless outer doings. Not realizing this power-

ful truth is why all the outer motion in which we invest in our attempts to change ourselves, invariably results in nothing but unnecessary expended energy.

Because of the examples set for us in the outer world, it is hard for us to comprehend that we can accomplish real change in our circumstances without outer drama. For example, as we enter this experience, we may already simultaneously be deciding to add unnecessary drama to our journey. In addition to entering The Presence Process, we may already be deciding to quit smoking or other addictions, or to go on a special diet, or to increase or initiate a workout program into our daily routine.

The main reason why we might be intending to supplement this experience with added outer drama is because we may have come to The Presence Process thinking it was a way to change ourselves. We may have come to The Presence Process still believing that we *are* our experience, instead of understanding that we are *having* an experience. When we mistakenly believe that we are the experience that we are having, then it is likely that we will attempt to restore balance to our life experience by attempting to change the nature of our behavior, our appearance, or our life circumstances. Yet our behavior, our appearance, and our life circumstances are not who or what we are: they are an experience we are having. They are the attributes of our ego. When we attempt to change these superficial aspects of our outer experience, we always resort to drama.

For the duration of *this* journey, all outer adjustments made to our appearance, our behavior, or our life circumstances are discouraged because they will amount to nothing but increased drama and wasted energy. They can only add drama to our experience of this Process because they will place the focus of our attention on fiddling with the effect and not the cause of our circumstances.

By the time we are old enough to read and understand this information, we can be certain of one thing: our appearance, our behavior, and our life circumstances as they are *right now* are the accumulated effect of the unresolved discomforts of our emotional body. Real movement (lasting change) is therefore only possible in our outer experience by adjusting the resonance of the inner cause of these outer experiences. Fiddling with our behavior, our appearance, or our life circumstances accomplishes nothing that lasts. The Presence Process will show us clearly that it is only by adjusting the cause, by activating real movement in the condition of our emotional body, that we will realize real and lasting changes to our outer experiences.

We must therefore not approach The Presence Process with intentions of simultaneously making any major outer adjustments to our behavior, our appearance, or our life circumstances. For the duration of this journey it is highly recommended that we focus on what is asked of us in each moment.

We must avoid all impulses to make any drastic changes or major life decisions for the duration of this Process.

We will feel impulses to do so, but we must abstain from such drama. Such impulses for drastic action will arise during the course of our journey as reactions to the unconscious issues that are surfacing for us to process. Our resorting to outer drama will be a manifestation of our unconscious desire to control or sedate what is happening to us. Reactions always breed drama and commotion. They will lead us to take on too much at once, which is an unconscious way of sabotaging ourselves. Therefore, let us give ourselves permission to take a break from outer drama as we journey through this inner process.

Let us keep in mind that this journey is not about changing ourselves; it is about changing the quality of our experiences. This is what The Presence Process will assist us to integrate through real experience. A good metaphor to capture the difference between this inner journey into present moment awareness and other outer journeys that we may have embarked on in a mistaken attempt to change ourselves is this:

Journeys that we have taken in an attempt to change ourselves are like moving a radio around a room to tune into a desired station. This journey, in which we are going to learn how to adjust the quality of our experience, as opposed to attempting to change ourselves, requires that we leave the radio exactly where it is. Instead, we are going to focus our attention and intention on turning the tuning dial. It is a much simpler approach than resorting to outer drama, and it enables us to successfully tune into the music that brings us joy.

The experience of present moment awareness that we seek is nowhere "'out there" in the world and cannot be achieved by fiddling with the outer world or moving frantically about in it. The experience of present moment awareness is an inner accomplishment. Once it is accessed through activating inner silence and stillness, it will automatically be reflected in our experience of the outer world. Activating an awareness of our Inner Presence requires no drama. It is free and effortless and available to all beyond the outer segregation caused by color, caste, creed, and by rites, rituals, and dogmas. Everything that we will be asked to attend to throughout the course of this journey is a procedure for laying a foundation in our life experience for the inner silence and stillness in which the experience of our Inner Presence patiently awaits.

Our journey through The Presence Process is very simple. However, we can make it complicated if we attempt to add to it—or if we try too hard. All our outer drama will be wasted energy. All that is required of us is that we attend daily to the trinity that makes up the structure of this journey: the breathing exercise, the Presence Activating Statements, and the reading materials which contain the various perceptual tools we will be trained to apply to our life experience.

<hr />

BEYOND ADDICTION & AFFLICTION

AS FAR AS THE PRESENCE PROCESS is concerned, addictions and afflictions (chronic illness/disease) are the same condition: they are both outer manifestations of unresolved discomfort within our emotional body. In addition, although we do not discuss the condition specifically in this particular discussion, we also consider all allergies to be the same as addictions and afflictions. An allergy is a condition that is the polar opposite of an addiction: when we are addicted, we are constantly pulling a specific outer experience into our field; whereas, when we are allergic, we are constantly repelling a specific outer experience from our field. However, the causes for both conditions are due to unresolved discomfort within the emotional body.

The Presence Process is highly effective in setting us on a path to completely neutralizing our addictions and afflictions—no matter how long we have entertained them or how acutely we have allowed them to color our life experience. The Presence Process does not accomplish this by promising "a cure", because a cure is a destination. It accomplishes this by teaching us how to enter an ongoing inner journey towards emotional balance that will automatically lead us beyond the manifestation of these outer experiences of imbalance. No one is immune to an outer experience of "living in balance"—no matter how acute their condition. It is a question of personal will, of commitment, and of consistency. If we truly intend to activate the power of our Inner Presence, and if we keep this intention in the forefront of our awareness, success is inevitable.

The Presence Process will demonstrate that all addictions, whether they are to illegal drugs, to alcohol, to food, to sex, to gambling, or to legal prescription medications, are self-medicating behaviors that manifest in an attempt to sedate or control a discomfort in the emotional body. In this respect, addictions and afflictions are the same condition wearing different outer masks. Without self-medicating, an addict will inevitably manifest an affliction. If an affliction is successfully suppressed by prescription medication, then the same condition will manifest as an addiction. Both conditions are an outer manifestation of an uncomfortable charge in the emotional body. The exact same emotional charge can manifest as an addiction or as an affliction depending on individual circumstances. We call this causal inner discomfort our negative emotional charge. We all have a negative emotional charge until we re-enter 100% present moment awareness.

When this negative emotional charge is neutralized sufficiently, there is no longer a foundation upon which the addictions or afflictions can stand; therefore, there is nothing left to medicate and so our addictive behavior or symptomatic condition automatically subsides. Based on this simple understanding, this Process takes what may be considered to be an unusual or controversial stance in restoring balance to those of us who have resorted to addictive behaviors or prescription medications as a means to sedate or control the discomfort in our emotional body.

We are not asked to cease our self-medicating behavior to commence the Process.

In other words, just as we are asked not to invest in any added outer activities (drama) while we move through this Process, we are also asked to not force ourselves to quit our addiction or to suspend our prescription medication before commencing this Process for the first time. We are asked to keep in mind that not only is our addictive behavior an effect, but up to this moment in our life experience, it is also a necessary act of self-medication. However, we are asked *not to self-medicate while we attend to our daily breathing practice or while we read the written materials for each session.*

If we attempt to quit our self-medicating procedure before we have begun successfully reducing the negative charge in our emotional body, we will find ourselves spiraling into a state of unconscious awareness in which it may become impossible to continue attending to our Process commitments. We may then find ourselves overwhelmed and discouraged and thus return to our addictive behaviors more intensely than before we entered the Process.

Medical Advisory: In the same light, those of us who are suffering from an affliction are asked not to change our prescription medication procedures or any other prescribed therapeutic practices when we commence this Process. We must continue as normal. Instead, we are asked to closely monitor the effects the prescription medication is having on our life experience as we move through the Process. If we discover that our response to our medication is changing, we must immediately consult our medical practitioner, request an examination and a review of our status. The reason for this is that as our negative emotional charge decreases, so does our necessity for medication. One of the ways this becomes apparent to us is that our medication starts becoming too strong. We can then contact our medical practitioner and request re-evaluation and a subsequent decreasing of our prescribed dosage.

The reason we are not asked to quit anything before starting The Presence Process is because we cannot change anything by fiddling with an effect. Remember that all our addictions and our afflictions are an effect, and therefore our addictive behaviors and our relationship with prescription medications are also an effect. Rather than putting energy into forcing ourselves to quit anything, it is more beneficial that we instead focus our energy on de-activating the cause of our condition by complying with the instructions of this Process.

However, this being said, it must be stated that it is not possible to benefit from The Presence Process if we are severely sedated to a point that we are completely unable to attend to our reading materials, Presence Activating Statements, and breathing exercises. Under such circumstances, it is advisable to first enter rehabilitation therapy in order to detoxify and to regain the level of clarity that enables us to attend to the above requirements of the Process. Rehabilitation therapy can deliver us into a state of "recovery" in which our level of perceptual comprehension is drastically improved. However, a state of recovery, as will be explained shortly, is nothing more than a precarious state of quiet desperation. Nevertheless, it does enable us to behave in a more lucid and therefore disciplined manner. Consequently, once we have completed our rehabilitation therapy, we can then immediately enter The Presence Process and take the steps necessary to adjust the *cause* of our imbalanced life experience.

By completing The Presence Process experientially once to the best of our ability, we will have automatically reduced our negative emotional charge significantly. We will have also learnt the perceptual tools that will enable us to live our life in a manner that constantly neutralizes our negative emotional charge. This journey, once initiated, inevitably restores balance to the quality of our life experience. How long we wish to take to restore balance completely to our outer experience depends on how much inner work we are prepared to embrace. The more we reduce our inner emotional discomfort, the less severe our outer afflictions are and the less we will require our various medications. At some point, our wine will metaphorically turn to castor oil, our smoke to ammonia, and our opium to acid. Self-medication only appears to have a pleasurable or healing affect when we need it. When we no longer need it, its pleasures sour and the comfort it provides turns to discomfort. Also, the more present we become in our physical, mental, and emotional bodies, the more we start to feel what our medication or drug of choice is *really* doing to us. There is nothing pleasurable about ingesting potentially toxic substances; it is only because of the discomfort in our emotional body that such a behavior appears to have benefits.

By reducing the negative emotional charge that drives our imbalanced condition, we automatically dismantle the foundations that uphold it. If we are long-term self-medicaters and prescription drug users, it is important that we enter this Process with clear intent to neutralize the *cause* of our uncomfortable experience and not become preoccupied with the *effects* of being uncomfortable. As addicts, we may feel great shame and guilt. This is unnecessary. We self-medicate because society as a whole is not physically present enough, not mentally clear enough, or emotionally mature enough to assist us. This is not a case of blaming society for our condition, as in the final analysis, based on the Law of Cause and Effect, we are responsible for our predicament. It is important to remind ourselves that:

All addiction is self-medication.
All addiction is an experience that we are having.
All experiences that we are having can be changed.

It is also important that a long-term addiction be given a compassionate amount of time in which to be unravelled and neutralized. Addiction programs generally convince addicts that they will *always be addicted* and that they must therefore attend group meetings regularly, forever, or else they will relapse into reuse. The Presence Process asks us to challenge this outdated belief system and the inevitable self-imposed perceptual prison of victim mentality that is supported and maintained by endless group meetings. It also asks addicts who already attend these meetings to observe how supposedly abstaining or recovering addicts have transferred their addictive behavior into other aspects of their life experience. Recovering alcoholics smoke more. Recovering cigarette smokers eat more. Recovering heroin users turn to painkillers.

"Recovery" (the act of covering up the suppressed issues that our life experience is attempting to expose) always leads to living in quiet desperation, while "discovery' (embracing our surfacing suppressed issues as raw material for emotional growth) always leads to life. Just like our medications, the need for attending endless support group meetings will automatically diminish and cease altogether as the negative charge is neutralized in our emotional body. Addiction is not a crime or a sin or a life-sentence. It is an experience, and all experiences can be changed.

The Presence Process asks us to embrace the possibility that we are standing right on the brink of an evolution in human healthcare. From having to run to another for insight into our own condition and for the possibility of making real changes to the quality of our life experiences, we are now being invited to realize that these capacities that we have automatically sought "out there" are actually found within each of us. Up to now, the group paradigm of the 12-Step Program has been a necessary part of our evolution. It has enabled many to tread water when they most certainly would have drowned. But now we have something to swim towards. Our Inner Presence is the rock of solid ground that will enable us to step upon dry land again.

What we are now being asked to consider is that there is a 13th Step, a step that is not found by moving outward into the world, but by moving deeper into ourselves. This does not negate in any way the experiences that have brought us to this point; this acknowledges them as a necessary part of our evolution. But like our journey up any stairway, unless we lift our foot off the step we are on, we cannot place it on the next step, one that invites us to evolve from "recovery" to "discovery" and from quiet acceptance of our predicament to a bold leap into the possibility of "no order of difficulty".

The Presence Process also asks those of us with chronic, incurable, or supposedly terminal afflictions to challenge the outdated belief systems of the allopathic and psychiatric communities. We must not believe that what we suffer from is incurable just because a doctor tells us so. In the language of authenticity, the word "incurable" means, "I do not know what to do for you." Yet doctors have used it to mean, "You are going to die, and there is nothing anyone can do about it." We must challenge the blind belief systems of those individuals who deal only with the surface of life as well as of those who have become increasingly cerebral about everything.

The allopathic profession is magnificent at coping with, controlling, and sedating physical symptomatic trauma. However, a large portion of this community does not as yet have much understanding about the causal aspect of addiction or affliction. For example, if we are in a car accident and physically injured, or if the symptoms of our diseased condition or our addiction are getting to a point that living has become unbearable, then going to a doctor or a medical specialist is absolutely necessary. They know how to mend bones and heal wounds. They know how to sedate and control physical, mental, and emotional symptoms so that we can function "normally". However, if we want to neutralize the causal emotional charge that is unconsciously driving us to manifest accidents that are injuring us or diseases that are physically, mentally, or emotionally debilitating to us, then a medical practitioner is possibly the last person that we may consider approaching. This is because their training has taught them to seek physical explanations for states of disease. Their specialty is in the realm of the effect and not the cause.

The Presence Process takes a confident step in a new direction. It demonstrates to all who are willing to dive into their own emotional abyss that by sincerely applying oneself to the journey of emotional growth, one can completely alleviate the cause of addictions and afflictions. It does not mean that this is an easy or a quick approach. Illegal drugs, pharmaceuticals, and operations *are* the easy approach. Emotional growth is one of the most challenging paths that we can undertake in this emotionally unbalanced, mentally confused, and physically distracted age. Yet, because of The Pathway of Awareness that we all share, it guarantees success.

As challenging as emotional growth may be for some of us, it is far more preferable than the dependency created by being condemned to a life sentence of support group meetings. It is also far more preferable than living with a physical disease that is made more unbearable by the side effects of prescription medication. The Presence Process is an invitation to move beyond these uncomfortable realities altogether. In the end, no matter what form it may take, an addiction is an affliction and an affliction is an addiction.

Society as a whole still thinks that addiction is caused by poverty, laziness, a lack of education, weakness of character, or drug pushers. These so-called causes of addiction are actually all effects and therefore cannot be the cause of anything.

All addiction is caused by inner emotional discomfort.

Depending on the severity of our condition, it can take moving through The Presence Process several times to completely neutralize the causal charge in our emotional body. Completing this journey once may initially assist us in neutralizing our negative emotional charge enough to comfortably disengage from our addictive behavior or to decrease our medication to a point that we do not have to endure the unpleasant side effects. The second time through this Process may then assist us in gaining a deeper conscious insight into the cause of our emotional discomfort in order to consciously begin the task of neutralizing it. The third time through may then assist us in taking our attention completely off our uncomfortable predicament so that we may begin exploring our life's purpose.

By accomplishing this, we will truly realize that our past—every little detail of it—served to bring us into the wholeness of present moment awareness. We will then realize that having guilt, shame, and regret for what we have been through is founded on misinterpretation. In the present moment, we are always greeted by the fragrance of gratitude. As we enter present moment awareness, we automatically feel gratitude for every aspect of the journey that spurred us on to re-enter the heart of our own Inner Presence. This is because the present moment is all-inclusive and thereby acknowledges every life experience as a blessing.

Addictive behavior or severe affliction bear no reflection on who and what we are; it is an experience that we are having. Once we have gained the insight that calls to us from within this experience, we can change it and move on.

TRADING IN RESULTS FOR CONSEQUENCES

IN LIFE, WE OFTEN do not say what we mean or mean what we say. For example, when many of us speak of abundance, we actually mean money; and when many of us speak of health, we actually mean our appearance; and when many of us speak of joy, we actually mean happiness. The difference between experiencing joy, abundance, and health, and acquiring money, a good appearance, and happiness is vast. The former are inclusive while the latter are exclusive. Joy is the state in which we allow ourselves to experience *everything* without judgment or concern. Abundance pertains to being grateful for *all* the physical, mental, and emotional energies that flow through our life experience. Health pertains to attending to the well-being of *every* aspect of our physical, mental, and emotional experience. However, happiness requires that "this" happens and that "that" does not happen, while money is just cash, and appearance is only skin deep.

The Presence Process is not concerned with happiness, money, or appearances. Instead, it is a means to prepare the garden of our life experience to plant, nurture, and bear the inherent fruits of present moment awareness: joy, abundance, and health. Because of our unconscious needs and wants, it is most likely that we will enter this journey with very specific and therefore exclusive intentions. This is natural. However, this Process is not about specifics; it is about opening the horizons of our life experience so that we may become inclusive and therefore all-embracing.

Oneness is inclusive and all embracing.

The Presence Process intends to remind us that joy is in everything, that abundance is in everything, and that health is in everything. Because this is so, joy *is* abundance, abundance *is* health, and health *is* joy. If we truly embrace one of these qualities in our life experience, we automatically embrace them all.

As we move through The Presence Process, it is natural that we will seek results. We have all grown up in a world where almost every aspect of our experience is a means to an end and where the outcome of almost all of our activities is held up to some form of measurement. It is unlikely therefore that we have learnt how to be unconditional. Because of this, it is natural that we will want to monitor our progress and measure our success through this Process by watching our outer life circumstances—even though we are asked not to. We are asked not to initially be preoccupied with results because initially we will not know where to look to see these results and will inevitably examine the wrong aspects of our outer life experience. There is no standardized measurement in this Process by which to gauge success. Our false expectations will always dampen our efforts and instill doubts. This is because our looking for results will always initially be motivated by our unconscious needs and wants. If we could take an honest look within, we would be able to see that:

*Unconsciously what we really need and want is for the big
black hole in our heart to be filled.*

The Presence Process is not about satisfying our unconscious needs and
wants because *they can never be satisfied*. That is what defines a desire as
being a desire; it is an emotional hunger that can never be satisfied. The
Presence Process is therefore not about satisfying our desires; it is about
teaching us how to deliver ourselves beyond them so that we can experience one single moment of real choice.

Of course we will need or want to know that something is really happening as a consequence of having entered this Process. This is natural and
completely acceptable. Following the easy instructions given to us at the
commencement of and throughout this journey will ensure that we will
receive ongoing confirmation that "something is happening". This
confirmation will occur because this Process is real and therefore has an
immediate impact on our inner and outer experiences. However, the initial consequences of entering this journey may not be what we desire or
expect. In fact they seldom are. They seldom are because:

*No matter how physically prepared we believe we are, no matter
how mentally agile we think we are, no matter how emotionally
mature or spiritually aware we may perceive ourselves to be, we
are all on some level entering a journey like this in hopes that it
will douse the flames of our unconscious needs and wants.*

The hard cold fact about living in this world is that since we departed
our childhood, the extent to which we have been able to subdue our needs
and wants has been our conscious and unconscious barometer for achievement. If we do not subdue these restless inner voices, we automatically
assume that we are not accomplishing anything. If we do, we feel successful. This is why we have consistently been led astray by the outer world:
because the outer world can only speak to our needs and wants—not to *us*.

In the past, we may have attempted to calm these inner cries for attention by adjusting our outer physical circumstances through fasting or
exercise routines, or through prescription medication and/or addictive
self-medication. We may have tried to quiet our needs and wants through

food, sex, work, or "helping" others. We may also have attempted to still these cries for attention by adjusting our mental circumstances through mind-control techniques, hypnosis, or positive thinking. We may have read many self-help books, attended New Age workshops, and gone through hours or even years of therapy. As we will have noticed, none of the changes initiated by these outer approaches are permanent. They are camouflage. They are like the act of treading water; they tire us and take us nowhere. They haven't achieved anything real and therefore lasting.

Through our efforts, we may have remained for long periods in a state of recovery, but unconsciously we would have had an awareness of the pre-cariousness of our emotional status quo. A recovering addict, even after sixty years, is always still at risk of betraying their sobriety. This is because the act of recovery is engaging in the artificial peace of quiet desperation. Recovery is not *discovery*, and without real discovery, there is no real and therefore lasting transformation in the quality of our life experience. Recovery places its attention on the effect while discovery dives into the depths of the cause. We cannot change a cause of anything by fiddling with the effect, so the only prize for engaging in recovery is inevitable self-deceptive quiet desperation. The Presence Process seeks out the cause knowing that *when the cause is taken care of, the effect is automatic*. This is why The Presence Process is not concerned with "results". We prefer to com-municate in terms of "consequences". Communicating in terms of results is to think in terms of an outcome that is not a certainty. Results cannot be guaranteed. Results must be graded and are too often attached to the seek-ing of acknowledgement and approval. Therefore, we prefer to approach this work in terms of consequences. A consequence is an effect. Consequences will happen automatically as a response to the causal nature of this Process. Everything about The Presence Process is causal and there-fore consequences are inevitable. Results are too often measured by the fulfillment—or not—of our unconscious needs and wants. A consequence is an effect of a causal action. A result is too often an opinion. Therefore, The Presence Process asks us to trade in result-mentality for consequence-mentality.

We have already discussed The Pathway of Awareness and The Seven-Year Cycle, and so there is no need to go into a detailed explanation as to why cleansing our emotional body is necessary to restore balance to the quality of our life experience. If we are not clear on this point it is advised we reread The Pathway of Awareness and the Seven-Year Cycle. What *this* discussion intends to bring to our attention is that the consequences of willingly entering our emotional body to neutralize our negative emotional charge through conscious breathing, gaining mental clarity, and "feeling" are not initially what we may expect. Actively allowing ourselves to become aware of our negative emotional charge is not an experience everyone willingly invites into his or her life because as we have already stated, initially it is not easy, and it may not cause us to feel "good". This is precisely because it does have a *real and immediate impact* on our life experience.

Consider what the word "impact" feels like.

The main reason we are not experiencing the quality of effortless joy, abundance, and health in our life experience right now is because of our negative emotional charge. This negative emotional charge is a blockage in our emotional body that causes resistance. Because we have not known how to deal with it, we have further resisted it by suppressing our awareness of it. All this resistance accumulates and creates heat and this heat causes us discomfort. To cope with this discomfort, we have tried to be happy, to appear fine, and to make enough money in an attempt to assist us to feel good about our life experience. While this negative emotional charge unconsciously dominates our thoughts, words, and deeds, we can only experience life as a constant laboring to fulfill the seemingly endless eruption of the needs and wants that arise from within us. Under such circumstances, *real* joy, abundance, and health are not a possibility. Unlike the endless quest for happiness, money, and a perfect appearance, real joy, abundance, and health are not a means to an end. They are only experienced therefore when we are truly at peace with the moment that we are in. Joy, abundance, and health are automatic by-products of present moment awareness. Like our Inner Presence, they are already within us. It is our attention that is elsewhere.

One of the reasons we may enter an experience like The Presence Process is because we are secretly hoping for a magical quick fix that will make everything alright by dissolving all our difficulties into nothingness. This is normal. We live in an instant gratification society. We have also suffered with our emotional discomforts for so long and are all on some level living in quiet desperation. Fortunately, as our past will have taught us, there is no quick or easy way around our present circumstances that has had any real and therefore lasting impact on the quality of our life experience. There are plenty of escape routes—but there is no peace in any of them. This is the hard cold truth about the emotional body: there is no way *around* it. The only way out is *through* and the only way through is *in*.

> *Only by looking deeply within yourself can you deepen*
> *your relationship with yourself.*

The Presence Process teaches us everything that we require to accomplish the task of looking deeply within ourselves. In hindsight, we will discover that very little is asked of us for what we achieve by completing this journey. However, our conscious participation and commitment are essential to empower us with the reward of being able to embrace the frequency of responsibility through understanding *and* experience. That is why this section has been written: because understanding the real nature of this quest as best as we can *right now* will save us from unnecessary drama, false expectations, and bowing out because of physical, mental, and emotional discomfort or resistance.

We must accept that if we are born into this world and have become "normal" citizens of our communities, then there is a storm raging within us. This is because what is accepted as normality in this world is a state of quiet desperation. As much as we might like to deny its existence, this controlled and sedated inner storm cannot be hidden. By gazing across the planet we can see the outer casualties of this inner condition everywhere. It is the storm of duality. It is the war between authenticity and the inauthentic. It is the great divide between Presence and pretence. It is the vast canyon of fear, anger, and grief between the adult and the child self. If we seek *real* peace, then we must enter this storm willingly and consciously. We do not have to take up the issues of the outer world to enter this storm because the doorway into its chaos is within each of us.

The Presence Process invites us to willingly step into our inner storm like a bungee jumper leaping into a canyon. Our Inner Presence will be the harness that will always guide our bravery and our foolishness. It will steer us into the eye of this storm and will facilitate us until we reach the other side. Entering this inner storm consciously will enable us to grow in ways we cannot yet imagine. Its winds will blast the fog of "living in time" from our life experience, and its torrential downpour will wash us clean of our illusions. Our inner emotional storm is a deliberate doorway. It prevents those not yet ready from taking the steps necessary to bridge the gap that enables our inner conflicts to dissolve into Oneness. It convinces those who still need their rest to stay in the dream of time. This inner storm is not an accident. It is both an invitation and a deterrent. It is a deliberate rite of passage for the Soul.

Although we have this book in our hands, The Presence Process is not an outer journey: it is an inner journey. We may not fully understand what this means yet, but through experience the full meaning of "an inner journey" will dawn in our awareness. An inner journey means that nothing is going to be adjusted out there in the world. We are going to leave the world alone. We are not going to clean the mirror in an attempt to remove the blemishes from the face of our life experience. We are going to use the mirror, or our experience of the world, as a means to see our blemishes more clearly. All adjustments to be made will take place *within* us because that is the only place a real and therefore lasting adjustment can be accomplished.

Our emotional body, although we can externalize it quite easily with our drama, is within us. The automatic consequence of entering this journey is that we are going to be making very real adjustments to our emotional body. Our consciously connected breathing, the reading materials, our Presence Activating Statements, and the perceptual tools all serve to accomplish this purpose gently and deliberately. What is important to grasp is this: whether we are aware of it or not, the focus of our attention and intention *is* initially going to be placed upon our negative emotional charge because:

By entering this journey, we are agreeing to consciously attend to our emotional blockages.

We must learn how to attend to our emotional blockages because it is the presence of *our* conscious attention and *our* compassionate intention that successfully neutralizes them. No one else can accomplish this on our behalf. Our present moment awareness alone will accomplish the task. *We must consciously feel what is out of balance to restore the balance.* In other words, we must feel it to heal it. In the same breath, it is important to remember that as we willingly approach this task we will not be given more than we can manage—but often not less. By intending to hold certain understandings in our heart right now, we will ensure a gentler journey. One of these understandings is this:

Our outer world experience right now is an effect—all of it.

Why must we keep this understanding in our heart? Because by deliberately placing our attention and intention upon our negative emotional charge, we are going to manifest outer physical, mental, and emotional experiences that mirror what we are focusing on internally. For most of us, the outer reflection (the effect) of consciously and willingly placing our attention on our inner negative emotional charge (the cause) is that we begin to feel unhappy, we do not "appear" to look so good, and we start struggling with our relationship with money. In other words, as we initially journey into The Presence Process, it may appear outwardly that our outer life experience is getting worse! It may appear that our needs and wants are not only being ignored, but that they are being exaggerated. This is not real. It is not true. It is a reflection of something from our childhood. However, because of our addiction to believing that the effect is the cause, or that the outer world is the reason we do not feel at peace within, it is likely that we will react negatively to this sudden change in circumstances.

We must therefore be vigilant. We must be aware. A chapter called "Confirmation" has been written and placed strategically in Part II of this book to empower us to consciously move through these sudden outer changes with greater inner awareness.

If our life experience appears to *seemingly* deteriorate or enter increased discomfort or "strangeness", we must remind ourselves that this is occurring because by entering The Presence Process, we are deliberately placing our attention on our emotional blockages. We must remind ourselves that these outer indicators of increased turbulence in our life experience are actually very positive! These are clear signs of progress. However, we must also keep in mind that there is a child within us, a child that is needing and wanting happiness, who is seeking to appear good, and is intent on making lots of money to buy stuff in order to feel more secure. To this childlike aspect of our Being, the sudden change in our outer circumstances may feel disastrous. It may feel like "the end of our world". On one level it is: it is the end of our world of pretence. Our pretence must dissolve in order for us to re-experience our Inner Presence. So as we go through these uncomfortable experiences, we must have patience and compassion for ourselves.

This is why we are asked to *trust the Process*. This is why we are told that the only way *out* is *through*. This is why we are told to complete the Process *no matter what*. It is better not to start this journey than to run away just as our focus begins zeroing in on our emotional blockages. This sudden outer experience of physical, mental, and emotional discomfort *will always pass* as long as we complete the Process because it is *part* of the Process. It is deliberately coming to pass. It is deliberately coming to the surface to be neutralized. This *is* how it is neutralized: not by suppressing it but by *allowing it to surface*. There is nothing "wrong" because we do not feel "good". Being confused and uncomfortable when intending to clear emotional debris is a favorable condition. Initially, it is a favorable consequence. Just because we are becoming increasingly uncomfortable does not imply that we are doing the Process incorrectly. In fact, the opposite is true: if we find that at times we are struggling physically, mentally, and emotionally, it is because *we are really doing the work*. This is opposite to what the world has taught us to perceive as accomplishment or as a barometer for success.

Only by witnessing firsthand how we move into, through, and out of these uncomfortable experiences do we truly come to *know* that we are completely responsible for the quality of our life experience. Only by accomplishing this do we *know* that taking care of our emotional growth is one of our greatest responsibilities. Only by witnessing this do we really *see* that our outer world is a reflection of our inner condition. Only by moving through this experience can we *witness* the awesome power of our Inner Presence. In this way, The Presence Process uses experience as a means of validation: not the experiences we want or need, but the experiences that are necessary to liberate us by showing us what is real and possible.

As we head into the completion phase of The Presence Process, the quality of our life experience will automatically move into a state of increased harmony. This time our restored sense of balance will not be quiet desperation, and it will not be because we are controlling or sedating our inner emotional condition. It will be because we have neutralized a portion of our negative emotional charge. From our point of completion, we will then be experiencing increased moments of spontaneous joy, natural abundance, and vibrant health. Then, if we seek to clear away yet another layer of emotional debris, we can re-enter this Process and again consciously take a deliberate dive into our emotional body. We can repeat The Presence Process as often as we feel inclined. Each time we enter it, it will meet us at our adjusted point of present moment awareness. Each time we consciously choose to dive into our emotional body with the intent of improving the quality of our life experience, our outer world will initially appear to move into discomfort *because* we are deliberately placing our attention on the inner discomforts. In other words:

It is our willingness to become aware of our imbalances that restores balance to the quality of our experience.

This is therefore the invitation being placed before us by The Presence Process:

To learn through experience not to fear or resist the inevitable discomforts that arise from emotional processing and hence from emotional growth. It is to learn through experience not to react to emotional processing by dramatically behaving as if our world is ending. Instead, it is to learn through experience to embrace the discomforts of emotional processing as a sign of our inner progress. The invitation being extended here is to willingly ride our inner dragon and to learn from experience that our inner dragon is only tamed when we consciously choose to ride it.

Anyone who tries to convince us that we can make any real and lasting adjustment to the quality of our life experience without experiencing what the mind perceives as discomfort is to be viewed dubiously. Our willingness to consciously interact with our inner discomfort is the very alchemy that fuels our transformation. This does not mean that we ever have to suffer unnecessarily or mindlessly; it means we must face what is real in a real way if we want to activate real movement in the quality of our life experience. If that is uncomfortable, facing the discomfort is what *being real* is, not pretending it away.

The Presence Process is therefore the battleground of emotional warriors. It is an opportunity to willingly step forward and unsheathe the sword that cuts us free of time. It quickly separates the wheat from the chaff. This work is not about easy or good. It is not about happiness, or appearances, or money. It is about getting real. It is about growing up emotionally. It is about authenticity and integrity. It is about grasping our life with both hands and raising ourselves up from being "the emotionally dead".

> *There are a million excuses to quit that the mind*
> *will find acceptable.*

The strange thing about our wanting to change the quality of our life experience is that there is a part of our life experience that really does not want to be changed: our mind. Our mind is the "better the devil you know" voice in our head. It always initially encourages us when we ask for change. However, it is always bluffing. It is just pretending to be on our side so that we do not see its ploy. It is just pretending because the mind actually prefers familiarity. That is why habits are so challenging to defuse. The mind does not approve of change at all! It encourages it and even willingly comes to our aid in suggesting the many wonderful and inventive ways which we can employ to change the quality of our present circumstances. Yet the moment we *really* attempt any of these suggestions and start to activate change in our life experience, the mind will play another tune. The moment our experience becomes unfamiliar, the mind will inject our thoughts with words like "bad", "wrong", "dangerous", "harmful", "evil", "uncomfortable", and so on. These words will cause us to feel afraid, and the fear will then cause us to doubt and question the new direction in which we are moving. The mind will encourage us then to scramble back to what is familiar so as to return to and thereby restore our sense of comfort—even if it is a habit that is literally killing us. Better the devil we know! So if we use the mind as a means to gauge the consequences of our attempts to make any real changes in the quality of our life experience, we are entering a catch-22 situation.

We ask for change.
We are given the opportunity to change.
We embrace the opportunity.
We start feeling different.
The mind tells us that this feeling is "wrong".
We become afraid.
We turn against that which is changing our experience.
We return to what is familiar and safe.
Nothing is accomplished.
We feel more frustrated and disillusioned than before.
The mind has grown stronger, and we have become weaker.

That is why we are advised to commit to completing The Presence Process—no matter what. As we begin, we must be clear that we intend to finish no matter what experiences we go through. We must finish every Session no matter what our mind tells us because our mind will be the last to embrace or encourage the changes we will initially perceive in our outer life experience by facing up to our inner emotional discomfort. Not finishing will give the mind added strength and dominance over our spirit.

PART II

PREPARING FOR THE JOURNEY

BEFORE TAKING ANY journey in life, it is beneficial to make careful preparations because it is the preparation for the journey that adds to its overall quality and that goes a long way to ensuring its successful completion. This is what Part II of *The Presence Process* enables us to accomplish. We have been thoroughly informed about what this journey intends. Now we must make final preparations before entering the experience.

THE PROCESS TRINITY

WE ARE NOW READY TO BEGIN taking a closer look at the structure of The Presence Process, at the nuts and bolts of the procedure. The trinity of this Process is the breathing exercise, the Presence Activating Statements, and the reading materials that contain our perceptual tools.

I. The Breathing Exercise

Consciously connected breathing is the heart of The Presence Process because it is our primary tool for accumulating present moment awareness. The Breathing Exercise, which will be taught to us during our first Session, is to be attended to twice a day for a minimum of 15 minutes—

no matter what. Consistency is where the power lies. This cannot be over-emphasized. Erratic attendance to this part of the Process will cause unnecessary difficulties along the way. By surrendering to this part of the Process, we are literally carried through the rest of it consciously. Avoiding this part of the Process means we will feel that we have to make unnecessary effort to carry ourselves. We will thus unconsciously resort to outer drama and commotion to feel like something is happening.

There are two main procedures unfolding simultaneously when we consciously connect our breathing:

1   **The first procedure is the gathering of present moment awareness.** This is an automatic by-product of breathing without pausing. For every moment that we spend focusing both our attention and intention on breathing without pausing, we are accumulating present moment awareness. Our intention during a dedicated breathing session must be *to not pause for the entire session* and in doing so to accumulate as much present moment awareness as possible. Our mind/ego will give us 101 good physical, mental, or emotional reasons to stop or to pause during our breathing sessions. Our task is to breathe without pausing no matter what. This in turn enables us to strengthen our personal will. For now, all we need to know is this: there is nothing more important in this Process than attending to our Breathing Exercises everyday.

It is interesting to note that we humans are the only breathing creatures who consistently and unconsciously embed pausing into our breathing cycle. Watch a dog or a cat and see how they breathe continuously without pausing. If they become alarmed or frightened, their connected breathing intensifies and speeds up to bring more present moment awareness and oxygen into their body. In comparison, we humans are continually pausing between breaths. When we become alarmed or frightened, we stop breathing altogether or enter an unbalanced breathing cycle that causes hyperventilation or asthma. This habit of pausing between our breaths occurs whenever we enter the illusionary mental realm that we call "time". Whenever we are absorbed by the circumstances of the past or the projected future, or whenever we exit the present moment by placing our attention beyond our present circumstances, we pause between breaths. Whenever we are not present, our breathing is not consciously connected because consciously connected breathing only occurs in the present moment. If we observe the people around us, we will see that they are consistently pausing. Breathing creatures that do not live "in time" do not pause unconsciously. One of the benefits of The Presence Process is that it automatically brings our attention to the disconnected condition of our breathing mechanism. As a consequence, we automatically begin restoring balance to our breathing pattern. The way we breathe, especially during our Breathing Exercises, is an exact reflection of the way we live our life. Are we connected and present, or are we disconnected and absent?

2   **The second procedure at work during a consciously connected breathing session is oxygenation.** Increased oxygenation occurs during a breathing session because our breathing pattern is normalized. All breathing creatures (aside from whales, dolphins, seals, crocodiles, hippopotami, and others that hold their breath deliberately) breathe fully and without pausing to maintain full present moment awareness and oxygenation. We humans, aside from pausing, are also in the habit of using less than 20% of our lung capacity. We live in a condition that is not only disconnected from the present moment, but that is also seriously oxygen-deprived. The benefits of increased oxygenation can best be summarized in the following statement: *Metaphorically, on a purely physical level, oxygen is life.* If we meditate on this for a few moments, we will integrate that it is in our best interest to oxygenate our physical form efficiently. Breathing deeply and fully with each breath throughout a session is therefore encouraged but by no means essential. It is not essential because The Presence Process pivots on the gathering of present moment awareness and not on oxygenation to achieve its objective. Present moment awareness accumulates automatically when we consciously connect our breathing. Increased oxygenation is an added bonus. Our thirst for oxygen automatically increases the more present we become.

Consciously connected breathing is certainly not to be confused with hyperventilation. Hyperventilation is usually a consequence of an imbalance between oxygen and carbon dioxide and results from forced, unnatural, exaggerated, and traumatic breathing. Consciously connected breathing instills balance and is not unnatural; it releases trauma as opposed to stimulating it. Any and all discomfort experienced from consciously connected breathing is unresolved past trauma surfacing to be integrated by our present moment awareness. All discomfort experienced during a consciously connected breathing session is deliberately coming to pass. It must be welcomed, not repelled.

During the initial stages of each consciously connected breathing session, we all face varying levels of personal resistance. This is normal. We either overcome it or it overcomes us. There are three levels of resistance that we may experience during breathing sessions.

1   **The first level of resistance is physical** and is evident when we say to ourselves: "I do not feel like doing this; it is too hard."

2   **The second level of resistance is mental** and is evident when we say to ourselves: "I do not feel like doing this because nothing is really happening."

3   **The third level of resistance is emotional** and is evident when we say to ourselves: "I think I can stop now because I feel alright, or fine, or okay (or any of the emotionally 'numb' words)".

We know we have passed through all resistance when, in the midst of a breathing session, we can honestly say to ourselves:

"This is fantastic; I feel like I can breathe like this forever."

Regardless of what experience we have during our breathing sessions, it is helpful to remember that just the act of keeping our breath connected to the best of our ability accomplishes the requirements of each breathing session. We must not approach these sessions expecting to have some sort of profound experience. We must not approach them with any other intention but to keep our breathing connected. Each breathing session we attend to will be different, and there is no prescribed experience that we are supposed to accomplish.

During The Presence Process, the breathing sessions are not intended to be the *experience—our life is.*

It is also important to be aware that there are going to be instances during The Presence Process when we feel unable to stay conscious during our Breathing Exercises: we keep falling asleep. This can be caused by our resistance to what is unfolding, but often it is not. What happens when we consciously connect our breathing is that we are deliberately anchoring ourselves to the present moment instead of unconsciously allowing our attention to drift into the past or the projected future. Consequently, instead of our attention leaving the present moment and journeying into time, these illusionary and unconscious places in time are drawn towards us. Until we have accumulated a certain degree of present moment awareness, some of these illusionary places can override our attempts to anchor ourselves in the present moment and instead drag us out into time. Our experience of this will be that without warning we will slip into a sleep state because in the present moment unconsciousness appears as sleep. We will only realize that this has happened when we awaken and discover that we have been sleeping instead of consciously connecting our breathing.

This is a normal experience for all of us when we attempt to begin extracting our consciousness from time. We must not beat ourselves up about it. We can, during periods of our journey through The Presence Process, get ourselves enmeshed in what appears to be a sleep-loop: every time we sit down to breathe, we almost immediately fall asleep! We must not be concerned. We must persevere. The only way out of this predicament is through it. We must continue to persevere until we break through the wall of unconsciousness. Through consistent daily attention to our Breathing Exercise, we will eventually accumulate enough present moment awareness to successfully anchor our attention in the present moment while we breathe. Then these unconscious places in time will not drag us into sleep. Instead, we will drag these unconscious experiences of the past into the present moment in which they will be integrated. They are all illusions, and no illusion can survive in the present moment. As each one of these integrates, we will gain more and more personal present moment awareness.

II. Presence Activating Statements

In each Session, we are given a Presence Activating Statement. These are directed at our conscious and unconscious mind-field. They are designed to realign our behavioral patterns and belief systems as well as to activate conscious awareness of aspects of our experience that are emotionally blocked and suppressed. By becoming conscious of these suppressed issues, we are able to integrate them. The more we apply ourselves to the mental repetition of these Presence Activators, the more efficiently they will serve us.

Our ego will at times resist and reject these Presence Activators. This is normal. Each instance that we realize that we have forgotten to repeat our Statement mentally and thus begin repeating it again is actually a necessary part of the Presence Activating process. We must therefore not lay negative judgments on ourselves when we appear to completely forget to attend to our mental repetition. The process of forgetting and then remembering is surprisingly beneficial to us because it strengthens the mental muscle that we use to bring our attention into the present moment. These Presence Activators are also designed to replace our "stinking thinking" (our unproductive thought patterns) with responsible mental processes. Therefore, whenever we are not mentally occupied, it serves us well to repeat our Presence Activating Statements.

These Presence Activators are not wishful or positive thinking. They are *causal*. This means they do not concern themselves with the effects of our emotional blockages, but with the causes. A person who goes around saying, "I am abundant" over and over to himself or herself because they have no money is using positive (wishful) thinking. They have derived their mental affirmation from an outer physical manifestation (effect) of their inner emotional blockage. Their mental affirmation is not touching the cause of their lack of finances. In other words, their lack of money, which is their apparent point of focus, is an effect of their emotional blockage, not the cause. Therefore, their mental affirmation will be impotent. The Presence Activators we are given throughout this Process are more than mental affirmations. They ignore the physical manifestations (effects) of our emotional blockages and instead directly target the unconscious causal points of the discomfort in the quality of our life experience.

These Statements are also aligned with the understanding that if we want peace, we must first become aware of the chaos in our life, because it is only by resolving the chaos that we truly are able to restore peace. Thus, the Presence Activating Statements are deliberately designed to bring our awareness to the unconscious aspects of our experience that are having a negative impact on the quality of our life experience. The nature of The Presence Process is that we do not "wish" our chaos away, and neither do we ignore it; we consciously bring it to our attention so that we can resolve it consciously and responsibly and thus gain wisdom from it. By consciously taking responsibility for the quality of all the experiences that do not serve us, we automatically liberate ourselves from waiting for the world to change so that we can enjoy the quality of our life experience.

Another name for these Presence Activating Statements could be "conscious responses" because aside from the applications discussed above, we use them as a mental means to consciously respond to the experiences that we would normally have reacted to unconsciously.

III. The Reading Materials & Perceptual Tools

The reading materials for each Session, as well as those we have been reading up to this point, are deliberate. Notice that the word "deliberate" includes the word "liberate". These reading materials are not written in paragraphs or pages or chapters; they are written in sentences. They contain a massive amount of information that is impossible to digest by brief or hurried scanning. They contain years of experiences and insights that have been placed in thought-packages to facilitate personal revelations. They are written not only for our conscious awareness but also for that aspect of our experience that is presently unfolding unconsciously. For this reason, they may at times appear to be repetitive. *This book is in fact one long deliberate series of Presence Activating Statements.*

It will not serve us to leave our reading materials until the last moment of each Session period. The reading materials assigned to each Session are designed to mentally activate present moment awareness. Each new Session contains Perceptual Tools that we are to begin using during the course of that Session, so although we must not hurry through our required reading, it is of vital importance that we make it a top priority. These written materials are designed to add gentleness to our process

83

by enabling us to be more conscious of what is happening to us during each step of the journey. Reviewing these written materials at regular intervals is also highly beneficial, as the insights to be gained from them will deepen as our personal level of present moment awareness increases.

The Perceptual Tools shared with us through our reading are designed to realign our behavior from being reactive to responsive and to simultaneously replace unproductive belief systems with those that will serve us and that will enhance the entire quality of our life experience. Like any new venture, the Perceptual Tools that we are introduced to in The Presence Process require repeated application to gain proficiency. Only through experiencing the outcome of repeatedly applying them to our life experience will we integrate their benefits. There is no "doing" involved in applying these Perceptual Tools; they are a way of responding internally to the quality of our outer experiences. However, they do require that we make an effort to wield our thought processes consciously and responsibly.

⌬

GENERAL GUIDANCE FOR A GENTLE PROCESS

THE FOLLOWING INFORMATION will assist us in remaining clear about the intentions of The Presence Process so that we can remain steadfast in our commitment. Some of what we have already read will be repeated here as a means to recap and place emphasis. This is one of the sections in this book that we are advised to turn to whenever we are unclear, feel confused, or have questions about what is happening to us:

1   **Before entering Session One, it is important and facilitating to set an overall intention as to what we would like to accomplish by taking this journey.** It is best if this intention can be verbalized in one simple sentence. This intention will be realized because The Presence Process is an intention-driven journey. However, our journey towards the realization of this intention may not necessarily unfold as we anticipate it. Our inner growth will always come from what we do not know and unfold in a manner that we may not anticipate.

2   It is equally important to accept that our initial intention for entering this journey will change and even drop away completely as the Process unfolds. This is
because we will enter this Process in a place of need (past issues) and
want (future hopes). However, as we progress, these needs and wants
will begin to dissipate, enabling us to begin experiencing this Process
unconditionally.

3   It is likely that during the course of our Process, circumstances may arise that
may cause some of our breathing sessions to be unavoidably postponed or
delayed. We must not make an issue or a drama out of these occurrences. We will only understand why this happens in hindsight. Once
we have set our intentions and made our commitment to complete
this experience as instructed, we must make the best of each moment
as it unfolds.

4   This Process will always unfold in our best interest. However, what is in our
best interest is not always in line with our personal agenda. Therefore, we must not under any circumstances "push the river" or assume
we know what is supposed to happen or how it is supposed to unfold.
It is beneficial to face the fact that if we really knew what we wanted
and how to accomplish this, we would have achieved it by now. Our
responsibility is to follow the instruction throughout the Process as
closely as possible.

5   This Process is not about trying. There is no one "out there" to acknowledge us, no one for us to impress, and no one to judge our progress.
There are also no reference points by which to compare our progress.
By following the instructions to the best of our ability, we will automatically be delivered to where we really choose to be.

6   We must complete the Process to feel complete.

7   It is best to dress comfortably in loose-fitting clothing whenever we attend to
our Breathing Exercises and to attend to these in the same place throughout the
Process if possible. As well, we must attend to our daily breathing sessions in complete privacy if possible. This Process is inner work and is

not to be used for show or as a means to attract attention. Such behavior is drama and will achieve nothing.

8   It is recommended that we do not attend to our Breathing Exercises on an empty stomach or after a heavy meal.

9   It is highly recommended that we drink at least one and a half liters of pure water a day throughout the Process because The Presence Process automatically stimulates detoxification. We should not drink too much liquid in the hour before breathing.

10   We are strongly advised to abstain from consuming medications that cause drowsiness before attending to a breathing session. Only take medications that are absolutely necessary or that have been prescribed by a medical practitioner.

11   Be aware that as we move through this journey, our physical, mental, and emotional experiences will adjust as we begin to re-establish balance in the quality of our overall life experience. *We must not react to these adjustments as if something is wrong.* Our body may at times feel uncomfortable, our stomach may flush toxins from our system, and we may experience various aches and pains from past injuries resurfacing to be integrated by our conscious attention. Avoid the drama of running to doctors unnecessarily. If a condition persists and requires assisted relief so that we can continue with our process, we should by all means consult the relevant practitioner. However, we must not be distracted by becoming unnecessarily embroiled in our physical, mental, and emotional drama. We must also avoid taking a pill just because we feel uncomfortable. Our awareness of our various states of surfacing discomfort is required for this Process to be successful.

12   It is strongly advisable that we do not consume alcohol at all during the duration of the process. Alcohol, even in small quantities, sedates our authenticity and exaggerates our drama. This is something that only becomes obvious to us once we have gained a certain level of present moment awareness. However, if we enter this Process believing that we are

addicted to alcohol, it is best that we take the advice given in the discussion Beyond Addiction and Affliction.

13 **In the same light, it is recommended that we do not smoke marijuana or take any mind-altering substances at all during the entire Process.** These substances, marijuana in particular, prevent us from having conscious access to and hence awareness of the condition of our emotional body. It is counterproductive therefore for us to use marijuana, as it is an obstacle that prevents us from successfully releasing the suppressed traumas in the emotional body. The traumas it masks are the very issues that are causing addiction to or the need for these self-sedation and self-medicating practices in the first place.

14 **Despite popular belief, both marijuana and alcohol are highly addictive.** Misconceptions about the addictive nature of these substances stem from misconceptions about what the real nature of an addiction is. In The Presence Process, addiction is not only defined as something one does uncontrollably or habitually; it is also a random activity that one is magnetized towards when faced with *specific* emotional triggers. The general rule is that it is best to attend to our Breathing Exercises when we are not altered by outside substances.

Sobriety is a prerequisite for achieving authenticity.

15 **The Presence Process excels in neutralizing addictions.** All addictions are behaviors that are fueled unconsciously by the desire to sedate and control the discomfort of a negative charge in the emotional body. The Presence Process does not seek to control the addictive behavior, as this is to tamper only with the effect. The Presence Process automatically accesses the suppressed emotional charge and gently releases it so that the underlying emotional discomfort, the cause of all addiction, is neutralized. This Process puts forward that there is no such thing as incurable addiction. The Presence Process in this respect invites us to liberate ourselves from our victim mentality perception. It also invites us to evolve beyond the mindset that having an addictive experience sentences us to a life of endless support group meetings.

16 **We cannot, on any level, enter and enjoy this experience if we are doing it to please someone else.** This point cannot be over-emphasized. If we attempt to enter this Process to please or manipulate someone else, we will find the journey exceedingly challenging. In the same light, we cannot neutralize an addiction because someone else asks us to. We cannot do inner work to satisfy someone else's outer demands or requirements of us. In most cases, individuals who do not complete this journey fail to do so because they entered it with an agenda other than seeking to sincerely make a change in the quality of their own experience *for themselves.*

17 **It often happens that even when we enter a process like this willingly, we still find ourselves resisting the prescribed tasks, just like children do when given homework they do not like.** This Process is not homework. But it is the work required to get us "home". Every facet and element of this Process is deliberately designed from years of personal experience. The manner and structure in which The Presence Process is delivered is intended to support and navigate us so that maximum consequences are achieved in the most gentle manner possible. When we commit to this Process, we must commit 100%. We will only understand the value of its structural aspects in hindsight.

18 **During this journey, our ego may decide to make changes to the way the Process has been constructed.** The ego may decide, for example, to change the wording in a particular Presence Activating Statement or not to read particular aspects of the Process because it disagrees with the content of the subject matter. The ego may decide that we do not have to wield certain of the Perceptual Tools because we have already "done stuff like this". If we feel compelled to change any aspect of this Process, there are two facts we must face. The first is that only our ego will attempt to make a change to this material. The second is that our ego is always in the dark. It may think or believe that it understands everything, yet in reality, it "knows" nothing.

19 **Like any endeavor, the more we give of ourselves, the more we will receive.** Often we do not do what we are asked to, even if we know it is in our

best interest, because it is the only way we can exert any control over the seemingly ongoing chaos in our life experience. Once we enter this Process, we must do our best not to resist doing what we are asked as an unconscious or even conscious means to feel some control over what is happening. This journey is an opportunity to realize what it truly means to surrender. In The Presence Process the word "surrender" does not mean "to give up". It means "not to give up, no matter what". The Presence Process is all about surrender.

20 **We cannot control the consequences of this Process, although we may most certainly attempt to.** We cannot control present moment awareness; we can only lay a foundation that enables us to reawaken to it as a conscious part of our daily awareness.

21 **The ego is allergic to being present because the ego is a time-based identity.** The substance of the ego is founded on the trinity of our behavior, our appearance, and our life circumstances. It is within the dynamics of this trinity that we will see changes taking place from our inner work. Therefore, The Presence Process is a powerful antidote to the antics of the ego. As already stated, when we find ourselves resisting aspects of this Process, it is because we are entertaining the intentions of or attempting to protect the structure of our ego. The only way out is through.

22 **TRUST THE PROCESS.** These three words will be a life raft in moments of doubt and confusion. We all experience moments of doubt and confusion during this journey because there will be aspects of this experience that we will not be able to navigate, control, or understand with our mind. So once we commit to this journey, we must do our best to trust the process no matter what. The only way out is through.

23 **We may have moments during the Process in which we experience levels of intense resistance to what is happening to us.** It is normal for this to occur when deeply unconscious issues start to surface. During a breathing session, this will manifest as a desire to sleep or not to breathe. Resistance can also cause us to avoid mentally repeating our Presence

Activating Statements. This is when our will to show up and be present in our life will be flexed and put to the test. The only way out is through.

24 **Resistance may also manifest as reluctance to attend to our daily Breathing Exercise, as delaying our breathing sessions, as anger and irritation towards the Process itself, or as a feeling of depression or hopelessness.** Our resistance may even manifest physically as cold and flu-like symptoms and various chest maladies that seemingly enable us to feel justified in cancelling or postponing our breathing sessions. We *must* attend to our daily sessions—*especially* if we do not feel like it. The only way out is through.

25 **We may only understand this in hindsight, but it is worth planting the information in our mind- field right now:** *everything* **that happens to us from the moment that we commence our first breathing session is part of The Presence Process.** Everything! We are going to be facilitated by our Inner Presence 24 hours a day and well beyond our tenth Session. How and why this works will be explained during the course of the Process.

26 **Throughout The Presence Process, our unconscious memories will begin to surface so that we can consciously neutralize their negative impact on the quality of our life experience.** Because we have turned suppressing unwanted memories into a fine art form, these unconscious memories will not surface as pictures or images in our mind but as unfolding outer circumstances or as the way people around us behave. In other words, we are going to become increasingly aware that the behavior of people around us and the outer circumstances that we are experiencing are *deliberately* reminding us of the past. During the Process, we will be taught how to consciously integrate these externally reflected memories so that their negative effect on the quality of our life experience is neutralized.

27 **Remember always that this is a** *process.* It begins when we commit to it, and it does not reach a noticeable point of completion until we have taken the entire ride. Even then, it is still only a beginning. We may feel like we are getting nowhere when we are in the middle of the Process: this is because *we are in the middle of the Process.*

28 When we have completed this Process, we will realize that we have been shown a door, taught how to open it, and that the rest of our life experience is an opportunity to enter consciously into this place we call our "Inner Presence". The Presence Process is therefore not an end to anything: it is a beginning and a continuation.

29 When we have completed this Process, we will be newly trained in a practical art form that will equip us with the knowledge, experience, Perceptual Tools, and physical practice that enable us to process and integrate the quality of any event that may occur in our destiny. This ability will remove anxiety from our life experience. By continuing responsibly along the path that this Process initiates, we will make increasing deposits of present moment awareness into the bank account we call "our consciousness". The more present moment awareness we accumulate, the more conscious we will become.

30 It will be of great benefit to slowly reread the entire book when we reach completion. This is because as we journey through The Presence Process, we will be gathering an ever-increasing amount of present moment awareness. Consequently, when we reread the book, we will be doing so from a different level of consciousness. Therefore, we will enjoy many insights that we did not "get" during our initial reading. We will definitely have a few "Aha's!" as well as a few chuckles at the extent of our dramas.

31 Nobody died from breathing!

THE INTEGRATIVE APPROACH

EVEN IF WE BELIEVE that our childhood was a good one, the nature of being born into a conditional world means that we all had physical, mental, or emotional experiences that were uncomfortable. Our authentic essence is that we are unconditional beings and so entering any conditional experience is on some level traumatic.

One of the revelations that The Presence Process demonstrates to us experientially is that in the first seven years of our life any and all uncomfortable experiences arising from our entry into this conditional world are imprinted into and affect the condition of our emotional body. Our emotional body is therefore where the record of these occurrences is kept. When the moment arrives in our growth in which we are ready to step beyond the limitations that these initial childhood experiences may still be imposing on our present perceptions, it is into the emotional body we must therefore journey. To accomplish this task gently and responsibly, it is strongly recommended that we take an integrative approach.

The integrative approach to restoring balance to the quality of our life experience is based on the understanding that when we change a part of any aspect of our experience, we simultaneously change the condition of the whole. It is also based on the understanding that the effects that these changes have on the whole unfold organically in a manner that best serves the well-being of the whole. The integrative approach is also based on the understanding that to activate efficient and lasting change in the quality of our whole experience, we must make causal changes and not fiddle with effects.

Throughout The Presence Process, the individual parts of our life experience that we are working with to activate changes in the quality of our whole life experience are our physical body (sensations), our mental body (thoughts), and our emotional body (feelings). During our discussion on The Pathway of Awareness, it was explained to us why the causal point of the quality of our experiences in this world is grounded in the emotional body. If we are unclear on this point, it is advisable that we reread The Pathway of Awareness and the Seven-Year Cycle.

In this particular discussion, we are going to explore this subject further as a means to introduce the necessity for having two levels of entry into The Presence Process as well as for underlining the importance of approaching this experience patiently, gently, and responsibly.

In the world that we live in today, if we are dissatisfied with the quality of our experience, we will most likely attempt to make changes in our life by working with our outer physical circumstances. This is because the outer physical aspect of our experience is the most tangible and immediately accessible to us. However, even though we may be able to make a relatively quick change to our physical circumstances, these changes do not last very long because the physical aspects of our circumstances are always effects, not causal. Also, change is constant in the nature of our physical experience, so whatever we change physically will inevitably change yet again in time. We may attempt to use force to change something quickly in our physical world, but this means we will have to consistently invest large amounts of energy to maintain the conditions that we have changed. Making and maintaining physical changes in an attempt to alter the quality of our life experience, therefore, requires control and sedation of our circumstances. Such changes require that we use constant force to hold any changes we make in place. This is an impossible task.

We may also attempt to change the quality of our life experience mentally, by changing our mind about something. Mind Power and Positive Thinking Courses aspire to accomplish this. Changing our mind about something will eventually lead to an adjustment in the quality of the experience we are having. However, it will take longer for us to see the effect of the mental changes that we have made appear in our physical world than if we took a purely physical approach. These mentally-driven changes will last somewhat longer—as long as we do not change our mind again.

The extent and duration of our ability to change the quality of our life experiences by making mental changes are haphazard because this approach has to continually defend its accomplishments from the nature and content of our unconscious thought processes. We only really know what our unconscious thought processes are up to by observing the circumstances that we manifest in our field of experience that appear to be contradicting the intent of our attempted "positive thinking".

Just because we consciously change our mind about our circumstances does not mean that we automatically *feel* differently about them. Therefore, even if our conscious change of mind eventually accomplishes adjustments in our physical circumstances, until we really *feel* differently, no amount of mind control will allow us to arrive at an authentic sense of peace. Our unconscious feelings and the unconscious thought processes they breed will continue to disturb our peace of mind. A peaceful experience is not the result of just a positive thought; it is also underlined by a feeling. The feeling and thinking process must harmonize intimately to achieve our intended state of Being. So, like attempting to make purely physical changes, making purely mental changes in an attempt to adjust the quality of our experiences is again fiddling with the effects and does not address cause.

Fortunately, we also have the option of going directly to the roots of our discomforts and making causal adjustments. We can accomplish this by activating changes in the condition of our emotional body. This is the most challenging but the only truly effective and rewarding approach. Although it is challenging to make changes in the condition of our emotional body, once achieved, the effects are lasting. To activate changes in the emotional body, we have to approach it with gentleness and consistency. This requires commitment and perseverance. It is much like chopping down a big tree. We chop, chop, and chop. At times the work may appear endless. It may appear as if nothing is happening. Then, without any warning, we hear a cracking sound, and in a few seconds, the tree falls. Once it is falling, nothing can stop it. Once it is lying on the ground, we cannot put it back up again.

Adjusting the condition of our emotional body is just like this. We work at it consistently, and sometimes it feels like we are getting nowhere. But then a shift suddenly occurs, and when it does, nothing can stop it. When this inner shift has occurred, it is literally impossible to return our emotional body to its previous condition. Because of the emotional body's propensity for sudden shifts, the shifting experience has the potential to be traumatic if not approached consciously, gently, and responsibly. Therefore, diving directly into the emotional body and activating shifts is not recommended. The key words here are "gentleness", "patience", and "responsibility".

The Presence Process is designed with this intent. We do not dive into the emotional body just because we know that this is where the causal points of the quality of our life experiences can be accessed. The Presence Process works hard at physically and mentally preparing us for this procedure so that we are able to absorb these sudden shifts in our stride. These sudden shifts in the emotional body, when approached responsibly, are wonderful experiences in that they lead to immediate perceptual shifts; we literally see our world differently from the moment of the shift onward.

The consequence of this emotional adjustment then gradually filters through and manifests in the quality of our mental and physical experience. When it does, it is lasting and requires no effort to maintain. Adjusting the condition of our emotional body literally allows us to step into a new world experience without going anywhere. Approaching the task at hand in this manner is what in this work we call "the integrative approach".

To gain a deeper insight into how changes made to our physical, mental, and emotional bodies affect the quality of our life experiences, let us examine the condition of an adult who is struggling with a body that is significantly overweight. Because the overweight individual in our example is a "normal" adult, they may, like all of us, have become completely *trans*fixed by the physical aspects of their world. This means they may initially perceive that the cause of the uncomfortable quality of their life experience is to be found in what they see on the surface of things. Because of this, they are likely to approach the task of losing their weight as a purely physical procedure, assuming that resolving their overweight condition simply entails the removal of excessive fat from their physical body.

If they pursue this physical approach, they may decide to go on a fat-free diet or take a diet formula that enables them to dissolve the fats in their system. Or they may decide to initiate an exercise program or step up their current one in order to burn excess calories. They may even attempt a radical physical procedure like stapling their stomach or wiring their teeth together. These are all physical approaches. These are all attending to the effect and not the cause of the overweight experience. These approaches differ in the time it takes for their consequences to be perceived, depending on how drastic the physical measure is to which they resort. These approaches take effort. Some of them literally take blood, sweat, and tears—and substantial financial resources.

However, even if the weight is lost, it does not guarantee the outcome the individual is *really* seeking. They may feel better about themselves for a while because their appearance will have improved, but this will eventually wear off because the cause of their initial overweight condition was never physical. All diets fail in the long-term. Stapling an intestine shut cannot seal off the discomfort of the emotional turmoil that an overweight person does not know how to stomach. Wiring teeth together does not empower the overweight individual to express themselves and thus address their suppressed emotions. Therefore, even though these procedures may be quick, depending on how drastic they are, the sense of well-being achieved through them is inauthentic and therefore temporary. When the inner pain finally returns, it can be devastating because then there is nowhere to run.

These physical procedures will not resolve unconscious negative mental activities relating to self-image, nor will they quiet internal emotional eruptions that manifest physically as bingeing. They may stop the person eating, but the addiction to food as a means of self-medication and therefore as a means of sedation and control of what is occurring in the emotional body will be transferred into other behaviors. For a while they may look good, but their thoughts will continually get tangled in negativity. No matter how much fat is removed, surgically or otherwise, beneath the surface they will not *feel* good. The long-term outcome will be proof of this.

The consequence of making drastic physical changes is that it does affect our relationship with our mental and emotional bodies. If anything, making purely physical changes exaggerates our mental and emotional condition: the more we cover up our suffering by resorting to physical procedures, the worse we feel inside mentally and emotionally. Eventually the illusionary bubble of a surgically beautiful body will burst into mental chaos and emotional catastrophe. It may take a while, but it will happen. The moment the newly improved physique does not have an outer admiring audience, it will become infected by rumblings of inner despair. Making purely physical adjustments to deal with discomfort in the quality of our life experience is to set an emotional time bomb ticking; one day it will go off.

By gaining some sort of understanding about this, our overweight individual, through consistent failure with the purely physical approach, may get to a point where they attempt to approach their condition mentally. In other words, they may attempt to change their mind about the food they are eating or about the image they have had about themselves all their life. They may get to a point where they identify self-defeating thought patterns that are not serving them. They may enlist in a Mind

Power or Positive Affirmation Course. This attempt at a change of mind will make a difference, limited though it will be. If they keep working consistently at the "mind over matter" approach, they will eventually start losing weight, but only to a point. The adjustment they are able to make to their physical condition will also be a lot slower than if they resorted to physical procedures.

Unfortunately, any change that they achieve through mental reconditioning will be also temporary because the individual is still fiddling with an effect: their thoughts. They are not yet making any real causal adjustments. Under these circumstances, they may lose weight, but they will not achieve optimal weight loss for their physique. If they do, they will struggle to maintain it. This is because even though they may have activated an adjustment in their conscious thought processes, they will not have been able to protect the quality of their experience from the negative impact of their unconscious thoughts.

Integrating unconscious negative thought patterns is only possible when we adjust the condition of the emotional body, the place from which these thoughts arise. The extent to which the overweight individual's negative unconscious commotion continues will be therefore the extent to which their body holds onto excess weight. The consequence is that they will still continually run the risk of going off the rails every now and then. Then, when this occurs, they will again eat too much of the wrong foods and consequently think poorly of their undisciplined behavior. This will occur even though they have made up their mind that such negative activities are not beneficial. This will occur because they will not be able to stop their unconscious thought forms from manifesting as self-sabotage. They may look a bit better physically; they may think a bit better of themselves mentally, but underneath it all, they will not really *feel* any better. Because they do not feel better emotionally, they will forever be in danger of resorting to food or other negative activities that are a catalyst to gaining weight as a means to console themselves. The changes they have made in their conscious mental processes will also have negative consequences on their emotional condition because changing the nature of their conscious thought processes without attending to their unconscious thoughts is simply mental control. Sooner or later this control will be lost, and they will find themselves overcome by erupting tides of emotional disarray. To cope with this, they will resort to detrimental physical behavior.

When our overweight individual finally discovers that s/he is unable to have any real and lasting effect on their condition physically or mentally, they may finally choose to tackle their weight issue emotionally. This is, of course, the most challenging route for many of us to take because it requires the will to become authentic. This is why it is usually the last approach to be considered. Making changes to the emotional body requires gradual and consistent "process work". This is not a quick fix, yet when accomplished, lasting transformation is a consequence. As challenging as it may be, because it is causal, any amount of emotional work that is accomplished has deeply rewarding consequences.

An overweight person who resolves their emotional baggage immediately feels better about him/herself, and this filters through into every aspect of their thinking processes and therefore their physical circumstances. Their eating habits and their approach to their physical interaction with the world automatically adjust. Thereby their weight condition automatically and effortlessly regains balance. They do not have to diet; they automatically begin eating healthy foods. They no longer use food to suppress unresolved emotions, so they automatically eat less. They do not have to initiate and maintain any extreme exercise program because they automatically seek to enjoy their world by physically participating in it. Because they have made a causal change in the quality of their life experience, they also do not have to live with the anxiety that their overweight condition may suddenly return.

As stated in the beginning of this section, the integrative approach to adjusting the quality of our life experience is built on the understanding that our physical, mental, and emotional bodies are all reflections of each other and that the experiences occurring in each are intimately interlinked. It is also founded on the understanding that if we are being authentic about making real changes in the quality of our life experience, then we must not waste time and energy focused solely on the effects of our unresolved childhood experiences. We must intend to make changes at the causal point.

Of course the most accelerated path to take in making quick, efficient, and lasting changes to the quality of our life experience would be to not waste time on any physical or mental procedures but instead to zero in on our emotional body. However, to zero in on the emotional body to the exclusion of all else is not *a gentle approach* and may lead to very traumatic experiences. The gentlest approach is always involves the most integrated approach—the holistic approach. This entails working simultaneously with our physical, mental, *and* emotional bodies with an intent to gradually move into and positively alter the condition of the causal point: the emotional body.

In other words, we do not rush to the causal point of our condition just because we know where it is. We gently and methodically approach it as we would a tiny kitten that has been frightened by a loud noise. We take into account that an uncomfortable emotional cycle that has been repeating unconsciously in our life experience since our childhood is not deactivated overnight. This is how The Presence Process is structured therefore and makes its approach: gently, methodically, consistently, moving deliberately along The Pathway of Awareness, integrating physical, mental, and emotional procedures with the overall intent to restore balance to the condition of the emotional body. This is the art of the integrative approach; it moves gently through the layers of the effect until it touches and adjusts the cause.

It is upon the foundations of this integrative approach that the two levels of entry into The Presence Process have been designed. Because of the varying conditions of our individual experiences in this world, The Presence Process has a point of entry and an approach that is comfortable and accessible to everyone who seeks to restore balance to the quality of their life experience. The concept of applying the integrative approach to restoring balance to the quality of our life experience is therefore both simple and deeply complex. It involves common sense and paradox; it accomplishes its intentions in the moment but allows the passage of time for the consequences to filter through and manifest in our awareness. As an approach, it is observable on the surface of things and it is simultaneously active beneath the surface.

The integrative approach is what we call "process work", and it unfolds organically. It calls upon the stamina of patience to flow as a conscious current through all its endeavors. The integrative approach works with all the parts of the whole but keeps its eye on the causal point. It knows with certainty that when change is activated at the causal point of anything that the effect will automatically manifest in the whole. It also knows and therefore trusts that this ripple effect will unfold at a pace that is best for the well-being of the whole. There is no purpose in hurrying, for every experience that is activated must be fully digested for the nutritional benefits to be completely absorbed and incorporated. Hurrying causes indigestion and constipation.

The paradox about living in time is that whenever we complete anything, we want to see the benefits, outcomes, and consequences *right now*. When we finish a job for someone, we want to be paid immediately. When we achieve something that is important to us, we want to receive acknowledgement for it straight away. This is our fast food, fast-paced mentality. We do not save up to buy our first car; we go to the bank, and they buy it for us. Teenagers expect to become adults overnight, and adults expect to be able to attain a four-year degree in a one-year part-time program. Modern day mothers and fathers at times no longer wait for their babies to birth naturally. Often, the moment the mother is due, she quickly pops into the hospital, between her business meetings to have it "cut out". Even our vegetable and fruit produce is genetically engineered to grow faster. If we cannot have what we want now, we will seek it elsewhere.

We are addicted to instant gratification. However, we are never gratified because although we are making everything possible Now, we are never present to enjoy it Now. The moment we receive what we desire, our attention instantly jumps out of the present moment into the plotting of our next acquisition. This has created a world that is comfortable about living in debt, on borrowed time, and on somebody else's energy. We no longer own our houses or cars or even our clothes; the bank does. We have robbed ourselves of the satisfaction of accomplishment. There is no more "rite of passage"; there is only the fast lane. Children want to be teenagers, teenagers we want to be adults, and adults want to immediately accomplish a life's work before turning 30. We spend each moment running ahead of ourselves, believing that there is a destination to arrive at which will be saturated in endless happiness, acknowledgement, ease, and luxury. We are continually running away from something and towards something, and because everyone is doing it, we accept this approach and the subsequent behavior it initiates as being normal. We mentally leapfrog over the eternal present moment in everything that we do. We ignore the flow of life.

The Presence Process and the consequences of completing it move at a different pace because this journey is about *process*, not about instant gratification. It is not about getting something done as quickly as possible. The consequences that we activate by completing this journey are made possible mainly because of its gently unfolding integrative approach. By following the instructions carefully, by taking one step at a time, by being consistent and committed to finishing—no matter what, we will enter and complete a rite of passage that will remind us what the word "process" means.

Awakening to the knowing of what a process is cannot be accomplished by a purely mental experience. It can only be accomplished through an integrated emotional, mental, and physical experience. Awakening to the value of process work is extremely rare in a world of instant gratification. It has a powerful impact on the quality of our life experience because life in the present moment is an organic process. Comprehending the power in the rhythm of process work may not necessarily impact or accelerate our ability to earn a living, but it will enhance our ability to open ourselves to the heartbeat of life.

A life experience that flows from present moment awareness moves gently. Because it is integrated and causal, it is therefore in a continual state of rest. It rests calmly and peacefully in the knowing that effects are inevitable. There is no need to hurry. Such a journey surpasses any destination we limit ourselves to in time.

OUR LEVEL OF ENTRY

THE PRESENCE PROCESS is a one-fits-all process because the cause of all our unbalanced physical, mental, and emotional experiences is the same: *our unconscious addiction to the mental habit of living in time in an attempt to escape the discomfort within our emotional body.* However, because some of us may come to this journey with varied intensities of emotional body discomfort and readiness, the Process is equipped with two levels of entry. Each varies in intensity.

For example, a person entering this experience who is already practicing a discipline like Pranayama Yoga or who has already explored other emotional cleansing techniques, may choose to enter this Process differently than a person who is commencing it as a means to neutralize a long-time heroin or alcohol addiction. The former, because of their accumulated experience in conscious breathing or inner emotional work, may be dealing with a less intense emotional charge than the latter. Because of this, they may be able to go deeper into their emotional body without triggering the sort of resistance that can cause one to terminate the experience altogether. They may choose therefore to dive in more intensely. So this option of entering the Process at different levels is built into the experience.

Making a choice at which level to enter this Process is a vital step and must be taken using both common sense and intuition. If we take on too much too soon, we are laying the foundations for the possibility of experiencing a massive internal resistance that will be reflected back to us as a sudden increase in external confusion and chaos. Unnecessary resistance may set us up to run from this experience. Consequently, we may fail to complete this journey. We must therefore not hurry into The Presence Process entertaining the illusion that "if we just get it done" or "get it over with as soon as possible" that everything will be alright.

The Presence Process is not only about the next few weeks of our life experience; it is about the *rest* of our life experience. It is about discovering how to live each moment responsibly for as long as we are given moments to fill with the power of our Presence.

The Presence Process has two levels of entry: the Introductory and the Experiential.

The Introductory Approach

The Introductory Approach is simple and easy: we continue to read this book as if it were a novel. We do not concern ourselves with repeating the Presence Activating Statements, with the Breathing Exercises, or with the Perceptual Tools. We read through the writings for each Session as if they were chapters in a book. In other words, we move through The

Presence Process mentally and abstain from any conscious physical and emotional participation. There is significant insight and benefit we can receive purely by reading, and the Introductory Approach will serve us in this way. This text is saturated with powerful insights and therefore reading and understanding it will automatically and quite effortlessly begin changing the way we are interacting with our life experience. It will gift us with wonderful insight into the nature of present moment awareness.

The Introductory Approach is perfect for those of us who are uncertain about whether The Presence Process is safe or who are first seeking an understanding of what present moment awareness is about, as opposed to an experience of what it is.

Once we have completed the Introductory Approach by reading through the book, if we wish we can then return to Part III which contains the 10 week Presence Process and commence the Experiential Approach from there. Or we may choose to start right at the beginning of the text again. The fact that we have already read the course material will not lessen the experience for us. On the contrary, it will enhance it greatly! We will then be entering the Process with a firm mental foundation and an awareness of the terrain ahead. By adding experience to this established foundation of insight, we will then discover further insights throughout the course materials that were not apparent to us during our initial Introductory journey through it.

The Experiential Approach

The Experiential Approach is designed so that we are able to gently enter the Process physically, mentally, and emotionally. It incorporates a gradual introduction to the full trinity of The Presence Process: the Breathing Technique, the Presence Activating Statements, and the Perceptual Tools. If we seek to enter The Presence Process as an experience and want to gain the most out of our journey through it, it is recommended that we complete it at least twice. In other words, it is recommended that we complete the Experiential Approach twice regardless of how we may perceive the current state of our emotional well-being. This is simply a recommendation. After our initial completion of the Experiential Approach, it is recommended that we take a few weeks break from our Session work to allow for physical, mental, and emotional integration. After a break, we may then choose to enter The Presence Process again.

When entering the Experiential Approach, by applying ourselves to these simple instructions with sincere commitment, we will achieve more than we ever have with all our many outer "doings". The Experiential Approach is very simple. All that is required as we approach each session is:

1   To attend to our 15-minute Breathing Exercise twice a day—no matter what.

2   To mentally repeat our weekly Presence Activating Statement whenever we are not mentally occupied.

3   To carefully read the written materials for each Session and apply the Perceptual Tools as instructed.

The only deviation from this routine occurs during Sessions Seven, Eight, and Nine. As we commence each of these Sessions, we are required to activate our new Session by submerging our body in a bathtub of warm water for 20 minutes prior to beginning our first 15-minute Breathing Exercise for that particular Session. We are not required to consciously connect our breathing while submerged in the water but to place our attention on the emotional experience activated by the warmth of the water and the experience in general. Session Ten then continues and completes the Process without any water segment, as in the earlier Sessions. Full instructions are given for this procedure in our Process materials.

During the break between completing the Experiential Approach and re-entering it, even though it is recommended that we do no conscious mental processing, it is crucial that we continue our 15-minute breathing routine twice a day. In fact it is highly recommended that we continue to attend to our daily Breathing Exercise for up to six months after completing The Presence Process.

When we have completed the Experiential Approach for the first time, have taken an integration break, and are ready to once again return to reenter the Process, we will make a wonderful discovery: it will be like entering a whole new experience. Because of the present moment awareness that we have accumulated, we will be reentering the Process from a different level of consciousness. Consequently, the reading materials and the Presence Activating Statements will greet us at a different place in our awareness. On occasion, it will appear as if we are reading the written material for the very first time. This is normal. Everyone who enters this Process more than once has this experience. This is why we can repeat this Process as often as we choose. The Process itself is neutral. It will therefore always meet us and reflect the processing requirements of our current level of consciousness.

The beauty of The Presence Process is that once we have completed both the Introductory and Experiential approaches, we can keep repeating the Process as often as we choose. Each time we reenter it, we will have a different experience, and each repeated experience will take us deeper into our emotional body. Many individuals have facilitated themselves through this experience numerous times, and in each case, all went to deeper levels of emotional cleansing. This enabled them to achieve progressively greater present moment awareness and balance in the quality of their life experience.

It may assist us to metaphorically think of The Presence Process as an instruction manual that teaches us how to drive our moment-by-moment life experience consciously and responsibly. The Introductory Approach may be considered as a theoretical overview of the task at hand. The Experiential Approach may be viewed as the most basic of practical instruction.

Once we have trained ourselves to consciously and responsibly drive the physical, mental, and emotional aspects of our life experience, then we are encouraged to take our newfound perceptions out onto the freeway of life to see what they are really capable of. In every facet of life, it is the understanding and the perfecting of the basics that establishes a thorough foundation for excellence. It is the same for The Presence Process. That is why we are encouraged to complete the Experiential Approach more than once.

We must not be in a hurry to "get somewhere". Being in a hurry is to miss the point completely. We must think "journey" and not "destination". The issues that distract us now from the present moment of our life may appear all-encompassing. Yet, if we gently move ourselves through the Experiential Approach more than once, we will gradually rise above these issues and make some truly wonderful discoveries. One of these will be that our personal issues are placed before us so that by resolving them we have an opportunity to learn the tools required to become conscious and responsible drivers of the experience called life.

By completing the Experiential Approach more than once, we will have gained enough present moment awareness to be able to take our attention and intention off our personal issues and begin placing them upon the world around us with an intent on being truly useful. Becoming available and therefore truly useful is the responsibility of those who choose to walk awake amongst those who are still tossed unconsciously by the sleep of time.

This is the invitation:
to embrace the art of living life consciously.

This is the journey:
to awaken from time and become present in this world.

This is the promise:
to become available and therefore truly useful.

This is the gift:
awareness of the power of our Inner Presence.

⸺⸺⸺⸺⸺⸺⸺⸺

Confirmation

THIS SECTION CONTAINS many of the answers to the questions that may arise as a consequence of entering and journeying through The Presence Process. It also contains explanations for many of the experiences we may encounter. This information is positioned just prior to entering the Process so that we keep it fresh in our mind. Subsequently, we are ensuring a decrease in the level of anxiety that we may experience as our inner and outer circumstances begin adjusting to the changes that we are deliberately making to the condition of our emotional body. It is recommended that we return to and reread this section of the book if ever we feel confused or find ourselves wondering if what is happening to us is supposed to be happening. This is why it is called "Confirmation".

Note: It is important to keep in mind that the following list details some of the experiences that may occur as we are moving *through the Process* and that may continue to persist for a while after we reach completion. However, this is not a list of what we are intending to accomplish by entering and completing this Process. The consequences of completing The Presence Process are revealed to us in depth after our journey in the section entitled "Fruit and Flowers".

1 **People may start behaving differently around us.** Just watch. This is happening because something is changing within us, and it is being reflected in our perceptions of others.

2 **Our body may develop aches and pains for no apparent reason.** Do not be concerned. Our body is using discomfort to attract our attention from where it is attached in "time". Pain is one of the ways our physical body assists us to bring our awareness into the present moment. By placing our attention on the discomfort without judgment, concern, or complaint, we will experience an increase of present moment awareness.

3 **Symptomatic conditions that we are already experiencing as we enter The Presence Process may appear to become heightened.** This occurs because as our attention enters our physical body our awareness of our bodily condition increases. This increase of awareness may appear to us as a worsening of our symptoms. It is not. It is often the first step in real healing.

4 **We may discover that we experience great resistance to attending to our Breathing Exercise, to mentally repeating our Presence Activators, to reading the written materials for the Session, and to applying our Perceptual Tools.** This is a sign that deeply unconscious and long-term suppressed memories are starting to surface. Do not be concerned: this is supposed to happen. We must keep in mind that we have spent our whole life experience keeping these unintegrated experiences hidden from our awareness.

Now we are allowing the opposite; we are intending that they surface because we are able to consciously neutralize them. Yet as they do begin to surface, all our conditioned instincts will tell us that what is happening "is wrong, uncomfortable, to be feared, and we are out of control." This is the voice of the ego. Naturally, as this occurs, we will feel resistance towards whatever is facilitating this sudden change of circumstances. We will therefore feel resistance towards everything about The Presence Process. We must embrace the feelings of resistance as being a positive indicator that the Process is succeeding. Instead of reacting to our resistance by backing away from our commitments, we must instead be motivated by these feelings to continue—regardless. By doing so, we will break through to the other side of the resistance and feel the release from an unconscious weight that we have been carrying most of our life.

5   **Old injuries may resurface.** They do so because we are now willing and able to attend to them with our present moment awareness as opposed to unconsciously suppressing, sedating, or controlling their symptoms. Again, it is our Presence with its concomitant compassionate attention that is being called for.

6   **We may have moments of feeling distracted or confused.** This occurs because we are gaining a new awareness of where we are not present in our life. These states of distraction and confusion have been occurring all through our life. Now that our present moment awareness is increasing, we are becoming acutely aware of them. Our awareness of them is what enables these states of distraction and confusion to be integrated.

7   **We may discover that we no longer appear to care about things over which we previously enforced control or that previously appeared to be of great importance to us.** Go with the flow and allow this to happen because it is a beneficial development. This occurs because many of our priorities are established for the benefit of others, not ourselves. As we become increasingly present, we realize that we can only be responsible for the quality of *our* experience. We cannot be responsible for the quality of the experience of another. We can believe we are, but this is an illu-

sion. As we become increasingly present, this illusion crumbles; consequently, we cease to use our energy to attempt to control the outer world and those who frequent it.

8   **We may begin speaking our mind in circumstances when we would normally have kept quiet.** This will happen when our authentic self begins to awaken. It is a wonderful development, though at first it may feel uncomfortable. It is wonderful when we learn how to say "no" when we mean "no" and "yes" when we mean "yes". However, getting to this point may initially cause us to feel as if we are doing something wrong. We must honor ourselves. "No" is a complete sentence.

9   **Our financial situation may change, and it may appear as if our resources are drying up.** This is temporary. Remember that money is a metaphor for our personal flow of energy and therefore for movement in our life experience. When we deliberately look at our emotional blockages, we are inwardly examining the disturbances in our personal energy flow. When we look directly at our emotional blockages, this is often automatically reflected in our experience of the outer world as a disturbance in our financial resources. This occurs especially if we have great attachment to money or if we judge our self-worth by our financial predicament. Once we clear this internal emotional blockage, our money situation will once again flow.

10 **Our family members, partner, or close companions may start discouraging us from being so "self-centered".** This is because we may for the first time in our life be taking steps to nurture ourselves as opposed to "helping" others, and they may not feel comfortable with the attention being taken off them. Do not be concerned; they will survive it. Some of them may even awaken to the necessity to grow emotionally because of it.

11 **We may feel very sleepy for no reason at all.** This is because our attention is being placed upon suppressed unconscious issues. As we place our attention on our inner unconsciousness, it is reflected outwardly as sleepiness. This is a good sign. We must do our best to rest when we are able to and to persevere when we cannot.

12 **We may find great difficulty in sleeping.** This is because our increasing level of present moment awareness is energizing us. It does not assist us in any way to toss and turn in bed all night. It is more beneficial for us to arise and be constructive or to sit and digest the alertness through being still with it. These moments of late night alertness are gifts of heightened awareness.

13 **We may begin experiencing vivid dreams.** Sometimes they are quite disturbing. Often they are very revealing about the nature of our process. Increased awareness of our dreamtime is due to emotional processing that is taking place while we sleep. Do not take any of these dreams literally, especially if they feature people that we know. For the purpose of The Presence Process, men in our dreams that are older than us metaphorically represent our relationship with our father and therefore what we have to learn about guiding ourselves. Women older than us metaphorically represent our relationship with our mother and what we have to learn about nurturing ourselves. Women the same age as us metaphorically represent our female side and therefore our relationship with our emotions and the healing we are being called to accomplish. Men the same age as us metaphorically represent our male side and therefore the condition of our mental activities and lessons we are being called on to learn. Individuals younger than ourselves represent our male and female sides at those ages. In a dream we must always embrace the images we see symbolically. They are messengers carrying metaphors. To interpret them, we are required to ask what the symbol means to us. The language of dreams is seldom literal; it is metaphoric.

14 **We may become grumpy and irritable for no conceivable reason.** We have probably been inwardly grumpy and irritable for most of our life; only now are we allowing these feelings to surface. We are allowed to be grumpy and irritable as long as we do not take it out on others. The Presence Process will teach Perceptual Tools that will enable us to integrate these feelings.

15 **We may not feel like being in the company of our regular social companions.** We must honor this when it occurs. This again is an opportunity to learn

how to say "yes" when we mean "yes", and often more importantly, "no" when we mean "no". It is an invitation to be authentic. It is an opportunity to claim our own quiet space in the world.

16 **People from our past or family members that we have not heard from for a while may phone or contact us in other ways.** Even though this Process is an individual journey, it affects our whole family and all who we are energetically connected to through our past experiences. Remember that our relationship with anyone is based on how we perceive him or her. As our perceptions alter, so do our relationships. These sudden contacts from people that we may not have heard from for a while are a positive sign that we are accomplishing something real. When we truly adjust the condition of our inner world, our outer world automatically shifts. Often these sudden communications from the past are invitations extended to us by the universe to make amends, to take responsibility for the quality of our past experiences, and to witness the outer accomplishments of our inner work.

17 **We may feeL melancholy.** We may start missing people or close companions from the past. These are memories stirring in order that our attachments to them can be integrated. As inner memories stir, the images we associate with them come into focus. We are not really "missing" these people or images: we are integrating the past. The past is gone and no longer exists. It is only us who are holding onto the illusion.

18 **We may find it challenging to be around our parents or our immediate family members.** This has absolutely nothing to do with them. These feelings arise because those closest to us are the clearest mirrors for reflecting the issues we prefer to hide from ourselves. The Presence Process will teach us how to read these experiences in a manner that empowers us to grow emotionally from them.

19 **Our children may begin behaving differently.** They may begin behaving exactly as we did when we were their age. This is because they will also start acting as mirrors so that we can see outside of ourselves the unresolved childhood issues that we are dealing with internally. This

is an invitation to watch but not to react. The behavior we are seeing is not real; it is a reflection, a memory. As we integrate our childhood memories, we automatically release our own children from having to carry our baggage. Their behavior will automatically transform. Each time we complete the Process, we will notice that our children become lighter and more joyful.

20 **Our children may become ill or experience colds and flu symptoms.** The nature of this world is that what we do not deal with is automatically picked up and carried by our children through an imprinting process. When we enter this journey, our children are already carrying our uninte-grated issues within their emotional bodies. Therefore, as we begin to cleanse our own emotional body, our children will simultaneously experience a shift in theirs. They may experience this through bodily symptoms, mental confusion, or emotional displays. As we complete the Process and regain a new level of emotional equilibrium, they will also reach completion. This does not apply only to our children; when we enter this Process, everyone in close proximity to us also begins to process. However, unlike us, they are going through this uncon-sciously. We must therefore be compassionate with those closest to us. We must also be unconcerned as they go through their emotional and thus mental and physical adjustments. Remember that they are mir-roring us. If we feel compelled to "do" anything, make sure that what-ever it is, we do it to ourselves.

21 **We may feel weepy for absolutely no reason.** When this occurs intend that a quiet uninterrupted moment open up in our daily experience so that we can be with these feelings. Then cry and cry and cry some more! Cry-ing detoxifies the emotional body like no other human activity. How-ever, it only accomplishes this if it is done with this intent, as opposed to being used as a tool to get outside attention and sympathy. Despite what many therapists may tell us, crying alone when involved in emotional processing is often more beneficial because then it is pure and authentic. Then it does not become a superficial drama or a tool in the hands of the ego. Weep! Sob! Every tear that we shed will wash the shallow coating of the pretence that is smothering our present moment awareness.

22 **Old issues that we had *thought* we had already dealt with may resurface.** This is because in the past we only controlled or sedated them. Now that we are regaining our present moment awareness, they are surfacing so that we can truly integrate them.

23 **Our eating habits may change.** This is because as we gain more present moment awareness we automatically become more aware of sensations within our physical body. The more present we become, the more aware we are of what food is actually doing to our body. Entering present moment awareness often causes a change in eating behavior from "dead" and heavy foods to "living" and light foods.

24 **We may feel cravings for foodstuffs we used to enjoy in the past.** This is because we are activating memories from those time periods. Enjoy, it will not last.

25 **We may go through moments when we feel overwhelmed.** It will pass. It is just a build up of energy in our emotional body. We will not have to deal with more than we can, but often we will not have to deal with less. Be strong.

26 **We may experience emotions that we cannot describe or recognize.** This will occur when our memories surface of experiences that occurred to us before we had a grasp of language. Therefore, they move through our field of awareness as feelings or sensations for which we have no explanation or means of description. Just feel.

27 **We may find it exceedingly difficult to explain to others what we are going through during the course of this Process.** The best course of action here is not to attempt to explain the mechanics of this Process to others. Rather, pass them the book to read or encourage them to investigate it for themselves. The Presence Process is an inner journey and therefore there are very few points of reference for what we will be going through to share with others in the outer world. Remember that everything we are experiencing will also be coming to us in context of our experience as a whole, and this makes its mechanics easily comprehensible only to us.

Therefore, if we attempt to explain certain isolated aspects of this Process to others, they will struggle to hold the individual pieces of information because they will not have a context in which to place them. Always keep in mind how much information we were required to read and digest before we even entered this Process. All the pre-process information in this book is an attunement: it creates a multi-dimensional internal pathway for us so that we can navigate through what is a very complex terrain in a very simple and gentle way.

PART III

THE PRESENCE PROCESS

WE HAVE NOW PREPARED OURSELVES mentally for an inner journey that is going to have a profound and wonderful impact on the quality of our life experience. It is perfectly natural and actually quite healthy that we may be feeling a stirring of anticipation or even a murmur of anxiety. As we now embark on this journey, let us be comforted and encouraged by keeping the following few thoughts in the forefront of our mind:

There is no qualification for entering The Presence Process—other than our willingness to do so.

There is no particular way that we are supposed to move through this experience—other than by following the instructions that we are given to the best of our ability.

There is no correct or incorrect experience that we are supposed to have. There is only our experience. And our experience will always be the most facilitating one for us.

We succeed purely by following the instructions and completing the Process. Completion is success. Success is completion.

INTENDING TO LISTEN

IT IS NOT NECESSARY to attempt to remember everything that we have read up to this point. The Presence Process is an "as-need-to-know-experience". In other words, we will know what we need to know usually just prior to or only in the moment that we need to know it. However, if we feel an inclination to re-read any of the previous sections before entering Session One, then we must honor this and do so now. This inclination is our inner voice speaking to us. This is our Inner Facilitator.

As we enter The Presence Process, we are encouraged to consciously set an intention to be receptive to our Inner Facilitator. By reading the first part of this book, our Inner Facilitator has already been activated. Whether we are aware of it or not, we have already been taught its medium of communication. We call this medium of communication "the language of authenticity". This language of authenticity is the conceptual framework that has been automatically constructed in our mind as a consequence of having read everything up to this point. This conceptual framework empowers us to have a deeper understanding of the Presence Activating Statements, the reading materials, and the Perceptual Tools that we encounter throughout the Process. This conceptual framework also enables us to accomplish very intricate and sensitive inner procedures gently and relatively effortlessly.

The silent voice of our Inner Facilitator communicates to us primarily through our intuition. We are now entering an experience in which we are consciously placing ourselves *in tuition*. Our intuition will always tell us exactly what we need to know exactly when we need to know it. However, we must now train ourselves to listen to it. We will learn how to do this by trial and error: by ignoring and obeying our intuition and witnessing the consequences. Along the way, we will learn to trust it implicitly because through our own experience, we will come to realize that it only has our best interest at heart.

Our Inner Facilitator does not attempt to mentally manipulate us or emotionally sway us. It does not interfere. It does not punish us for not paying attention to it or withdraw from us because we do not accept its guidance. Our Inner Facilitator does not entertain drama. It is clinical in its expression. It says what it has to say and will not metaphorically shout above the voice of the ego. It provides us with instant "knowings", not long drawn-out procedures of attempting to understand. When we go against our inner knowing, we will stumble, and in our stumbling, we will realize that we ought to have listened. When we obey this inner knowing, we will succeed, and so we will gradually begin to embrace it without being suspicious of its motives. By learning through trial and error to trust it, we will automatically begin transforming our entire life experience into effortless gentleness.

The instructions coming from our Inner Facilitator will often not make sense to us; they will just be "knowings". This is because our Inner Facilitator speaks to us from beyond what we call "time", and so it knows "ahead of time" what is going to occur in our inner and outer life experience. For this reason, its communication does not always logically appear to be in synch with where our conscious attention is anchored in time. We must therefore trust our sense of knowing, especially when we appear to have no logical understanding to back up what it is telling us. Listening to our Inner Facilitator is the key to unlocking the door to the experience that we call present moment awareness.

The Presence Process deliberately sets out to dismantle the barriers created by the endless beckoning of our arrogant ego so that we may once again awaken our inner ear to the sweet silent voice of our Inner Presence. It intends this because to establish this inner communication is to accomplish everything.

A PERSONAL NOTE

DEAR FRIEND,

I commend you for coming this far, and I encourage you to go all the way. I have walked this pathway myself—many times. This pathway was uncovered by walking it, not by talking it, or reading it, or thinking it. By walking it myself I have ensured that if you follow the simple instructions your journey will be safe, gentle, and full of profound insights and confirmation. I have paved this journey with my integrity. Many others have also contributed to the efficiency of this experience by successfully walking it themselves. Many more are walking it right now with you. All who have succeeded have done so by completing it. As you enter and commence The Presence Process, please therefore intend to do whatever it takes to complete it.

Please accept that you do not have to resolve everything that is causing imbalance in the quality of your life experience in the short time it takes for you to complete this journey. You can walk it several times to gain a sure footing upon the pathway that is your life. In The Presence Process "completion" does not mean "being finished"; it means arriving at a point in your journey where you are ready and equipped to take full responsibility for the quality of your unfolding life experience.

Everything you could possibly require to bring the quality of present moment awareness into every step that you take is between the covers of this book. Read, apply, and practice it well, and you will deliver yourself to where you really choose to be.

Remember that your life is your divine destiny unfolding deliberately according to a sacred blueprint that in each moment invites you to show up and fulfill your highest potential. Your life experience is a beautiful gift revealed by your conscious unwrapping of it. Your point of freedom in it all is accessed by your attitude towards it. Choose to be aware. Choose to be present in each moment of it. Choose to walk with grace and gratitude through every experience.

From the center of my heart to the center of yours I bid you well. The Presence within me is the same Presence within you. As such we depart together, we journey together, and we reach completion together. Thank you for having faith in what we share. Thank you for your company along this most beautiful way.

Kindest regards,
Michael

ACTIVATING OUR PROCESS

WE ARE NOW READY TO ENTER Session One and to consciously activate our journey through The Presence Process. Activation is a simple procedure:

1   Firstly, we memorize the given Presence Activating Statement.

2   Then we read through all the written materials for Session One.

3   Then we sit still as instructed in the Session One reading materials and connect our breathing for at least 15 minutes.

Please note: Due to the length of some of the Session reading materials, it is important to ensure that we have a generous amount of uninterrupted time for reading before we activate each Session. It is important to review the reading materials for each individual Session as soon as possible without hurrying or approaching them with a sense of urgency. The reason for this is that the reading materials for each Session are imbedded with Perceptual Tools that we are required to practice during the seven days of each Session. It does not benefit us in any way therefore if we leave our reading materials to the last possible moment. Once we have completed reading through them once, we can then review them slowly during the seven days before activating our next Session.

⬤⬤⬤

MAINTAINING OUR MOMENTUM

DURING THE SEVEN DAYS between activating each new Session, we are required to:

1   Attend to our 15-minute Breathing Exercise twice each day as the first thing we do after we are fully awake and as the last thing we do before we climb into bed at night.

2   **Repeat our given Presence Activating Statement for the Session whenever we are not mentally engaged.** Once we activate a new Session and receive a new Presence Activating Statement, we must immediately cease to use the Presence Activator from the previous Session.

3   **Review our reading materials and apply the Perceptual Tools as instructed.**

Entering this journey believing that we will find the time to attend to our process commitments as we go along is to automatically invite failure and unconscious self-sabotage before we even begin. We must therefore make a commitment to follow and stick to the instructions we receive throughout our journey *no matter what* because the power of The Presence Process is greatly enhanced by our commitment to consistency.

> *Consistency is always more powerful and productive*
> *than sporadic and drastic activity.*

Inevitably, circumstances will occur that may prevent us from following through on our intentions for a particular Session. This is where we must also learn to surrender to the process. If, against all our good intentions, the activities around us unfold in a manner that prevents us from sticking to our commitments, then we must not fight the situation. We must merely surrender to it. However, we must not confuse surrendering with being in resistance or making excuses.

The golden rule in discerning between surrender and resistance is this: if we are relieved that we have been prevented from attending to our process commitments, then it is most likely that we are in resistance and that we have unconsciously manufactured these circumstances to sabotage our progress. If we are honestly disappointed that we are not able to meet our process commitments, then it is most likely the intelligence of our Inner Presence rearranging our routine because it is in our best interest to do so. In hindsight, we will always be able to tell which was the case.

Our egos will give us many reasons why we cannot fulfill our process commitments, especially when our unconscious memories are surfacing for integration. This is where our true level of self-discipline and personal will becomes apparent to us. By keeping our daily commitment to this Process, we automatically strengthen and accumulate self-discipline and personal will.

We must not beat ourselves up mentally or emotionally if we fall along the way. Falling is not failing if we get up and continue. Falling is only failing if we stop before we reach completion.

Let us begin.

SESSION ONE

Our Presence Activating Statement for the next seven days is:

I choose to experience this moment.

OUR INNER PRESENCE

FROM BIRTH WE ARE TAUGHT that our identity is that which makes us different from everybody else. In other words, we are taught to believe that our real identity is based on our appearance, our behavior, and our individual life circumstances. Therefore, we mistakenly believe that we are our body, the sum of our behaviors, and the circumstances that we are experiencing. Yet these outer attributes simply constitute passing experiences that we are having; they do not and cannot tell us who and what we *really* are. It is more accurate to say that our body, our behavior, and our life circumstances are, in fact, the trinity that makes up the structure of our ego: that which we show the outer world and that which the outer world sees of us.

Yet who and what are we really?

The nature of all our experiences is that they are all constantly changing. They are changing in form and quality. The form of any given experience takes shape based on our previous thoughts, words, and deeds, while the quality of our experiences are entirely dependent on our interpretations of them in any given moment.

Our body, our behavior, and the circumstances in our life are constantly changing. Experiences come and go and yet "we" remain. Realizing that change is what remains constant throughout all our experiences is a massive insight because then we know for certain that if we do not like the quality of the experience that we are having, that we have the real possibility of changing it.

This realization goes right to the heart of The Presence Process. This adventure is not about attempting to change ourselves; it is about making immediate changes to *the quality of our life experience.*

The Presence Process works from a standpoint that it is impossible to change who and what we really are because we are a Presence that is eternal. For now, we are invited to accept our immortality as a concept or as a good idea. However, once we learn how to consciously detach from our experiences, we will see clearly that even though our experiences are constantly changing, we, the experiencer, remain unchanged.

What remains unchanged must of necessity be eternal.

Throughout The Presence Process, we are therefore invited to realize and remember that that which most reflects who and what we are is to be found in the silent, still, and invisible quality of our own Inner Presence. Some have called this aspect of our Being "the observer". This is because it watches everything and therefore knows everything that has ever happened to us. When we fully enter present moment awareness, we will also discover that our Inner Presence appears to know everything that is to occur to us as well. As we develop a conscious relationship with our Inner Presence, we will realize the following:

- **That our Inner Presence knows no order of difficulty.** There is nothing that it cannot accomplish.

- **That our Inner Presence truly has our best interest at heart.** It knows us better than we presently know ourselves. It knows what will restore our authentic joy.

- **That the Presence within each one of us is One and the same as the Presence in all other living creatures.** In other words, our real identity is shared with all life.

- **That the Presence that is within us and also within all life is intimately, consistently, and eternally connected.** Our Inner Presence is our connection with all life.

- **That the Presence within us will not interfere with our life.** It will only attend to those aspects of our life experience that we consciously surrender to it. Learning to surrender is our ultimate challenge and one of the most powerful lessons our journey through The Presence Process can teach us.

At first the above realizations may be mental concepts that we may choose to accept—or not. However, as we gather more and more personal Presence (which is the same as saying as we become more present in our own life), we will also be given the experiences to assist us in knowing firsthand that all this is true. These revelations will then stay with us forever, for present moment awareness, once consciously accumulated, seldom decays.

By developing a relationship with our Inner Presence through the Breathing Exercise, the Presence Activating Statements, and the Perceptual Tools, we will be able to see clearly that what we have come to accept since childhood as our personal identity is inauthentic. As opposed to our inner authentic Presence, our adult identity is our outer inauthentic pretence. This Process will enable us to begin seeing that that which makes us different from others is actually the part of ourselves that is the most limited and separated. It will also help us to realize that by identifying only with these outer attributes (our appearance, our behavior, and our life circumstances), that we are severely limiting and separating ourselves from the unlimited vibrancy contained within all life.

When our identity is solely anchored to these outer attributes, then it is based on an interpretation. In other words, it is a manufactured idea of who and what we are that is based upon past circumstances, future projections, and the opinions and interpretations of others. We are not our body or our behavior, just as we are not the circumstances of our life experience. Our entire outer life experience is a temporary and constantly changing physical, mental, and emotional journey. It shall pass, yet we shall remain. Therefore, it is not a true reflection of who or what we are at all. A more accurate definition of who or what we are is "that which we share with all life".

What is it that we share with all life?

THE WILL TO BREATHE

THE PRESENCE PROCESS is initiated when we sit down for the first time with the intent to consciously connect our breathing. Initially, we may, like many others who have embarked on this journey, find it very challenging to attend to our daily 15-minute Breathing Exercise. In fact, we may discover that there are moments when we have an immense resistance to it. The first 15 minutes that we sit alone and breathe can often stretch out and become the longest 15 minutes we have ever experienced. Understanding why this occurs and that this is not unusual will assist us and even motivate us to break through this psychological barrier. For this is all it is. We must break through this barrier, when and if it occurs, because everything we are seeking lies on the other side of this resistance.

The reasons why it can be indescribably hard for us to sit down for a minimum of 15 minutes twice a day and connect our breathing are not because the practice is difficult. When we follow the instructions for the Breathing Exercise, we are breathing correctly. We are breathing normally. No exertion and no special postures are required. In fact, we are not actually being asked to do anything. It is more accurate to say that we are being asked to undo or enter an experience of not doing. The physical act and effort required to consciously connect our breathing for 15 minutes twice a day is therefore not the issue at all. The core reasons why it is initially challenging are different than what we may think. There are two main reasons which are actually two halves of the same condition:

1 **The first reason is that we may be consciously or unconsciously entering The Presence Process because someone else told us we should do it or because we believe that by doing it we will gain something from someone or from the outside world.** In other words, someone may have thought they should or could "help" us by introducing us to this Process, and we may have gone ahead and began doing it to please or appease them. Or we may have other externalized motivators. For example, we may believe that by entering this Process our partner will come back to us because we will have then dealt with the issues that caused our separation. Or we may think that if we complete this Process, we will suddenly start making lots of money. These arbitrary examples are merely mentioned to demonstrate situations in which our intention in entering this Process may be motivated by someone or something outside ourselves. If this is the case, we may initially struggle because if we are doing this for anyone or anything other than ourselves, we may find it challenging to initiate the will to move through this experience. The will to complete The Presence Process must come from us and be accessed by us. We cannot do inner work for someone else.

We cannot breathe for someone else.

2 **The second reason why we may struggle to attend to our Breathing Exercise twice a day is because this may well be the first time in our life that we have ever done anything "real" for ourselves.** As you can see, the first and the second reason are two halves of the same whole: the predicament and consequence of a lack of personal will. Everyone who enters this Process is in this predicament to some extent. We all bear the scars of taking the cue for our behavior, appearance, and expectations we have about life from external sources.

As children, we entered the world of order, routine, and "appropriate" behavior through the guidance, encouragement, and insistence of our parents. Initially, this predicament of lacking personal will was the consequence of our intimate relationship with our mother. We ate, dressed, bathed, and behaved in a manner that was first initiated and spoken for by our mother. Then we acted according to what we perceived as appropriate in the eyes of our mother and father. The consequence is that today, on an unconscious level, our motivation for the way we eat, dress, bathe, and behave is almost solely sourced from the reflected presence of others. We unconsciously use these "others" as ongoing reflections of our mother and father. Through the presence of others, we are still attempting to please and appease our mother and father in order that we may gain their approval and unconditional acceptance.

This initial motivation to do this and that for mommy and daddy was inevitably transformed and transferred as we moved through our childhood, teenage years, and into adulthood. When we were young, this compulsion to act in a manner that we believed would enable us to gain our parents' love and approval was automatic. During our teenage years this behavior transformed into an automatic desire to "fit in" with our peer groups. By the time we entered our adult experience, this need for outer validation became cloaked as a desire to be responsible, or to "get ahead". Therefore, let us call most of our behavior what it is: a desire to get a reaction, a drama staged for the purpose of gaining outer attention. For some of us this desire may have manifested as its polar opposite. In other words, we desired "not" to fit in or get ahead. This resistance is also a reaction and can be traced to our initial interactions with our parents (or their substitutes).

No matter how we cloak our desire for attention and no matter how we justify it, deep introspection will always reveal the inauthenticity of our predicament. The tragedy is that we can go through our whole life and never stop for a moment to accomplish anything "real" and therefore lasting for ourselves. Even the thought of investing in so-called "self-orientated behavior" may be enough to cause us deep feelings of guilt. We may even think taking care of ourselves is being selfish. This is because in the time-based experience of our modern day society, we are expected to function like "clockwork". We are expected to live our life as a dependent piece of the overall societal mechanism, and any behavior in which we appear to disconnect from the machinery to nurture our individual evolution is not encouraged, as its value for the whole cannot be initially perceived.

The act of living for the approval and acknowledgement of others is so much part of the experience of the society in which we live today that for the most part we cannot even see the true nature of our predicament. We cannot see that we possess very little and often absolutely no will of our own. Everything we do is for someone else or because of someone else. Most of us, if we were taken out of our present environment and placed alone on an idyllic desert island with all our heart's desire, except the presence of other humans or pets, would perish. The reason for this is that from the beginning of our life, our entire motivation to act has been sourced from the presence of others. If we did not perish, we would undergo a profound internal transformation.

We have not been given the opportunity to develop the muscle that powers our will to act independently of what we perceive to be happening outside of us.

The only conscious sign that this is really so is our proficiency at saying "yes" when we mean "no" and "no" when we mean "yes". This is the telltale symptom of having no personal will and as a consequence having our behavior dictated by our outer circumstances. If we catch ourselves behaving in this manner just once in our life, we can be sure that unconsciously we are doing it everywhere. We can also be sure that if we are indeed living for the acknowledgement and approval of others, then when we take the first step towards doing anything "real" for ourselves, like attending to our daily 15-minute Breathing Exercise, we may hit a massive wall of resistance. The wall will be invisible, but it may turn out to be seemingly impenetrable at first.

What this really means is that we live in continual reaction to our experience of the world. When we live in reaction, the only activity that will appear to have any real value is activity that is supported, acknowledged, and rewarded by the outside world and the people in it. If we are like most people in this world, then the act of accomplishing something real for ourselves, something "responsible", something from which only we will initially seemingly benefit, and for which *we* must encourage, acknowledge, and reward ourselves will seem pointless. We will have no point of reference for such self-orientated behavior nor have any memory with which to gauge its outcome. Such an activity will initially appear meaningless to us and so our resistance towards doing it will be massive. We may even feel that we are being selfish or self-indulgent.

Any resistance to attending to our daily Breathing Exercises will likely increase when we tell others about our intentions. This is the risk we take in talking about work we are doing on our experiences and for ourselves, because in most cases, we would only be talking about it in an effort to gain outside support, or to confirm and validate our efforts as being worthy and appropriate. This is the predicament we face when we enter The Presence Process. At first we will be inclined to tell others about it, disguising our desire for validation as casual conversation. The universe has a sense of humor and will often meet our instinctive desire for validation with comments like, "Breathe? But surely you know how to breathe already, ha-ha." Other comments we may have to endure include:

> "Oh, I have done that before. It doesn't help."
> "Oh, I know all that already. It doesn't work."
> "Why go into the past? Just get on with your life."
> "I would love to do stuff like that too, but right now
> I have to deal with the real world."

Then we will feel even more resistance to doing our daily breathing because nobody has confirmed the validity of our intentions as being relevant. On the other hand, if everyone stood around and told us how great and noble an undertaking The Presence Process was, then it would be different; it would actually make attending to the daily breathing exercises quite easy. It would be easy because we would be able to report back and receive the accolades for our valiant efforts. But then we would gain nothing "real" from our efforts because anything we gain would only appear to have any substance in the company of others. Inevitably, we will make the mistake of telling others what we are doing to seek their validation because this is habitual behavior. Hopefully, we will not

waste too much energy in this pointless pursuit. In the end, our validation of ourselves has to be sufficient.

To accomplish anything real from The Presence Process, we must
make a conscious effort to make this journey for ourselves, knowing that
our inner successes will inevitably benefit our whole world. But to start
with, we are the ones who must reap the rewards of our efforts because *we
cannot give away what we do not have.* The first reward we must intend to
gather for ourselves is to build the muscles of our own personal will to
act, a will to act in spite of what is happening outside of us. This is one of
the fruits automatically accomplished when we diligently connect our
breathing twice a day for a minimum of 15 minutes no matter what.
Every added session steadily builds the muscles of our personal will
because when we breathe we must initially do so by ourselves, for ourselves and no "other". No one can breathe for us. Consistency in this
endeavor is the right recipe for the gathering of personal will.

No one needs to understand why we are doing this. It will only make
clear and obvious sense to those who are ready to make real movement in
their life experience from reactive to responsive behavior. At times even
we will struggle to understand why we are doing the Breathing Exercises.
Or why we are doing any of this. This is normal because the ego cannot
comprehend the idea of being responsible for the quality of all our experiences. The ego only understands blame. So we must intend to apply ourselves to this course of action above and beyond the need to understand
why. We must attend to our breathing every day—no matter what—
because throughout The Presence Process, it is the most important act of
"not-doing" that we can master for ourselves.

*Our daily Breathing Exercise is the seed of the plant
that will bear the fruit we seek.*

We can begin by making our daily breathing times special for ourselves.
It is *our* time. We must find a place, preferably the same place, and a time,
preferably the same time, to attend to this special task everyday. Familiarity
tames the unruly mind and consistency strengthens the will to act. For the
duration of this Process, we will make the entire experience gentler for ourselves if attending to our Breathing Exercise is how we choose to start our

day and how we choose to end it. Let it be the opening and the closing of the inverted commas of our waking moments. By elevating our relationship with "the breath of life" to this status in our daily routine, we will be laying the foundation for a rebirth of our personal will to live. This personal will to live is not based on anything or anyone outside of us. It is within us, and within it is the power that surges through all life.

CONSCIOUSLY CONNECTED BREATHING

WE INITIATE OUR JOURNEY through The Presence Process the moment we sit down and consciously connect our breathing for the first time. It is as simple as that. Yet the power of this simple exercise is that through this daily practice we will make profound discoveries. We will begin unraveling all our real life challenges, challenges that we have so successfully hidden from ourselves. Through this simple exercise, we will gently penetrate parts of our awareness that have appeared inaccessible. Through this simple procedure, we will begin automatically attracting what we require in life to restore balance to the quality of our life experience.

The reason all this and more is made possible by this simple exercise is because consciously connected breathing is one of the most accelerated ways for us to re-awaken a conscious relationship with our Inner Presence. Without consistent application of this simple exercise, this Process is just a stream of clever words and ideas. It is our consciously connected breathing that assists us to activate the power of our Inner Presence, thereby enabling us to enter present moment awareness experientially.

To add to what has already been stated about it, the functions of this Breathing Exercise throughout The Presence Process are:

- To assist us to become more conscious of our breathing,

- To assist us to consistently gather and maintain present moment awareness,

- To assist us to remain present throughout the day so that we respond instead of react to the experiences that come to our attention for processing,

- To assist us to enter sleep consciously,

- To relax and calm our physical body through increased oxygenation,

- To energize us (morning) and calm us (evening),

- To assist us to gain deeper insights into the Presence Activating Statements, Perceptual Tools, and written materials,

- To introduce us to the practice of meditation, if we are not already meditating,

- To enhance our present meditation practice.

Throughout this Process, we must therefore commit to practicing our consciously connected Breathing Exercise every morning as soon as possible after we feel awake and every evening as our last activity before climbing into bed.

Our Consciously Connected Breathing Excercise

1 **We begin by sitting in a comfortable posture with our back straight and eyes closed.** Cross-legged on a cushion or sitting conventionally on a chair are both good. *Preferably not in or on the bed.* The object is to adopt a posture that encourages both alertness and the opportunity to forget the body.

2 **We must ensure we are comfortably warm.**

3 **We connect our breathing naturally.** In other words, we breathe in and out without pausing between our breaths. We breathe gently applying slight effort only to our in-breath. The out-breath is automatic and relaxed. It is useful to visualize a fountain: energy is only required to push the water into the air because gravity will automatically bring it down. Our in-breath is the water being pushed up and our out-breath is the water effortlessly returning to earth. Even though we apply slight effort to our in-breath and relax during our out-breath, it is important to make sure both our in-breath and out-breath are evenly lengthened in duration and that there are absolutely no pauses between them. We must intend to breathe with our inhale and our exhale being

one continuous breath—one continual flow. We must not in any way breathe abnormally or attempt to exaggerate our breathing pattern.

4   **Nose breathing is best, but if our nose is blocked, we may use our mouth.** We must *not* use both our nose and mouth. In other words, we must not use our nose for inhaling and then our mouth for exhaling, or vice versa. Using both our nose and mouth may cause an imbalance between the oxygen and carbon dioxide levels of our body.

5   **We may, if we choose, synchronize our breathing with our current Presence Activating Statement.**

6   **Once we connect our breathing, we immediately begin entering present moment awareness, and so our concept of clock time will automatically alter.** Therefore, we may initially require a clock or a watch to assist us to keep accurate time.

7   **After we have completed our session, we are encouraged to take our attention off our breathing, to sit quietly and enjoy the stillness and peace within.** Inner stillness and silence is the foundation of present moment awareness.

As we progress, we may feel inclined to breathe for longer than 15 minutes during our twice-daily sessions. This is encouraged. However, it is important to set an intention not to accomplish less than 15 minutes per session—no matter what. The mind/ego is unlimited when it comes to finding excuses to justify why we cannot put this small amount of clock time aside for ourselves. Do not buy into this nonsense. The golden rule for all our breathing experiences is this:

Whatever happens physically, mentally, and emotionally during our breathing sessions is supposed to happen.

There is no exception to this rule. This rule especially applies when these experiences appear to us as physical discomfort, mental confusion, or emotional distress. No matter what the nature of our experience, whether we perceive it as comfortable or uncomfortable, we must keep our breathing connected, remain relaxed and as still as possible, and continue our session until whatever is unfolding reaches a point of resolution.

By keeping our breathing connected and remaining as relaxed as possible, all discomfort that arises during a session will pass. Tingling sensations may remain in the extremities of our body after a session. This is normal and positive. There is a big difference however between these tingling sensations and the experiences related to mild or even extreme discomfort.

We must intend never to end a session in the midst of physical, mental, or emotional discomfort. By remaining relaxed and by continuing our connected breathing any uncomfortable experience that we are having, no matter what it is, will unfold to a point of resolution.

Any discomfort that we experience during a consciously connected breathing session is a positive indicator that unconscious emotional experiences are coming to the surface to be neutralized by the presence of our conscious and compassionate attention. All perceived discomfort that we experience during our breathing sessions is always *the past coming to pass*. Always trust the process and complete the session. By ending a session in mid-discomfort, we then take our unintegrated experience into our outer daily life and unconsciously manifest it as challenging external circumstances.

The Presence Process is extremely gentle for what it accomplishes, and it is 100% safe when we pay attention to these simple instructions. Let any discomfort that we experience not steer us into imaginary fears but instead be a powerful confirmations that what we are experiencing is having a real effect.

In all circumstances we are encouraged to trust the process. No one has ever been hurt by breathing normally and naturally.

At times during our breathing sessions we may find ourselves lapsing into states of unconsciousness. This unconsciousness manifests as seemingly falling asleep without warning during our breathing sessions. This is a normal aspect of the process. It occurs when deeply unconscious memories become activated and begin surfacing.

It is recommended that when we enter a re-occurring loop of unconsciousness (when we seem to lapse into sleep every time we sit down to breathe) that we double-up the tempo of our breathing pattern until we feel present again. In other words, we double the speed of the particular breathing rhythm we are in that keeps leading us into the unconscious experience. Even though we double up the speed of our breathing pattern, we must still keep our inhale and exhale evenly balanced.

What this doubling-up procedure accomplishes is that it minimizes the occurrence of any pauses in our breathing. We will notice that the point at which we lapse into sleep is always at the end of an out-breath. Doubling-up the tempo of our breathing assists to minimize the possibility of this occurring. Once we feel more conscious, we can then return to the tempo of our normal breathing pattern. The more present we become, the less our surfacing unconsciousness will overwhelm us. In other words, when we are feeling deeply unconscious, the only way out is to breathe our way through.

EXPERIENCING INNER PRESENCE

THERE IS NOTHING TO MATCH experiencing the power and wonder of our Inner Presence. Our simple Breathing Exercise empowers us to begin entering the state of consciousness in which this experience becomes accessible to us. However, our ego is allergic to present moment awareness and therefore will literally do anything to distract us from having such an experience. To train ourselves to bypass the antics of the ego and to successfully lay the foundations for a personal experience of our Inner Presence, two golden rules must be kept in mind as we attend to our Breathing Exercise:

1 **We must breathe without pausing, no matter what.** This point cannot be over-emphasized. Our personal experience of present moment awareness during a session is accumulative based on the length of time we breathe without pausing. We must therefore keep our breaths

connected throughout our Breathing Exercise, no matter what. Our experience of present moment awareness builds exponentially with each moment that our breathing remains connected. The moment we pause, even if it is just for a few seconds, our growing connection with and awareness of this experience begins waning, and we may feel as if we have lost the awareness we have accumulated. It is important to know, however, that *we do not lose the accumulated processing effect of the breathing session* because we paused, but we may lose our personal awareness of being "in the Presence". During our session, we must therefore intend not to pause no matter what. If we need to go to the bathroom or to place a blanket on ourselves, we must do so without disconnecting our breathing. If we need to blow our nose, cough, yawn, or take a sip of water, we must complete the task swiftly and immediately return to our breathing. If our suppressed emotions surface for release and we feel the need to cry, we must allow ourselves this experience of release, but as soon as it passes, we must immediately return to our breathing.

2   **Physically we must remain as still as possible throughout the session.** Present moment awareness is not only generated by consciously connecting our breathing, but also by maintaining physical stillness throughout our session. Everything physical that occurs during our session, aside from our breathing, is either a releasing of past dramas or the ego's attempt to distract us from the stillness in which our Inner Presence makes its home. It is always in our best interest to ignore our desire to move about and instead keep our attention focused on our Presence Activating Statement and our breathing. We must not itch, fiddle, scratch, rock or shift our body, entertain a sudden desire to do yoga postures, hum, or talk during our session. All of this is unnecessary drama. Drama instantly dissolves present moment awareness.

To experience the wonder and power of our own Presence, we must train ourselves to sit as still as a statue and to connect our breathing as if one pause meant sudden death. For the purpose of our journey through The Presence Process, there is no other physical body movement aside from the natural and balanced inhale and exhale of our own breathing that can generate a sense of present moment awareness for us. All other physical movement, no matter how relevant it may be to our mind, is ego-drama. For the purpose of this Process, we are encouraged to keep the following in mind:

*Silence, stillness, consciously connected breathing, and a mind focused on our Presence Activating Statement provide the most accelerated pathway to the present moment.
– All else is interference.*

We cannot force an experience of present moment awareness. We can only lay the foundation for it. The awareness of our Inner Presence enters our consciousness when *we least expect it*. Let this also tell us something about the disadvantages of having expectations.

From this moment onward …

Every moment of every day of this Process counts. Every consciously connected breath in every breathing session makes this Process gentler (more conscious) for us. We are therefore encouraged to make the most of every moment of this opportunity to intimately connect with the magnificent power that we call our Inner Presence. When we accomplish this connection, we accomplish everything.

By sincerely committing to applying ourselves to every aspect of this Process, we will be enhancing the quality of our entire life experience. In essence, the opportunity within this experience is for our own emotional rebirth into the life that we always suspected existed but somehow remained at an unobtainable distance. The Presence Process is our opportunity to reach within and set in motion the causal events that will enable us to reclaim our authentic state of joy, creativity, and peace. Nobody can accomplish this for us. Nobody ever did. Nobody ever will. We are and always will be 100% responsible for the quality of our life experience.

*In life we are all given choices and opportunities. But it must be our own footprints that lead us into what is real —
and therefore lasting.*

It is facilitating to consciously set an intention every morning after our Breathing Exercise to strive to maintain our sense of present moment awareness throughout the day. We can achieve this practically by applying the following simple technique:

During the course of our day, when we become aware of our breathing—and we will—let it remind us to mentally repeat our Presence Activating Statement. In the same manner, when we remember to say our Presence Activator—and we will—let it remind us to consciously connect our breathing.

By remaining as physically and mentally present as possible throughout our day, we are more likely to emotionally respond rather than to react to what we are processing. We will also be more present in every aspect of our daily activities. We must keep in mind, however, that we will go through periods when we will appear to be completely distracted no matter how ardently we apply ourselves to our process. This is a sign that deeply suppressed memories are surfacing because we are ready to process them. Allow these moments to be acknowledgements that the Process is unfolding exactly as it is supposed to. As this Process is being orchestrated by our Inner Facilitator, we will not be given more than we are able to digest. Often we will find that we are also not given any less.

FOR THE NEXT SEVEN DAYS WE ARE REQUIRED TO:

1 Attend to our 15-minute Breathing Exercise twice each day as the first activity we attend to after we are fully awake and as the last activity we attend to before we climb into bed.

2 Repeat our given Presence Activating Statement for this Session whenever we are not mentally engaged.

3 **Review these reading materials.** The best time for our daily reviewing of these reading materials is directly after our morning or evening breathing session because this is when our level of present moment awareness is heightened. SPECIFICS: When we attend to our Breathing Exercise, let us observe how much movement occurs in our body aside from the increase and decrease in the size of our lungs. When we are breathing, there is no need for any other part of our body to move in tandem with our lungs. Let us train ourselves to remain completely still. Also, let us listen carefully to the moment our inhale transforms into an exhale and also when our exhale transforms into an inhale. Is the flow of our breath being interrupted at all during these transitions? If it is, then we are still imbedding pauses in our breathing pattern. Let us be patient with ourselves as we learn to consciously connect our breathing. Our breathing mechanism has been habitually disconnected most of our life. It is also a good idea to re-read our breathing instructions after our first few breathing sessions to make sure we are attending to this procedure correctly.

THIS ENDS SESSION ONE.

SESSION TWO

Our Presence Activating Statement for the next seven days is:

I acknowledge my reflections in the world.

TO ACTIVATE THIS SESSION:

We memorize the given Presence Activating Statement.
We then read through all the written materials.
We sit still and connect our breathing for at least 15 minutes.

IDENTIFYING THE MESSENGER

ONE OF THE MOST POWERFUL transformations that we will automatically experience as a consequence of completing The Presence Process is our evolution from reactive to responsive beings. This one inner causal adjustment to our perception of the world, and hence our outer interaction with it, will improve the quality of our entire life experience. The consequences of choosing to be responsible for the quality of all our life experiences are eternal.

Whenever the effects of our thoughts, words, and deeds are significantly delayed by time, they appear to us to occur independently of any cause. The consequence is that we then assume that many of the circumstances of our life are happening *to us* and not *because of us*. This enables us to enter victim or victor mentality. Being a victim or a victor means that we are either complaining about our experiences or competing with the experiences of others. Because of the pauses between cause and effect manufactured by time, it never occurs to us that we are actually complaining about ourselves and the consequences of our own actions, or that we are actually competing with ourselves because of the obstacles that we have placed in our own way. Being a victim or victor is no different than the behavior of a dog chasing its own tail. The only difference is that the dog has more fun.

Reactive behavior is founded on a belief that the world is happening *to* us and that it is therefore our duty to enforce our will upon it. This illusion appears to be real to us only because we are "living in time". Living in time is an unconscious state in which our attention is almost exclusively focused on our past and on the future that we have projected for ourselves. The consequence of this unconscious state is that, for the most part, the distance between our thoughts, words, and deeds and their inevitable physical, mental, and emotional consequences is just long enough for us to be able to convince ourselves that we are not the cause of most of our present life experiences.

In other words, while living in time, we cannot clearly see the connection between cause and effect. This is because the energetic connection between all causes and their inevitable effects takes place in what we call "the present moment". The present moment, when we are not consciously aware of it, becomes a blind spot in our awareness. This blind spot, or lack of present moment awareness, makes it impossible for us to perceive the connection and continuity of all life. To perceive the connection and continuity of all life requires that we are aware of the intimate relationship between cause and effect. If we cannot see the connection between cause and effect, our life experience appears to be unfolding chaotically, randomly, and devoid of meaning or purpose. Hence, when we live in time, we spend our life seeking the meaning of life. In the present moment, we enjoy a life saturated with meaning.

Time is an experience in which there is therefore an appearance of a delay or a pause or an empty space between any thought, word, or deed and its inevitable consequence. For the most part, this apparent delay or pause or empty space between any thought, word, or deed and its inevitable consequence makes it appear as if the two events are not connected. This delay or pause or empty space is an illusion because all thoughts, words, and deeds and their consequences are intimately connected and can never be separated. They are connected energetically. This is the Law of Cause and Effect upon which the tide of our entire universe rises and falls.

One of the obstacles that prevents us from perceiving this law of the universe in action is that our attention has become *trans*fixed upon the surface of things. The consequence of seeing everything as having a solid surface, and interacting with it solely according to what we perceive on its surface, is twofold:

1 **We cannot see into anything and therefore have no awareness of the real and vibrant inner content of life.** Consequently, we cannot see how everything intimately interacts with everything else. This is because all authentic interactions between life forms occur inwardly.

2 **The solid surface of whatever we focus upon appears to us as a barrier and thus seems to separate whatever we are focusing on from all other objects or life forms.** Hence we cannot see the connectedness of life. Once again, the connectedness between all life forms is an inner experience.

The outcome of this perceptual addiction (which is what it is) to being *trans*fixed by the surface of things is that we no longer see the energy that flows within and between all life. To begin rekindling our ability to perceive the content and connection of all life, which is essential to perceive the play of cause and effect of every experience in our life, we must once again relearn or remember how to perceive life as "energy in motion". We can initiate this adjustment in our perception by consciously training ourselves to redirect our point of focus to the emotional content of our own experiences. In other words, we must first become aware of our own energies in motion, and this awareness will then automatically be reflected by the world around us.

The "effect" of The Presence Process is that once we activate our present moment awareness by consciously connecting our breathing, we initiate a journey that awakens us from the unconscious physical and mental state of living in time into the conscious emotional experience that enables us to perceive our personal flow of energy.

The consequence of this gradual shift of consciousness is that the distance between many of our thoughts, words, and deeds and their inevitable physical, mental, and emotional consequences appears to become increasingly shorter. This shift often gives us the sensation of time speeding up. What in fact is occurring is that we are becoming aware of the emotional undercurrent of our experiences, of the energetic chord that connects all the causes and effects that flow through our life. This energetic chord is the threshold of the present moment, and our ability to perceive it is the rebirthing of our present moment awareness.

The consequence of entering present moment awareness is that it starts becoming apparent to us that when we are living in time, the quality of the life that we are experiencing is mostly an effect. As we further awaken into present moment awareness, it becomes clearer to us that the quality of our life experience right now is a reoccurring effect of belief systems that are generated by the unintegrated experiences of our childhood. It is only at this point that we truly realize that our unintegrated childhood emotions are the causes that we normally cannot see of the physical and mental circumstances that are unfolding as the quality of our adult life experience.

Aside from the blind spot created within our perception from lack of present moment awareness, the reason why these causes, these emotionally-rooted belief systems, are unconscious to our normal everyday physical and mental awareness is twofold.

1   **Most of them were imprinted into our emotional body before our awareness consciously entered the mental realm, so they are not located within us as thoughts, words, and concepts, but as feelings.** The nature of our adult life in time is

that we interact with our past mentally and not emotionally and so these emotional causal points are no longer visible to us.

2   **The core emotional experiences of the past that are having a negative affect on our life right now are by their very nature uncomfortable to us, so our automatic impulse has been to place them out of our conscious awareness so that we can "get on with our life".** This is called "suppression". We are masters at the art form of hiding from ourselves that which we do not know how to cope with.

To get on with our adult life, we literally had to put these uncomfortable emotional experiences "behind us" and in doing so we successfully hid the causes of many of our present- day discomforts from ourselves. The consequence is that we are now unable to consciously make the connection between these causal events and their ongoing impact on our present circumstances. This is what generates a life that appears to be happening chaotically. Being a victim or a victor is a behavior pattern rising out of the inability to make a connection between the unfolding circumstances of our life right now and the unconscious belief systems that are activated by the suppressed emotional discomfort of our past.

By entering The Presence Process, it is our intention that these suppressed childhood emotions and the negative belief systems that they have spurned begin to surface into our awareness. This becomes our intention now because we are simultaneously being taught how to integrate them and to neutralize the negative effect they are having on our present life experience.

A good metaphor to illustrate this procedure is to think of a jar containing oil and water. The water is who and what we really are while the oil is the sum of our uncomfortable physical, mental, and emotional experiences. When we are living in reaction, in victim or victor mentality, it is the same as shaking the jar endlessly in an attempt to make a change in our circumstances. Yet all that happens is that the oil and the water get so mixed up that it becomes impossible to tell one apart from the other. All that our endless "doings" accomplish is a murky mixture.

The Presence Process is all about "not doing". It teaches us to place the jar of our life experience down and leave it to "be". This automatically allows the oil to rise to the surface and to separate from the water.

This rising oil is our unconscious childhood memories and the negative belief systems they have spurned. They will automatically rise to the surface of our life experience when we engage in "not-doing".

The Presence Process, while simultaneously introducing us to the arena of "not-doing", instructs us how to gently begin scooping the oil of our suppressed emotions off the surface of our life experience. As we accomplish this, the jar of our life contains less and less oil. Simultaneously, the water, our life experience, regains clarity. In other words, by moving through The Presence Process, we automatically start becoming aware of who and what we really are as opposed to being endlessly distracted by the experiences that we have manufactured as a reaction to our inner discomforts.

Fortunately, we will not have to re-experience, re-live, or re-witness all these suppressed childhood experiences. Most of them have no real value to us. Most of them will re-enter and then flow out of our awareness as feelings that we cannot seem to pin down to anything. We will only be required to become aware of the details of suppressed memories from which we are deliberately meant to gain wisdom at this time. This is usually because the wisdom gained from these past experiences will facilitate our emotional growth and be useful in assisting us to set an example that will facilitate the emotional growth of the people in our environment.

As these suppressed emotions come to pass, which is all that is occurring when we start re-experiencing them, we may at first perceive them to be experiences that are unfolding for the very first time. Yet as we gain more present moment awareness, we will realize that these are the emotions that we have been unconsciously holding onto and hiding within ourselves all our life. We will be instructed how to use our attention and intention to allow them to integrate. Our undivided attention and our compassionate intention are all that are required to facilitate this task.

Because these suppressed memories and their corresponding emotions are so deeply imbedded in our unconscious, they are often only apparent to us, if at all, as nameless sensations. Because of this, it is not possible for us to recall them as images in our mind's eye, as we would the memory of a recent event that has happened in our life. Therefore, this is not the manner in which they will surface into our awareness. Now, as we intend them to surface in our life experience so that we may consciously integrate them, they will do so as *reflections* and *projections*.

A reflection is the occurrence of an experience in our life that reminds us of something, while a projection is the behavior that we adopt when we react to such a memory. For example, if someone reminds us of one of our parents, this is a reflection. If we then start behaving around that person as we would around the parent they remind us of, this is a projection. A reflection occurs first and is then quickly followed by a projection. This process is often called "being triggered", or "having our buttons pushed". What is really occurring is that we are seeing ghosts from our past (reflections) and then chasing them (projections).

Before we begin accumulating present moment awareness, these reflections and projections will initially appear as if they are happening *to* us, independently of our behavior. Initially, they will appear cloaked in the guise of seemingly random and chaotic external circumstances or as the unprovoked behavior of people around us that cause us emotional upset. But as we accumulate present moment awareness, we will also attain the ability to see that whenever we are triggered in a manner that causes us emotional discomfort, we are deliberately being "set up". We are deliberately being visited by ghosts of our past so that we can have the opportunity to consciously exorcise them from haunting our present.

To recognize the reflections of our own unconscious memories in the world around us, we need remember this golden rule:

> *Whenever anything happens that upsets us emotionally,*
> *whether it appears to us as an event or as another person's*
> *behavior, we are seeing a reflection of our past.*

> *Whenever we react physically, mentally, or emotionally to such*
> *a circumstance, we are projecting.*

Unfortunately, there is no exception to this rule. If we are emotionally upset by anything, we are actively remembering something that has been unconsciously hidden from us until that moment. We are energetically attached to it because of past emotional circumstances. We are being haunted by it. This is why we react to it.

One of the reasons why we may not initially be able to recognize the upsetting circumstances in our present life as surfacing emotional memories of the past is because in "time" our tendency is to focus our attention on the physical aspects of the upsetting circumstances. In other words, our attention is usually *trans*fixed by the physical event or the physical behavior of the person that is emotionally upsetting us instead of the emotional reaction we are experiencing as a consequence. We are *trans*fixed by the surface of our life experience. So now we must train ourselves to go beneath the surface because it is always the emotional signature of the upsetting circumstance that is the surfacing memory, not the physical event or the person's behavior. Our earliest memories are only available to us as emotional signatures and so to gain the skill required to recognize them, we have to learn how to see beneath the surface of unfolding physical circumstances of our life as it is right now. We have to teach ourselves to become aware of the emotional currents that flow behind the scenes of our physical world experience.

The nature of the physical world is that it is in a constant state of change; therefore, by focusing on the surface of any event, we are more than likely to assume that what is happening to us in any given moment is something new. The physical circumstances of life, because they are always changing, appear on the surface to be brand new occurrences. Yet the fact that we are upset emotionally by certain circumstances, and not by others, and that we then automatically emotionally react to these specific circumstances is evidence enough that what is occurring in that moment is not something new. It impacts us emotionally because it is reminding us of something. It triggers us emotionally because it is a reflection, and it is usually reflecting something we would rather not remember, hence our innate annoyance with it. Such an occurrence is always a reflection and our reaction to it is therefore always a projection.

> *Any occurrence in our life that emotionally triggers us in*
> *a negative way is always a message from the past being*
> *communicated to us in the present. Throughout The Presence*
> *Process, we call the triggering event "the messenger".*

Herein is one of the most awesome aspects of The Presence Process: throughout this journey our Inner Presence will set us up (upset us) by deliberately sending outer "messengers'" (reflections of our past) to assist us to recall the unintegrated childhood memories that we have long since suppressed. Our Inner Presence does this because the use of reflections (or messengers) is the only way for us to "see" our deeply suppressed past in a way that we can consciously work with it. We are "set up" in this manner because unless these suppressed memories are able to surface and be consciously integrated, they will continue to fuel the negative belief systems that do not serve us. The nature of these setup experiences is that they are initially uncomfortable; however, they occur to liberate us not humiliate us.

To encourage us to embrace and make the most of this setup procedure is why we are asked not to approach this Process with an intention that it initially be easy or that it make us feel good. Such intentions cause us to steer away from the very experiences that are deliberately occurring to facilitate our emotional growth.

But how, we may wonder, is our Inner Presence able to deliberately send these "messengers" and thus initiate these opportunities for us to reflect on our unintegrated past? It is very simple. Session One introduced us to the attributes of our Inner Presence. One of these is that the Presence within us is intimately and constantly connected with the Presence within everyone else. There is a great benefit to this particular attribute as far as The Presence Process is concerned. It enables the Presence within us to activate the people and circumstances in our life experience into replicating behaviors and conditions that remind us of interactions and incidents that we have long since suppressed. In other words, this omnipresent attribute enables Presence to "set us up" when, where, how, and with whom it sees fit. It is important to keep in mind that this only happens to facilitate our emotional growth.

The procedure of unconscious memory activation through the use of "messengers" (reflections) is an integral part of The Presence Process. It is what enables us to accomplish what is impossible through conventional verbal therapeutic procedures. We can be sure that by the end of this journey we will have experienced enough of these deliberate "setups" to eliminate all doubts as to whether this procedure is being done deliberately or not. It is. By the end of this Process, we will know through our own personal experience that every time we are emotionally upset, we are deliberately being set up to clear our blocked emotions. We may not want to acknowledge this at the time our setups occur, but we will know it to be true.

Unfortunately, the humorous aspect of being setup is usually only available to us in hindsight. However, the profound consequence of repeatedly having these setup experiences is that we will come to know for certain that the Presence within each of us is consistently and intimately connected with the Presence in all of us. Our Inner Presence can literally act through anything and anyone to assist us in our emotional growth. And it does.

Initially, this realization may be somewhat daunting, because we will then realize that this awesome omnipresent power is paying close and personal attention to us in every moment. This realization is eventually extremely comforting, however, when it becomes obvious to us that we can never be, nor have we ever been alone, lost, or without assistance. We have simply been asleep and in "the dream of time". While we wander through the haunted corridors of time, we render our awareness numb to the experience of our Inner Presence.

One of the most profound insights we gain during The Presence Process is the awareness that all the circumstances of our life have quite literally been a play that is being deliberately staged for our benefit. This has occurred so that we can see reflected outside of ourselves what we have suppressed so deeply within.

Along the way, we will also have the opportunity to realize that the reflections (memories) that cause us to project (react) are our own personal suppressed memories and therefore only have any real meaning to us. We will know this to be true because if we approach "the messenger" (someone who has been activated by Presence to emotionally upset us) and ask him or her why they behaved like that towards us, they will most likely look at us in confusion. We may have already had such confusing and utterly frustrating experiences in the past. Usually, if approached and interrogated, the messenger will look at us as if we are crazy because the whole event and its implications *for us* are completely unconscious to the person who our past memories are being reflected upon. They are being unconsciously activated by Presence to facilitate us. The biggest players in this staged drama of ongoing setups are our immediate family, our intimate and our working relationships. However, anyone or anything in our outer world can be used by Presence to direct our attention to an unintegrated inner condition.

Another important realization to digest throughout these setup experiences is that our reflections are not real, but that our projections have a very real impact and consequence. This is why the following instruction will serve us well throughout our experience of The Presence Process:

> *For the remainder of this journey, we must endeavor to sit back and watch our life experience as we would a play in a theater.*

When we are watching a live play, we do not get up from our seats and confront the actors just because they utter lines and exhibit behaviors that emotionally upset us. We remain in our seats because we accept that what is unfolding in front of us is part of the play and that the actors are only emotionally triggering us because they are reflecting something that is "close to our hearts". This is exactly how we will be experiencing the surfacing of our unconscious emotional memories during the course of The Presence Process and beyond. This is how it has always occurred. It is just that we cannot see this in a time-based experience. When we really see how this procedure of being set up works, we will laugh at how well and how often we do get set up. On one level, life is a complete setup. This is the so-called cosmic joke. When we really learn to laugh at how well and how often we get set up and how we react unconsciously to these experiences, we will then have access to endless laughter.

To react to the people or circumstances that are emotionally triggering us is to "shoot the messengers" sent by Presence. Instead of reacting, we are now going to begin teaching ourselves the perceptual steps that lead to "responding". The core difference between a reaction and a response is as follows:

A *reaction* is unconscious behavior in which our energy is directed outwards into the world in an attempt to defend ourselves or to attack another. A reaction is a drama that is played out in an effort to sedate or control the nature of our experiences. The theme of all reactive behavior is blame or revenge.

A *response* is a conscious choice to contain and constructively internalize our energy with the intention of using it to integrate and liberate our unconsciousness. The theme of all responsive behaviors is responsibility.

From this point onward, as we go about our daily experiences, certain circumstances will unfold that will magnetically attract our attention. These are the circumstances that we want to pay attention to so that we can work with them internally. This magnetic pull on our attention occurs because these particular circumstances are energetically connected with our suppressed past. These specific circumstances will isolate themselves from all the others that we are experiencing in that we will have a powerful emotional reaction towards them. Often we will perceive this emotional reaction to be uncomfortable or unpleasant. Initially, we are going to react unconsciously to these setups until we gain the present moment awareness to behave consciously and responsibly. Therefore, it is important for us to keep the understanding of how deeply suppressed memories surface in the forefront of our awareness: not as images in our head but as unfolding circumstances and as the way people behave in our outer world experiences.

Our task for this Session is to identify the "messengers" as they appear in our life experience. By being able to accomplish this task, we will be awakening a quality of "seeing" that enables us to begin perceiving what is really happening beneath the surface of the physical circumstances of the world. Developing this skill of discernment teaches us how to use our mental capabilities to see beneath the surface of our physical experiences and into the emotional currents of our predicament. This skill is essential because it enables us to differentiate what is *really* happening from what is a reflected memory. Only when we are able to accomplish the task of efficiently identifying the messengers in our life experience will we be ready and able to exorcise the ghosts of our past. Being able to identify the messengers will enable us to become our own ghost-busters. We can then begin navigating our awareness out of the illusions created by the dream called "time".

FOR THE NEXT SEVEN DAYS WE ARE REQUIRED TO:

1   Attend to our 15-minute Breathing Exercise twice each day.

2   Repeat our given Presence Activating Statement for the Session whenever we are not mentally engaged.

3   Review our reading materials. SPECIFICS: As we move through our daily life experience, we are now asked to pay attention to what magnetically grabs our attention, to watch for "the messengers": those people or circumstances that push our buttons. DO NOT SHOOT THE MESSENGER!

THIS ENDS SESSION TWO.

SESSION THREE

Our Presence Activating Statement for the next seven days is:

I respond consciously to all my experiences.

TO ACTIVATE THIS SESSION:

We memorize the given Presence Activating Statement.
We then read through all the written materials.
We sit still and connect our breathing for at least 15 minutes.

GETTING THE MESSAGE

WHEN WE ENTER THE PRESENCE PROCESS, we are asked not to react to our
life experience, but to watch it as if we are watching a play. This instruction is not as easy as it sounds because while "living in time", we are all

addicted to reacting to our life. Being reactive appears to us to be normal behavior because just about everyone on this planet is to some extent living in a state of reaction. So initially, by being asked not to react, it appears as if we are being asked not to act "normally".

In Session Two, we were asked to begin acknowledging the reflections of our unconscious memories and belief systems in the world by watching our life with the intention of identifying "the messengers" sent to us by our Inner Presence. These messengers are easy to identify because they materialize as any event or person's behavior that emotionally upsets us. We were then asked to do our best not to shoot the messenger but instead to watch the event unfolding in our life as if we were sitting in an audience and watching a play. In this way, what we are doing is dismissing the messenger and in the same breath acknowledging that the value of the experience is in *the message* and not its carrier. We do not blame the mail person for the bills delivered to us, and we do not blame the mirror for anything we do not like about our appearance. Likewise, it is pointless reacting to our reflections in the world.

Reacting to our reflections in this world is what true insanity is.

In this Session, we are now asked to take this procedure one step further. Having dismissed the messenger, it is essential we now receive the intended message. Initially, it may be challenging for us to accomplish this because up to this point we may be used to reacting automatically whenever we are emotionally triggered. However, because we are consciously connecting our breathing twice every day and thereby consistently accumulating present moment awareness, we are becoming increasingly more conscious. This present moment awareness enables us to become conscious that anything in our experience that emotionally upsets us is a deliberate tool being wielded by our Inner Presence to reflect our unconscious emotional issues back to us. It accomplishes this by transforming our world experience into a mirror so that we can see reflected outside of us the memories of emotions that we have suppressed deeply within us. To succeed at the task of getting the message we must be willing to:

1   Take our attention off the messenger (the physical event or person's behavior).

2   Step back from the voice in our head urging us into reaction (the mental event).

3   Instead place our attention on *how we are feeling* as a consequence of the trig-gering interaction (the emotional event).

We can begin accomplishing this task by asking ourselves the follow-ing question each time we are emotionally triggered:

> "What specific emotional reaction did this event or person
> trigger within me?"

In answering this question, it is advisable to describe the emotional reaction we are experiencing using a simple word. To assist us in search-ing for the relevant word that describes exactly what we are feeling when we are being set up, we may say out loud:

> "I am feeling.... " (Describe the emotion in one simple word.)

In completing this sentence, we may use words like "angry, sad, hurt, alone, scared, afraid, shy," and so on, until we connect with a word that resonates with our triggered emotional state. We will know when we have connected with the right word because our body will literally res-onate physically to the emotional reaction we are verbally describing out loud. By "resonate" what is meant is that we may feel our hands buzzing, or our solar plexus tightening, or our heartbeat increasing, or our face flushing, or any number of other body indicators. Once we have used this simple technique to identify the word that describes the emotional reac-tion we experienced as a consequence of being triggered by the messen-ger, then we have officially received the message from the messenger.

We are now ready to take the next step: to gather the information imbedded in this message. We are ready to see that the particular emo-tional reaction that was triggered within us by the external world is not something new in our life but that it is a reaction that has reoccurred repeatedly in the past. To see this clearly, we ask the following question:

> "When last did I experience the exact same emotional reaction?"

We will discover that our mind will mentally guide us to a previous incident. (Remember that if we cannot recall the answer immediately we must remain open-minded and allow the answer to be given to us by our Inner Facilitator when we least expect it.) Without getting hooked into the physical details of the previous event that is shown to us or into a mental conversation with ourselves about it, we acknowledge the occurrence of the identical emotional reaction that we have recalled and continue to seek further into our past. To do this we ask:

> "And when before this incident did I experience the exact same
> emotional reaction?"

As we continue to ask this question, we will gradually uncover a reoccurring emotional pattern that extends all the way back to our childhood. If we find it difficult to trace this emotional pathway, it may be because our mind is too focused on the physical aspect of the trail. The physical circumstances trailing back into our past that have triggered these same reoccurring emotional reactions may not look alike at all. Metaphorically, they will all be identical, but until we gather a certain amount of present moment awareness, we may not be able to decipher the symbolism. We must therefore make sure our intention during this exercise is to focus our attention specifically on recalling *similar emotional reactions* as opposed to scanning the past for the appearance of *similar "messengers"*.

A useful insight in assisting us to trace a specific reoccurring emotional pattern comes from the understanding that all core emotional circumstances repeat in our life approximately every seven years. So if we have difficulty retracing the pathway of similar emotional reactions, we can jump about seven years back from the most recent occurrence and seek out the familiar emotional signature.

By applying the above simple technique, we will be able to journey backwards through the circumstances of time to a point close to or within our childhood experience. It is normal that we will struggle to access the initial causal event that set up the repeating seven-year pattern because it will have occurred before we had a grasp of language with which to express or to create a concept around any of our experiences. The core event may have occurred at birth or in our first year or two of life when we were interacting with our world purely on an emotional level. As such, it will be recorded as a feeling that is hard for us to verbalize.

There are two more questions that we can ask ourselves in order to access even more information about the reoccurring emotional reaction that has been brought to our attention by the messenger. This requires that we metaphorically take a step back from our upsetting event or interaction and the specific reoccurring emotional signature that we have identified and now look at the entire scenario as we would view an act in a play. In other words, we must step out of this whole event completely and observe it as an outsider. Then we can ask:

"What does this remind me of?"

And/or

"Who used to behave like this towards or around me?"

The answer to these two questions will most likely initially point to events occurring right now in our most current relationships. But if we keep searching our experience, these two questions will lead us on a journey that extends back into our past relationships, all the way to our initial relationship with our mother or our father, or with both of them. Asking these two questions will assist us in seeing that the unintegrated emotions that we have been carrying, whether they are fear, anger, or grief related, were initially imprinted within us by our parents either through their interaction with us or by our witnessing their interaction with each other. This is because *all behavior is learnt*. This includes all our emotional reactions.

Whenever we are emotionally triggered, we perform an act that we originally copied from somebody by observing their behavior when they were emotionally triggered. These are our dramas, dramas that we re-en-act whenever the right buttons are pushed. We all have our learned dramas that we automatically perform whenever certain emotional buttons are pushed.

That is why everyone in this world to some extent lives in reaction. While we "live in time", this world is an unconscious drama in which the past and the projected future write the script for our ongoing life experience. The Presence Process is an opportunity and an invitation to awaken from this drama. The first step in awakening from this drama is learning how to take the cue for our behavior from what is unfolding in the present moment, not from what happened in the past or what we think may happen in the future. Being able to discern the present moment from the ghosts of time requires an ability to distinguish reflections from real occurrences.

This is why we must now train ourselves to step back from "the messengers" and instead use our energy to access "the messages" that they are bringing to our attention. By inwardly asking the series of questions below whenever we are emotionally triggered, instead of projecting our attention outward in reaction, we will start to accomplish this and consequently gain profound insights into the source of our own repetitive emotional behavior.

1 **"What specific emotional reaction did this event or person trigger within me?"** We answer this by saying out loud to ourselves, "I am feeling...." (Describe the specific emotion in one simple word.)

2 **"When last did I experience the exact same emotional reaction?"**

3 **"And when before this incident did I experience the exact same emotional reaction?"** We keep asking this over and over until we approach the source of the event.

4 **"What does this remind me of?"** and/or **"Who used to behave like this towards or around me?"**

During The Presence Process, this procedure of accessing information from the messenger using the following series of questions is called "getting the message". By choosing to take our focus off the physical event in front of us (the reflection/messenger) and instead place it on the emotional reaction triggered within us (the message), we take a massive step away from being a victim or a victor. This choice to respond immediately starts neutralizing our seemingly unconscious and automatic impulse to react. What we initially perceived to be random events happening chaotically to us become gems of insight into our own behavior patterns. They become the raw material for emotional growth.

By consciously choosing to follow our reoccurring emotional reaction as it extends back into our past, we take another massive step away from "reacting" and towards "responding". By applying this procedure, we will quickly become aware that all the physical, mental, and emotional discomfort in our life right now is not at all random. By "getting the message", we will clearly be able to see that everything that negatively triggers our emotions is part of a recurring pattern that is anchored in the distant past and perpetuated unconsciously by our unresolved and suppressed childhood memories.

Until we can clearly see this for ourselves, we are unable to neutralize this ongoing pattern. Just being able to see it changes everything because it elevates what was unconscious and therefore unseen to being consciously visible. For a while, we may still continue to act out these learned dramas in our life, but we will not be able to do so unconsciously. We will realize that we are reacting when we are reacting, or very soon thereafter. Eventually, we will be able to see the messenger coming a mile away and be able to catch ourselves before we react.

"Getting the message" changes everything because by doing so we realize that the emotional reactions we feel as a consequence of being triggered have nothing to do with our life as an adult. They are the unintegrated emotions that we have been suppressing for years. They are unresolved feelings related to our childhood that leak unconsciously into our adult life experience. They deliberately come to our attention as external circumstances and the behavior of others so that we have the opportunity to see, acknowledge, and integrate them. Until we allow ourselves the opportunity to consciously integrate them, they will diligently keep reoccurring in our adult experience in some form or another—often in a manner that seemingly sets out to sabotage our best intentions.

The Presence Process invites us to begin maturing emotionally. What this means is that instead of reacting we choose to respond. We choose to metaphorically take a deep breath, to gracefully move out of the triggering situation and in doing so to keep ourselves cool and conscious. If it is not appropriate for us to do any emotional processing work in the moment that we are being triggered, then we can "bank" the incident. We can then intend a quiet time to open up for us so that we can spend a few moments alone asking the relevant internal questions. When that opportunity arises, we can then recall the setup and the emotional reaction that was triggered by it and begin tracking its reoccurrence backwards into our past until we can access the initial causal event.

Remember that it is the asking of the questions that is important. The answers will automatically come to us if we keep an open mind. Also, keep in mind that even though the asking of these questions appears to take our attention into the past, this is not what is actually occurring. The past does not exist anymore as something behind us or something that we can go back to. The unintegrated experiences of the past do, however, exist as conditions within our emotional body that require our compassionate attention. In essence we are not going "back", we are going "in".

A good reason for applying ourselves to this inner work is because these unintegrated childhood experiences will continue to surface in our adult life as physical, mental, and emotional imbalance until we evolve to a point where we have the capacity to wield the Perceptual Tools required to resolve them. By teaching ourselves to metaphorically look beyond "the messenger" to "get the message", we begin to accomplish this.

Note: If we have had any difficulties with this Session, it may be due to the approach we are taking to the questions. Rereading The Consciousness of Questions in Part I will remind us about the approach that we are asked to take to questions asked throughout The Presence Process.

FOR THE NEXT SEVEN DAYS WE ARE REQUIRED TO:

1 Attend to our 15-minute Breathing Exercise twice each day.

2 Repeat our given Presence Activating Statement for the Session whenever we are not mentally engaged.

3 Review our reading materials. SPECIFICS: Our task now is to train ourselves how to "get the message" whenever a "messenger" crosses our path. Each time we are emotionally triggered, we can accomplish this task by asking ourselves the list of questions revealed to us in this Session's material.

THIS ENDS SESSION THREE.

SESSION FOUR

—————

Our Presence Activating Statement for the next seven days is:

I restore my inner balance with my compassionate attention.

TO ACTIVATE THIS SESSION:

We memorize the given Presence Activating Statement.
We then read through all the written materials.
We sit still and connect our breathing for at least 15 minutes.

⊖⊗⊗⊖

FEEL IT TO HEAL IT

LET US NOW CONSIDER the experiences that we call pain and discomfort. Throughout this Process when we refer to "pain and discomfort" we are including all states of imbalance, whether they manifest physically, mentally, or emotionally.

The consequence of "living in time" is that we will all experience pain and discomfort, whether it is physical, mental, or emotional. Pain and discomfort are words that we use to describe an energetic condition in our emotional body that we mentally and physically perceive as being wrong, unpleasant, unproductive, uncomfortable, against us, harmful and/or unnatural. Due to our conditioned mental and physical perception of this emotional condition, our automatic reaction to it is usually founded on fear and therefore fueled with resistance.

From the moment we enter this world, we are taught by the example of others to fear and therefore resist pain and discomfort by controlling it, sedating it, distracting ourselves from it, numbing it, drugging it, and even going so far as to cutting it out. By the examples of others, we are led to believe that pain and discomfort are enemies and that when they manifest in our experience, we must escape or conquer them at all costs. We are led to assume that pain and discomfort are always indicators that *something is wrong*. In this world, it is very rare that we are invited or encouraged to respond to our experiences of pain and discomfort by listening to them instead of running from them.

During The Presence Process, we are asked to consider the possibility that the experience of pain and discomfort is deliberate and therefore on purpose. In other words, when these experiences occur to us, it is because they are supposed to happen. We are asked to open our mind to the idea that pain and discomfort are essential forms of communication that have a necessary and valuable function in our life experience. We are being invited to change our perception of what pain and discomfort are and what the nature of our relationship is with them.

We are being invited to consider that pain and discomfort are our friends, not our enemies, and that they have come to assist us, not hurt us.

Consider what the experience of pain and discomfort automatically accomplishes. It always obediently brings the focus of our attention to a specific place in our physical, mental, or emotional experience. Why?

Consider how we impulsively react to this experience? Metaphorically we run in the opposite direction by pulling our attention away from the area that is experiencing pain and discomfort. We do our best to annihilate our awareness of this experience with tablets, alcohol, or various medical procedures. In other words, we automatically attempt to resist and suppress the experience through control and sedation. What are we assuming?

Our reactive behavior never resolves the pain and discomfort; it merely suppresses and postpones it for a time. Inevitably, the pain or discomfort will reappear at a later date and continue its attempt to gain our attention or show up in another form elsewhere. Consider this possibility:

The most painful thing about pain and discomfort may well be our resistance to it.

During The Presence Process, our suppressed memories are going to be surfacing deliberately so that they can be integrated by our compassionate attention. Pain and discomfort in the body, mind, and heart are our physical, mental, or emotional bodies calling for our attention so that we will attend to them. Yet our impulse is always to run away from these experiences or find someone else to attend to them. What we are now being asked to consider is this: maybe our lack of success in resolving our pain and discomfort in the past is because *it is not possible for someone else's attention to integrate our experiences on our behalf.* What we are being invited to consider is that because it is *our* physical, mental, or emotional body that is in a state of imbalance, that it is therefore *our* attention and only *our* attention that can really restore balance to our experience.

All our prophets, spiritual masters, and sacred texts tell us that the omnipresence that we have named God resides within us all. If we can on some level begin to accept this, even initially only as a concept, then we can also begin to accept another possibility—that in our life experience, our direct link to the intimate presence and unlimited healing power of what God is to us is to be found in *the presence of our consciously wielded attention.* However, the possibilities contained in this realization remain mental gymnastics until we begin exploring them experientially. The only way we can *know* if this is true is to consciously and compassionately wield our own attention with the intention of resolving our own states of physical, mental, and emotional imbalance. In other words, our experience must become our own laboratory, our own testing ground.

During The Presence Process, we are deliberately using the breath as a tool to bring our attention back into our physical, mental, and emotional bodies and to temporarily anchor it there. One of the consequences of this practice is that we become aware of pains and discomforts that have been with us since we were children, but that we have very successfully suppressed from our awareness. The following metaphor illustrates how long-term suppressed conditions of pain and discomfort can come to our attention as the consequence of increased present moment awareness:

We may have a friend who we visit once a week for tea. Each time we go and see them, we spend an hour or so in their home. After a few years of visiting this friend once a week, we may assume that we are very familiar with their home. One day this friend informs us that they must go away for three weeks and asks us to take care of their home. We agree and move in for this duration. After only one full day in their home, something strange starts to occur: we start to notice things about the interior of their home that we did not see before. It may be a crack in the ceiling or a picture in the hallway that somehow escaped our attention all these years. As the days pass by, we discover that we notice even more details that had somehow escaped our attention during all our previous visits.

This exact scenario unfolds when we choose to consciously connect our breathing. Instead of flitting in and out of the mental paradigm called "time", we are deliberately choosing to anchor our awareness in our body. As a consequence, physical, mental, and emotional experiences are going to come to our attention that may initially appear new to us. However, they are not. They have been going on most of our life. We have not been aware of them because we have not been present long enough to perceive them. Initially, many of these experiences will come to our attention as pain and discomfort. Why? Because pain and discomfort are tools the physical body uses to capture and focus our attention.

If we now choose to run from these dawning experiences, or to numb them with drugs, or even to consider cutting them out, we will be defeating the object of choosing to become aware of them in the first place. This really is a "no pain no gain" predicament. Instead of resisting our pain and discomfort, we are being invited to explore the experience. We are being invited to resist the automatic reflex of seeking to hand this experience over to someone else or to suppress it. We are being invited to step beyond any behavior that masks it and that allows us to go on pretending that we are "fine". We are being invited to bravely answer the call of our body: to take the power of our own attention into our own hands with the intention of wielding it compassionately to restore balance in the quality of our life experience.

In other words, The Presence Process is asking that we now choose to stand our ground and not hide from our hurt or pass our pain onto someone else. For the first time in our life, we are being asked to believe in the inherent power of our Inner Presence. We are being invited to overcome a powerful reactive reflex to instinctively run from our physical, mental, and emotional pain and discomfort. Instead, we are being asked to embrace it with our full attention and with our most compassionate intention, to keep our breathing connected, and to gaze deeply into it. Instead of running from it, we are being encouraged to face it and to willingly seek out its center so that we can open ourselves up to insight.

Learning to restore balance to our own physical, mental, and emotional experiences of pain and discomfort is a simple procedure:

We choose to "be" with our pain or discomfort with a clear intention to compassionately soothe it with our full attention.

This choice gradually and gently changes our entire relationship with what we consider to be pain and discomfort. Instead of treating them like invading enemies, we are choosing to approach them just like a mother gently comforting a distraught child. This transformation of our approach releases within us the energetic tools of healing instead of the armor and weapons of war. War within ourselves cannot and has never enabled us to realize the inner peace we seek. However, the power inherent in the nurturing love of a mother guarantees it. This nurturing power is inherent in all human beings. It is our birthright. It is within our Presence.

Our Inner Presence is a power that knows no order of difficulty. It is ours to wield through the conscious direction of our own attention and intention. It is futile to consistently run to and depend on the attention of another to restore the balance in our own experience when the entire force of the universe waits quietly and patiently within us. We are now being asked to commit to reversing our intentions entirely. We are being asked to choose to compassionately *feel* the physical, mental, and emotional sensations that we have so long been taught to suppress and run from.

This is a crucial step in enabling us to release the ghosts of the past. Like every aspect of The Presence Process, this step is something no one else can take for us. Restoring balance to our experiences is a pathway that can only be established by our own footprints. No matter how qualified or experienced another human being may be, they will never be able to truly feel our physical, mental, and emotional pain and discomfort. Without being able to feel what we are experiencing, there is no way that another human can truly restore balance to our experiences. Having another human being achieving such a feat on our behalf is called "magic", and magic is an illusion in the mind of a believer and a delusion in the hands of the practitioner. These "magical" illusions, though initially appearing to have validity, always collapse with the passage of time. Time will always reveal that they have no lasting foundation. Real and lasting change can only be made within us by consciously wielding our own attention and intention. We were born fully equipped with the tools to restore balance to the quality of our experiences. We do not have to, nor can we, use someone else's equipment.

Restoring balance to any experience requires being able to gauge exactly how out of balance that experience is. This is not possible unless the imbalance can be consciously felt. Machines, tools, and qualified practitioners cannot feel on our behalf and will never achieve such a feat. Feeling and healing are the two halves that make the whole procedure that empowers us to restore our inner balance. Until we accept and act on this insight, we will not be able to restore balance to the quality of our physical, mental, and emotional experiences.

RESTORING BALANCE TO THE QUALITY OF OUR LIFE EXPERIENCE

WE ARE NOW GOING TO BE TAUGHT the procedure for restoring balance to the quality of our life experience. We are asked to apply this Perceptual Tool whenever the messengers of pain and discomfort call upon us to do so.

Commencing the journey of regaining the ability to restore balance to our pain and discomfort requires sincerity, laced with splashings of patience, compassionate intention, and our full, undivided attention. By keeping our full compassionate attention on our pain and discomfort, we will notice that the nature of the sensations that we are experiencing will begin to change. We are asked to notice the changes with curiosity and non-judgment. We must not expect pleasure from the following procedure; we must expect change in condition. Then, we must acknowledge these changes in whatever form they take. Sometimes our condition initially appears to worsen; sometimes it changes form; sometimes it appears to literally move within our body, sometimes to wane, dissolve, or transmute.

Once we are consciously playing our part with our attention and our intention, we must allow the sensations of pain and discomfort to take their course. Anything else is to return to the ancient and hostile behaviors of sedation and control. Our Inner Presence knows no order of difficulty. Let it determine the outcome.

As our pain and discomfort change, we must continue to attend to it like a loving parent would a hurting child. Consistency is key. Just because a child's fever begins to subside does not mean it no longer needs its mother's attention. Our consistent attention will enable our condition to begin gradually returning to a state of balance.

It is important to keep in mind that we have ignored and suppressed our pain and discomfort for most of our life. We have treated it as a hostile enemy and not as the facilitating messenger it really is. So we must be patient with it. A child that has been ignored by its parents for years does not immediately soften towards them just because they suddenly open their arms affectionately. There is hesitation. The child first watches for consistency and sincerity. So we must not be in a hurry, and we must not give up because we do not realize immediate consequences. This procedure is not about applying a "quick fix"; this is about changing our entire approach to a lifelong hostility that we have had towards our own physical, mental, and emotional imbalances. Through patience and perseverance with our own pain and discomfort, we will inevitably discover that:

Nothing outside of us will have any real and lasting effect on what is happening within us.

It is *our* intimate and loving attention that is being called for when our experience sends us the signals of imbalance that we call pain and discomfort. By keeping ourselves present through consciously connecting our breathing and by placing our own loving attention within the center of our pain and discomfort, we are fulfilling our part of the process of restoring balance to our experiences. We are making a causal impact on our experience. Our Inner Presence will take care of everything else. We are asked to initiate the procedure and then to *trust the process*. This is how we activate the task:

1 **We begin by sitting in a comfortable posture with our back straight and eyes closed.** Cross-legged or on a chair are both good. The object is to be in a posture that encourages alertness.

2 **We make sure we are comfortably warm.**

3 **We consciously connect our breathing.**

4 **We place our full attention on any pain and discomfort we are experiencing, whether we perceive it as physical, mental, or emotional.** We do not judge it; we watch it compassionately with our attention.

5 **Our intention is to fully experience the pain and discomfort.** If it is physical in nature, we can seek out the center of the sensation and be with it. If it is mental confusion we are experiencing, we sit and watch the nature of our thought processes. If it is emotional turmoil we are experiencing, we sit and feel the emotions, allowing them to flow as they choose. We do this without judgment, without concern, and without agenda.

6 **Initially, the condition may appear to worsen or become exaggerated in some way.** This is an automatic consequence of our placing our attention on it. This is a positive indicator. It does not mean the condition is worsening; it means our awareness of the condition is growing. We must keep in mind that whatever we are feeling while we perform this task is coming into our awareness so that our Inner Presence can transform

it. We must do our best to allow the pain or discomfort to follow its own path.

7 Throughout the experience, it is important to keep our breathing connected.

Whatever occurs as a consequence of this practice is supposed to happen. It will be different for everyone and different every time we apply this procedure. We are encouraged to stay with the experience until the sensations we perceive as pain and discomfort subside. For acute and long-term conditions, it may take repeated sessions to accomplish a sense of completion. Patience is key. The more we wield this tool, the more efficient it becomes.

It is healthy and beneficial to spend a few moments each day placing our attention on those aspects of our experience that we perceive as painful or uncomfortable. Each time we nurture ourselves in this way, the power of our attention and intention will increase. Each time we experience the beneficial consequences of tending to ourselves in this manner, the power of our faith in our Inner Presence will increase. This tool automatically activates our ability to nurture ourselves.

FOR THE NEXT SEVEN DAYS WE ARE REQUIRED TO:

1   Attend to our 15-minute Breathing Exercise twice each day.

2   Repeat our given Presence Activating Statement for the Session whenever we are not mentally engaged.

3   Review our reading materials. SPECIFICS: Whenever any pain and discomfort enter our field of awareness, instead of resisting it, let us attend to it compassionately as instructed in our reading materials for this Session.

THIS ENDS SESSION FOUR.

SESSION FIVE

Our Presence Activating Statement for the next seven days is:

I compassionately embrace my innocence.

TO ACTIVATE THIS SESSION:

We memorize the given Presence Activating Statement.
We then read through all the written materials.
We sit still and connect our breathing for at least 15 minutes.

ACTIVATING INNER COMPASSION

DORMANT WITHIN US ALL is the trinity of the father (guidance), the mother (nurturing), and the child (innocence, joy, and creativity). Setting an intention to reestablish a relationship with our child self activates this trinity and allows us the opportunity to remember how to actively give to ourselves the quality of unconditional love we asked for as children but did not receive. The intent to reestablish a loving relationship with our child self activates the procedure of learning how to become our own parent. Connecting with our child self calls us to step onto the pathway of self-nurturing, a pathway that is paved with compassion. This pathway invites us to overcome the issues we unconsciously have with our own parents by reaching into a place where only forgiveness can take us. Every effort that we make to reestablish a loving relationship with our child self is rewarded with an ever-increasing sense of present moment awareness.

Many of us in this world appear to be very helpful, but when it comes to the necessary ability of knowing how to nurture ourselves, we discover that we are at a loss. We also realize that we tend to feel a deep sense of guilt whenever we attempt to do anything real and loving for ourselves. This is because it is only our unconscious sense of helplessness and neediness that drives us to sacrifice ourselves in the name of helping others. The behavior of running around and trying to help everyone to our own detriment is always fueled by the reflection we see of our own helpless plight mirrored in the world around us. We cannot give away what we do not have, so only when we have learned how to truly nurture and unconditionally love ourselves do we develop the propensity for authentic service. Unless we consciously step into the present moment and own our life, our ability to be truly of assistance in this world will remain shallow and ineffectual. The first step in learning how to nurture and unconditionally love ourselves is to understand which aspect of our being is really suffering and needing our attention.

As adults, we experience myriad physical, mental, and emotional states of imbalance, and when we do, we usually do everything in our power to numb or distract ourselves from our plight. Or else we run to someone for attention. When we live in a time-based paradigm, what we are unable to see is that none of our physical, mental, and emotional difficulties stem from what is happening to us right now, even though they are clearly reflected in and by what is happening to us right now.

During Session Four, we were encouraged to allow ourselves to feel all our pains and discomforts without fear and judgment. By allowing ourselves to have this experience, the realization to which we are opening ourselves is that all our pains and discomforts carry an emotional signature. The identity of this emotional signature will be one of the many emotions that arise from the trinity of fear, anger, and grief.

Throughout The Presence Process, we call this emotional signature "the emotional charge". We may identify this emotional charge by a variety of names ranging from fear to rage to grief. This emotional charge is an unpleasant feeling that we will literally do anything not to feel. As we progress through The Presence Process, it will become clearer to us that it is the emotional charge crouched behind our pains and discomforts that fuels our compulsion to metaphorically run from the present moment and into distraction. By reacting to this emotional charge, we lunge from Presence to pretence. We sidestep from authenticity to drama.

We also know by now where this emotional charge is really anchored. We have already been shown how to track it back in time. To recap: if we look back over our life, and instead of viewing our past experiences as physical circumstances we choose instead to see them as a re-occurrence of emotional signatures, we will see a clear pathway of similar emotional signatures extending all the way back into our childhood. This pathway reveals to us that the imbalances that we feel today, be they physical, mental, or emotional, have nothing to do with our present adult life. They are merely *reflected* in it. This pathway shows us that all our experiences of imbalance were initiated by encounters that we had before we turned seven. And so one of the biggest revelations we can have at this point is:

It is not our adult experience that requires healing:
it is our childhood.

From the moment we turned our backs on our childhood so that we might become acceptable in the adult world, our child self has been using physical, mental, and emotional states of imbalance to attempt to attract our attention. Our child self has been attempting to attract our attention so that we can consciously and compassionately attend to the unintegrated emotional state in which we left it. Until we consciously attend to the unintegrated experiences of our childhood, our adult experience will continue to be an unconsciously unfolding "effect" of our unintegrated childhood.

In "time", our adult experience is an echo of our childhood.

Until we integrate our childhood, our adult life will continue to be a seemingly chaotic and disconnected experience sewn together with what appears to be randomly occurring physical, mental, and emotional imbalance. It is crucial at this point in The Presence Process that we understand that an unbalanced adult experience is "an effect", not a cause of anything. It is crucial that we understand this because it is futile tampering with an effect of anything, as it is only at the point of cause that any real change can be initiated. The only value of our adult symptoms of imbalance is that we can use them as clues to successfully navigate our awareness to their childhood causes. Unless we embark on such a journey, we remain ineffectual.

The pursuit of happiness, in other words, the drive to control and sedate external circumstances so that we can feel at ease within ourselves, is nothing more than a behavior that stems from attempting to fiddle with an effect to adjust a cause. This is impossible. Such behavior leads us further and further away from the inherent joy that is already available and waiting for us within our child self. The child self is our harbor of innocence, joy, and creativity. When we ignore its state of imbalance, we trade in our inherent innocence, joy, and creativity, and instead invest our energy in attempting to be happy by "making something of ourselves". And so we are faced with another major revelation:

Unless we are prepared to reach back through time and space
and rescue our child self by bringing it into the safety of the
present moment, where we can give it the unconditional love and
attention it is calling for, we as adults will never experience
authentic peace.

The intention to metaphorically reach back and rescue our own child-self can be thought of as a form of time travel. However, this form of time travel is not science fiction. It does not take place "out there", and its purpose is not to visit other far-off places. It takes place within us, and its Soul purpose is for us to compassionately reconnect with a particular attribute of our own Being from which we have become separated and alienated. This is an inside job that consciously connects our present moment with our past. It invites unconscious behaviors triggered by our past experiences to the surface of our present life so that we can consciously attend to them *right now*. If approached with commitment, consistency, and sincerity, this inner work releases our child self of its pain and discomfort. The unfolding consequence of rescuing our child self is that our present adult self will gradually be released from the emotional charge that is the source of all our distraction and imbalance. In other words, it is our child self that is the caretaker of our emotional charge. Emotionally it is in charge.

Like any innocent child, our child self accepts everything to be true, real, and possible. It does not know the difference between the authenticity of what it sees on TV (through our adult eyes) and what it experiences through us in our every day life. It also does not know the difference between what we visualize in our imagination and what it experiences through us in our every day adult life. This means it is both vulnerable and gullible. It listens to everything we think and say, and through our eyes, it watches everything we do. It learns by our example. It watches how we behave with others. If we say "no" when we mean "yes" and "yes" when we mean "no", it becomes mistrustful of our ability to take care of its needs on all levels. Because it is a child, it does not view our present adult self to be part of who it is. Instead, it assumes our adult self to be a parent-figure quite separate from itself. Therefore our intention in approaching it must be impeccable. We must attend to it with unconditional love, devotion, and consistency.

If we have not done work with our child self prior to this moment, then it is important to realize that our relationship with our child self right now will be similar to that of a parent who has for many years abandoned their own child. At about the age of seven, most urbanized humans begin preparing to enter the adult world. This requires a willingness to turn around and walk away from our childhood. As the years unfold, it is very unlikely that we choose to look back or even consider the state of the child we once were. In most cases, we lay a blanket of forgetfulness over that aspect of our Being and openly admit that we cannot remember much of what happened when we were children. We can no longer see our child self, yet it sees everything. We seemingly no longer feel its pain, yet all our adult pain is a mirror of its unresolved feelings.

We may ask, "Why must we now go back and deal with the past? Can we not just leave it alone and carry on with our life?"

Our unfortunate predicament is that the pain and suffering of our unresolved childhood issues follows us as an emotional trail of imbalance that pollutes our adult experiences in an ongoing pattern that is as regular and as punctual as a timepiece. And this timepiece is not neutral, as are the mechanical watches we wear on our wrists. The ticking of this childhood timepiece and the effect it has on our present life is what may be thought of as "emotional time". Wearing a watch and using it as an instrument to navigate the present moment of our life is different. It is a conscious experience. We can choose to remove the watch at any moment and no longer be exposed to its influence. However, the debris of "emotional time" is constantly invading our present moment and distracting our attention. For years, we can sedate and control the effects of the childhood debris which leak out into our adult experiences, but sooner or later it will rear up like an angry snake and challenge the very fiber of our Being. It is not necessary to get to a crisis point in our life before we begin paying attention to it, but sometimes a crisis is exactly what it takes for our desperate and abandoned child self to harness our attention.

Yet the moment we turn inward and start sincerely attending to our child self with the unconditional love, compassion, and the devotion it deserves, our physical, mental, and emotional states of imbalance gradually begin subsiding. This is the real work, and it realizes very real consequences. Once our child self comes to peace, so do we. It is that simple and that powerful. If we are not at peace, it is our child self that is in conflict. There is nowhere else to look, and there is no other solution but to compassionately reach inward and lovingly attend to this precious part of our Being. Only when we begin to accomplish this task, will we be able to truly understand what is meant by the words:

> "Only when we become as children again, can we enter
> the Kingdom of Heaven." (Matthew 18:2–4.)

Translated this means: Only when we bring peace to our child self, can we regain and maintain emotional balance in the quality of our life experience. Our desire to reconnect with our own child self and to develop a conscious relationship with this precious part of our Being is what separates the wheat from the chaff. It is never too late for a happy childhood. Especially when it dawns on us that there are no adults in Heaven.

RESCUING OUR CHILD SELF

DURING OUR JOURNEY through The Presence Process, there have already been and are going to be numerous moments when we feel anything but present. During these moments of distraction, we may feel irritable, anxious, annoyed, or even full of fear, rage, and grief. These are the moments when we are being called upon to consciously attend to our child self. These are the moments in which we must strive to remember that the states of imbalance that we are feeling have nothing to do with what is happening *right now*. They are a call for assistance from a very emotional child-like part of our self that is trapped in a mental concept that we have called "the past". So what do we do? How do we destroy this concept and inject present moment awareness into our relationship with our child self? It is very easy; it takes more heart than mind.

We find a quiet and comfortable space or wait until we have an opportunity to be alone and undisturbed. We then close our eyes and imagine our adult self (the person we are now) standing in front of our child self. We then mentally picture the child that we once were going through the exact same level of emotional imbalance that we are presently feeling in our adult experience. This seemingly imagined scenario is quite real because the feelings that presently drive us to distraction are really the surfacing of suppressed memories echoing from our childhood experiences. Symptoms are echoes. Phonetically the word "symptom" when spoken out loud can be heard as "some time". This is what a symptom is: a piece of our unintegrated timeline.

Once we have this imagined scenario in mind, it is then up to us to respond compassionately to our child self as a loving and devoted parent would. We must allow and even encourage our child self in this imagined scenario to express its feelings without any censorship or judgment on our behalf. We must metaphorically take it in our arms and unconditionally love and comfort it. *We must do whatever it takes — for heaven's sake.*

Through this imagined nurturing of our child self, we automatically activate our inner parent and access a state of being called *compassion*. As its loving parent, we must ask our child self what happened and why it is feeling troubled? We must confidently and sincerely assure it that we will take care of it from this moment onwards and that we will give it all the unconditional love it deserves. Most of all, we must assure our child self that we lived on well beyond the fear it is experiencing. We must tell it about our adult life and invite it to once again become a conscious participant in what we are experiencing from day to day. In this way, we allow it to escape its imprisonment in this mental concept of "the past" and to enter the very real experience of our present circumstances.

We will know when we have been successful in our attempts to communicate with our child self because we will have an emotional response to the experience. Our child self will often respond to our sincere compassion towards it by crying with relief. For the child self, our sincere intent to restore balance by consciously communicating with it is the answering of its prayers. Crying is the commencement of the release of the negative emotional charge that has caused so much discomfort in our adult experience. The tears we cry will not be adult tears but the tears that we as a child could not cry. We must let it all out. These tears represent blocked and stagnant energy that has only served to unconsciously pollute our life with imbalance. We must let the tears flow so that we can get back into the flow. This emotional response means that the energy pathway is being restored between our adult self and our child self.

We must not be concerned if we do not initially experience an emotional response when contacting our child self. Often our child self has become numb from neglect and emotionally deadened by abandonment. Our duty is to persevere regardless of the outcome. Our intent must be unconditional. Our task is to be there for our child no matter what. The tears will often come when we least expect them, and great relief will follow.

Once our child self truly realizes that we have returned to rescue it, we will begin to receive the fruits of our unconditional love, compassion, and devotion: increasing bouts of spontaneous peace, joy, and creativity. We will discover that all those little things that annoyed us and irritated us do not matter anymore. We will spontaneously enjoy playfulness with others and experience an ongoing decrease of physical, mental, and emotional imbalance. We will trade a life of walking around and carrying a charge for a life in which we will confidently feel in charge. Our dramas or states of pretence will gradually be replaced by a growing radiance of Presence.

Like all activities, to reap the rewards of rescuing our child self takes practice, commitment, and consistency. It also takes sincerity and integrity. Remember that nobody gives up attempting to drive a car just because they cannot achieve a high speed on the freeway during their first lesson. We must not give up on our child self or our ability to make contact with it just because it is reluctant to immediately come forward and confide in us. As we approach our child self, it is important to keep in mind how long we have ignored its cries for assistance by sedating and controlling its attempts to gain our attention. We must be patient, sincere, and most of all, we must be consistent.

If we keep in mind that any distracted adult experience is the call for assistance from our past, and if we commit to responding to this call whenever possible with self-directed unconditional love, compassion, and devotion, then we will automatically set into motion a process that will begin restoring balance to the quality of our life experience. We will begin liberating the best part of who and what we are from the conceptual prison of the past. Then, we will begin to understand why it is said: "The present is a gift". There is no greater gift we can give to ourselves than reawakening the child-like joy and creativity inherent in our shared Inner Presence.

FOR THE NEXT SEVEN DAYS WE ARE REQUIRED TO:

1   Attend to our 15-minute Breathing Exercise twice each day.

2   Repeat our given Presence Activating Statement for the Session whenever we are not mentally engaged.

3   **Review our reading materials.** SPECIFICS: Whenever we feel mentally distracted or emotionally and physically uncomfortable, it is a signal and an invitation from the past to establish a connection with our child self in the present moment. The more often we reach out to this aspect of our Being, the more successful we are at restoring balance to the quality of our entire life experience.

THIS ENDS SESSION FIVE.

SESSION SIX

Our Presence Activating Statement for the next seven days is:

I neutralize my negative emotional charge.

TO ACTIVATE THIS SESSION:

We memorize the given Presence Activating Statement.
We then read through all the written materials.
We sit still and connect our breathing for at least 15 minutes.

———— ⌾⌾⌾ ————

DECREASING OUR NEGATIVE EMOTIONAL CHARGE

WE HAVE NOW ARRIVED at a point in The Presence Process where we have familiarized ourselves with the various procedures of the Perceptual Tool that is designed to empower us to begin consciously decreasing the intensity of what we call "our negative emotional charge". This tool is called The Emotional Cleansing Process. The beauty of this Perceptual Tool is that we begin applying it automatically by simply understanding its mechanisms. This is because its application is not "a doing"; it is a state of Being. Before we explore it further, let us first take a closer look at the nature of the emotional body in and out of time and the origin of what we call "our negative emotional charge".

In the present moment, the highest application of our physical body is that it is used as a means and focal point for us to consciously anchor the full power of our present moment awareness in this world. Life in a physical body is an opportunity for our Soul to achieve full consciousness, or what we may call 100% present moment awareness, while in this world. In other words, life is an opportunity to show up completely in our life experience. To accomplish this, our mental and emotional bodies must also be aligned with their highest application.

The highest application of our mental body is when we use it to consciously navigate the focus of our attention. The highest application of our emotional body is when we use it to fuel the momentum of our intentions. In this respect, our mental body is the navigation system of the craft of our Beingness, and our emotional body is a fuel tank containing the various emotions or different grade fuels that are intended to activate various intensities of real movement in our life experience.

However, while "living in time", we do not fulfill these structural potentials. Instead, we use our physical body as a vacant lot, or at the most as a pit stop between mental excursions into the nonexistent past and future. It is a place to pause in between the distraction of making plans. We also use our physical and mental body to "do" a lot of stuff— endless stuff, stuff that has very little and often absolutely nothing to do with our Soul purpose. We spend most of our life experience focused on accumulating stuff that we cannot ever take with us on our journey beyond the borders of our present circumstances. Or else we are "doing" stuff to get attention so that our presence in this world is somehow acknowledged and verified. To accomplish these distractions, we use our mental body as a tool for thinking, analyzing, and controlling our experiences and our emotional body as a means for sedation, projection, and all manners of drama. This is why we often feel like we are "going nowhere", because in actuality, we are not. Fortunately, The Presence

Process automatically begins rectifying this predicament. It accomplishes this by:

1   Instructing us how to use our breath to activate immediate physical presence.

2   Supplying us with the Presence Activating Statements and reading materials that activate and encourage mental navigation.

3   Assisting us to begin consciously unblocking our fuel supply by introducing us to The Emotional Cleansing Process, thus instructing us on how to consciously de-activate our drama.

While we live in time and are still attempting to have "a good time" or at least "an easy time", we are in an experience of polarities. We are attempting to have a good time because we feel so bad, and we are attempting to make things easy for ourselves because our life experience feels so hard. The only problem is that while we spend our time chasing one experience so that we can flee another, all we are "doing" is essentially bouncing off the walls of a self-created perceptual prison cell. This commotion may initiate a lot of outer activity, and we may experience a variety of physical, mental, and emotional circumstances, but in essence, we will not really get anywhere. That is why we were asked not to enter or to judge our progress through this Process based on how good we feel or how easy it is. When it comes to accomplishing emotional growth, good and easy are not barometers for success; they are usually indicators of avoidance, resistance, and denial.

To activate real movement in our life, we must elevate our perception to a point where it is no longer necessary to label our emotional experiences as being either good or bad. In present moment awareness, there is no good or bad emotion: there is just energy in motion. There are just varying grades of fuel for different intensities of inner movement. To achieve full throttle and to make the most of the potential distance we can cover in our life experience, we must be prepared to use the entire range of fuels that are available to us. This is what real joy and creativity are. Achieving the frequency of real joy and creativity requires that we become inclusive, not exclusive.

In "time", we confuse joy with the outer changing experience of happiness, and we confuse creativity with the outer busy-ness of making or accumulating "stuff". Yet joy is not about feeling good; it's about *feeling everything.* Creativity is not about rearranging the content of the physical world to make life easier or more convenient for us; it is about embracing it all as the raw materials intended to assist us to realize our highest potential.

However, while we are still in a time-based and polarized experience, it is necessary that we communicate in polarized terminology. We will therefore describe the uncomfortable condition of our emotional body in terms of our having a "negative emotional charge" because it adequately communicates a condition in our emotional body that does not serve us in terms that we can understand. We can therefore think in terms of having both a positive and a negative emotional charge. We can think of the negative charge as that which inhibits real movement in our life experience and the positive charge as that which encourages it. Both these negative and positive emotional charges can be thought of as having been initiated in our experience through the process of emotional imprinting that took place during our first Seven-Year Cycle.

Emotional imprinting is the term that we use in The Presence Process to describe the unconscious procedure of entrainment in which a photocopy of the emotional content of our parents' (or their substitutes) emotional bodies is passed onto us. By the time we reach seven years old, we are then emotionally picking up where they have left off. This imprinting process occurs through a whole range of interactive physical, mental, and emotional experiences. The unavoidable consequence of childhood is that we all receive this emotional baton from our parents so that we can enter and commence our part in the human race. This is an unfolding of a sacred agreement we have with each other. This is a consequence of the relationships we have had with each other extending beyond the borders of this life experience. In the East, this is referred to as a karmic relationship. It is "consequence" that keeps individual Souls bound together in groups that we call families. This is not because we are actually related to only those specific Souls. The Presence within us is shared by all life. Our close interaction in this life with any other Soul is determined purely by our past interactions with each other.

The positive emotional charge carried by our parents and activated by experiences we have with them before the age of seven is also passed on to us in this manner, but these positive charges do not lead to what we may perceive as physical, mental, and emotional discomfort. The positive emotional charge we receive from them does not inhibit our ability to experience real movement; instead, it gives rise to creative urges, inspiration, and a desire to manifest an experience of living with purpose.

This initial seven-year period of passing the emotional baton from the parents to the children can also be regarded as the deliberate process of destiny downloading. This is because the content of our first seven-year emotional cycle establishes a pattern that initiates the unfolding and cyclic emotional, mental, and physical circumstances of our life experience.

Our destiny for each life is downloaded vibrationally during the last seven months of our womb life, emotionally during the first seven years after our birth, mentally between seven and fourteen-years-old, and then physically by the time we turn twenty-one. In each case, it occurs through imprinting. In the first seven months, we are mainly imprinted by the vibrations of the activities we experience within our mother's womb. This occurs deliberately through our experience of her heart beating, her lungs breathing, her blood pumping, her body movement, the resonance of her voice, and so on. In the first seven years, we are imprinted primarily by our interaction with our parents and our immediate family. During our teenage years, our schooling and our peer groups imprint us. From fourteen to twenty-one our first lovers and our interactions with our broader physical world experience imprint us. By the time we are twenty-one, our destiny has been imprinted vibrationally, emotionally, mentally, and physically into our experience.

While we are "living in time", these imprinting experiences appear to be occurring randomly and haphazardly. However, they are not. A barometer of the extent of our entry into present moment awareness is the level to which we perceive how deliberately each and every life experience we have had has unfolded.

As discussed in The Pathway of Awareness and Our Seven-Year Cycle, we do not at present have a shared vibrational language in this world that we can use to consciously access and resolve experiences imprinted into us at a vibrational level. This language will surface naturally in our awareness when we are ready. Integrating our vibrational body is not therefore a task that we can accomplish without personal facilitation. That is why we presently choose the emotional body as the causal point as far as making real and lasting changes in the quality of our life experience. Even though it is still relatively suppressed, immature, and dysfunctional, we do have an emotional language that we share; we can feel our way through our experiences. Unearthing, developing, and exploring the consequences of becoming well-versed in the language of our emotional body is one of the primary intentions of The Presence Process. Accomplishing this assists us in evolving to a state of Being that automatically makes us vulnerable to our vibrational awareness. Present moment awareness is the platform we must arrive at to catch the train that carries us into our vibrational paradigm.

Until we awaken to the point where we can consciously interact with and adjust this Seven-Year Cycle at an emotional level, we live unconsciously enslaved by it. It is our willingness and ability to awaken to the awareness of the mechanisms of our imprinted destiny that empowers us to participate in and direct its pathway consciously and responsibly. Only at this point do we begin to reestablish and explore what we now only *think* of as free will.

Participating consciously in our destiny is exactly what is occurring when we begin to consciously neutralize the imbalance in our emotional body by decreasing our negative emotional charge and increasing our positive emotional charge. Once these two come into balance with each other, our sense of experiencing emotional polarities dissolves, and our relationship with our emotional body is restored to its highest potential. This is how we begin to take charge and to consequently live on purpose. In this light, taking responsibility for the quality (emotional content) of our life experience is the doorway to real personal freedom.

For the first Six Sessions of The Presence Process, our focus is therefore on gaining awareness about and learning how to consciously decrease the effects of our negative emotional charge. From Session Seven, we then begin placing an increased emphasis on activating conscious awareness on our positive emotional charge. In this way, we begin consciously laying the foundation for our return to balance.

Ideally, we seek to achieve a balance between our negative and positive emotional charge so that we experience emotional harmony no matter what our life circumstances. This emotional balance is only possible when we have decreased our level of pain and discomfort to a point that we can begin viewing all emotions as energy in motion, instead of perceiving some of them as threatening experiences we need to react to. Emotional balance requires achieving a state of acceptance within ourselves in which we no longer have an agenda about what emotions we desire to experience.

In other words, to experience real emotional balance requires a complete departure from polarity in which we move beyond the perception of favoring one emotion over another. Remember that before we started naming the energy, before the energy "mattered" to us, it was purely energy in motion. This was before we started attempting to make sense of it all—when we were in a state of *pre-sense*. Our return to present moment awareness is an adjustment to our perceptions that will begin restoring our neutral relationship with energy. Then energy in motion will become a fuel for us to initiate real movement in the quality of our experiences. Then we can live on purpose.

Joy is only possible when we greet all energetic
circumstances equally.

In the most simplistic terms, the main characteristic of the negative emotional charge is that it is uncomfortable. It is trapped, blocked, sedated, and controlled energy. Our resistance to its inherent compulsion to move causes friction, and this friction causes heat to seep into every aspect of our experience. This internal heat literally causes our life to become hell. We are so used to this inner heat that, for the most part, we do not even know that it is occurring.

Yet outwardly, we manifest a reflection of this inner heat in our outer world. Our outer experience has become a veritable cesspool of combustion. We mould our outer circumstances by heating them up, by boiling them, and by burning them. We practically heat all our food, and many of the liquids we drink, from coffee to alcohol, generate heat in our experience. Many of the substances we are addicted to eating, like sugar, cause heat in our body. We even created cigarettes, a means to burn and heat up the air we breathe. Our outer forms cannot move through this world without this process of combustion. This gradual heating up of our outer world is a manifestation of our unconscious internal combustion. Our intense resistance to being authentic fans its flames. While we feel more comfortable entertaining pretence instead of Presence, we will feel more comfortable living in a world that is on fire. When we cannot perceive our own internal heat, we also cannot perceive what the nature of "hell" really is.

We mentally describe this emotionally generated condition of inner heat by a variety of names, but the trinity that represents them all is fear, anger, and grief. Fear, anger, and grief are mental definitions of the consequences of our internal heat. Understanding the relationship between heat and our negative emotional charge, as well as understanding that the emotional body is metaphorically associated with the element of water, gives us a whole new appreciation for many of the expressions in our language that encapsulate emotional overload:

"In the heat of the moment"
"Hot under the collar"
"Going to blow my top"
"Letting off steam"
"Losing my cool"
"I'm in hot water now!"

The level of our internal heat, or our emotional body discomfort, is determined by the intensity of the initial childhood experience that imprinted it. Aside from the metaphoric hellfire that we have made of our outer world experience, this internal discomfort manifests behaviorally in two main ways:

1 **Drama.** The first consequence of carrying an excessive negative emotional charge is the manifestation of outer drama. Our dramas are the "acts" we use to gain attention and acceptance from others. We all have a range of tried and tested acts that we conceived when our authentic behavior was discouraged, when we were entrained to resist being spontaneous. These are our "re-act-ions" to the world. During childhood, as part of our emotional imprinting, we all went through experi-

ences in which our authentic behavior was discouraged and reshaped through various degrees of discipline into calculated appropriateness. This occurred so that we could be socially acceptable in the adult world. A spontaneously joyful and creative child is pure energy in motion. To be introduced and incorporated into the adult world, or into "living in time" as we have called it in The Presence Process, the parent and the environment in which the child lives will deliberately begin to weed out the child's spontaneous behavior. The reason for this is that although spontaneous behavior is deemed cute for a two-year-old, it becomes inappropriate for an eight-year-old, and maybe even illegal for an eighteen-year-old. For example, running around naked in public is okay for a two-year-old, but running around naked in a public school is seen as quite inappropriate for an eight-year-old, and in most societies it is illegal for an eighteen-year-old. Whether or not spontaneous behavior should be tempered (note the pun) is not the issue we are discussing here. What we are focusing on are the consequences of it being accomplished.

The reshaping of our spontaneous behavior is usually initiated and accomplished by our parents using words like "stop" and "no". What is not apparent to the world is that *spontaneous behavior never stops when interrupted by enforced discipline. It merely transforms into something else.* It becomes calculated drama. It becomes resistance. The child's Presence is replaced by an adult's pretence. Our calculated drama is successful in that it makes us acceptable to the adult world, but in the same breath, it renders our authentic self unacceptable to us. This inner condition creates conflict, and this conflict is then reflected outwardly in all the ways we conjure up to gain attention and acceptance in the world. This is the inspiration for most of our drama. Our ongoing resistance to being authentic is also a catalyst for continually adding more heat to our emotional body because resistance, by its nature, causes friction, and friction causes heat.

Once we realized that certain aspects of our authentic behavior were no longer acceptable, we created little acts to find ways to remain acceptable. Our gauge on whether these acts worked for us was based on how much attention we got from our parents and immediate family when we performed them. Often, any attention, even if it was negative and had uncomfortable consequences, was better than no attention at all. Consequently, our repertoire of "acts" was designed to contain behaviors that led to negative and positive attention. These inauthentic acts became part of the dramatic repertoire that we bring out and perform right up to this moment in our life experience whenever we seek attention or acceptance from our world.

This desire for attention and acceptance can be positively and creatively channeled as is accomplished through many aspects of the performing and creative arts. However, this entails first learning how to give ourselves the attention we are seeking from others.

Underlying all our desire for attention and acceptance is the thirst to have the discomfort or the heat created by our negative emotional charge reduced. Our drama is the belief that someone "out there" can relieve or remove this discomfort for us.

2 **Self-medication—sedation and control.** The second consequence of carrying an excessive negative emotional charge is also a type of dramatic behavior that arises out of a reaction to our inner discomfort. This behavior, however, as opposed to being aimed outwards at others to achieve acceptance and attention, is aimed inwards at ourselves in an attempt to decrease the experience of our inner discomfort. Throughout The Presence Process, this behavior is called "self-medication". It manifests as sedation and control.

Whenever circumstances arise in our experience that cause our negative emotional charge to begin seeping into our conscious awareness, in other words, whenever we start feeling very uncomfortable within ourselves, we either attempt to sedate or control our experience. Let us take a closer look at these two behaviors:

i) **Sedation** is a dysfunction of our female side and is the attempt to numb our discomfort. For example, the habitual need and use of alcohol is the intent to sedate our inner discomfort; we are drowning out our real feelings. The term popularly used is "drowning our sorrows".

ii) **Control** is a dysfunction of our male side and is the intent to gain power over our discomfort, or to overpower it. The habitual use and need to smoke cigarettes is the intent to control this discomfort. Whenever we do not know what is happening and start feeling out of control, we reach for a cigarette, because by smoking we at least know what is going on and therefore appear to have control over the uncomfortable moment we are moving through.

Smoking marijuana is such a powerful and popular self-medication tool on this planet because it simultaneously combines and achieves both sedation and control. Sedation and control behaviors range from being blatant to very subtle. Until we substantially decrease our negative emotional charge, we are all self-medicating on one level or another. Our quest for "happiness" is self-medication. Our quest to have it "good" is usually control-based. Our quest to have it "easy" is usually sedation-based.

We can discover the identity of the negative emotion beneath the charge that we are carrying by stopping our habits and/or addictions. The emotions that consequently erupt will reveal the nature and intensity of the negative emotional charge that unconsciously drives our self-medicating behavior. All addictions are self-medication, and all are passed on through vibrational, emotional, mental, and physical imprinting. Effectively decreasing our negative emotional charge is the only causative treatment for addiction that has any real and lasting effect. The outer physical self-medicating habit is an effect of an inner emotional condition, so quitting our self-medicating behaviors without releasing the attached charge accomplishes nothing real. It is ineffectual. All that will occur is that our self-medication will be transferred from one behavior pattern to another.

The extent of the negative emotional charge is what separates a person who is "in charge" of his or her life from a person who is "carrying a charge" through his or her life. When a person enters our sphere of awareness, it is not immediately apparent whether they are in charge or carrying a charge. However, observing their behavior over a period of time will tell all. Everyone who is carrying a substantial negative emotional charge will exhibit physical, mental, or emotional drama sooner or later. It will manifest automatically in their outer life experiences. They will also lace their life with self-medication behaviors; they will have established their means of sedation and control through habits and addictions. Society's acceptance of alcohol and cigarettes enables us to self-medicate openly without feeling awkward about our inability to integrate our uncomfortable inner emotional condition.

The good news is that this is not a predicament that we have to be imprisoned in for life. Since the beginning of The Presence Process, we have been training to consciously empower ourselves so that we can begin consciously decreasing our negative emotional charge by applying a Perceptual Tool called The Emotional Cleansing Process. We are already familiar with the components of this tool because for the last four Sessions we have been working with each of its four procedures. It is a powerful yet gentle tool that is designed to physically, mentally, and emotionally steer us away from reactive and towards responsive behavior. This is important because all reactive behavior causes and adds heat to our emotional body.

By diligently applying The Emotional Cleansing Process whenever and wherever possible, we gradually transform the quality of our entire life experience. We transform it from one in which we are attempting to achieve happiness or to feel good, to one in which we are giving ourselves the opportunity to lay the foundations for authentic joy and creativity. Consistent application of this tool will automatically turn every challenging experience into an opportunity for emotional growth. All friction, instead of being a catalyst for the buildup of heat, will then become an opportunity for movement. This is how it is meant to be. Mastering our application of The Emotional Cleansing Process will end all our anxiety because its consequences will show us beyond any doubt that every life situation that we perceive as uncomfortable can be integrated consciously.

THE EMOTIONAL CLEANSING PROCESS

UP TO THIS POINT in The Presence Process, we have been taught four perceptual procedures:

195

1   In Session Two, we were taught how to see the surfacing of our inner uninte-
    grated memories as outer reflections in the world. This we called identify-
    ing "the messenger".

2   In Session Three, we were taught how to access information from the emotional
    content of these surfacing memories. This we called "getting the mes-
    sage".

3   In Session Four, we were taught how to compassionately feel and thus attend to
    the pain and discomfort contained within these surfacing memories. We
    referred to this as "feeling it to heal it".

4   In Session Five, we were taught how to re-establish our energetic connection
    with our child self—the causal point of these surfacing memories.

The Emotional Cleansing Process is a procedure that entails combin-
ing these four individual steps into one complete Perceptual Tool. When
used consistently, this tool actively charts a new pathway for our awareness that automatically transforms us from a reactive to a responsible
human being. This tool also honors The Pathway of Awareness.

The implications of applying this tool passionately is that with every
application we will be gently decreasing the negative charge that was
imprinted in our emotional body during the first seven years of our life.
As the heat and therefore the discomfort in our emotional body decreases,
our negative belief systems about ourselves and the world we experience
around us will automatically begin dismantling. In turn, this will automatically decrease the drama that we manifest in our life experiences to
gain attention and achieve acceptability. It will also gradually and gently
unplug the causes of our self-medicating behaviors. The consequence of
this is that our internal and external experiences will automatically
become more comfortable. This comfort will blossom as growing inner
peace and outer harmony.

By consistently applying this tool, we will realize once and for all
where our power lies: within our Inner Presence. By continual application of The Emotional Cleansing Process, we will realize immediate consequences, and this will confirm that the quality of all our outer experi-

ences is determined by our internal state. The moment we really get this will be the moment that we have consciously regained our freedom because we will then truly know through our own experience that we are 100% responsible for the quality (emotional content) of our life experience. This knowing is inevitably accomplished through repeatedly experiencing the outcome of applying this tool.

Applying The Emotional Cleansing Process requires a willingness to be responsible. We are already trained to use it; we have been training for the last four Sessions. Its methodology is already part of our perceptual approach. Now all that we require is initiative and patience. We did not learn to walk in one step. Learning to wield this tool is metaphorically like learning to walk again. It is metaphorically that act of learning to get up and stand responsibly on our own two emotional feet for the first time in our adult life. So we are asked to be patient and committed. We must commit to applying this tool whenever we have the opportunity and be patient as the consequences of wielding it unfold in the quality of our life experience.

*The power of The Emotional Cleansing Process is that it is
100% causal. As such its benefits are inevitable.*

The mechanisms of this tool will appear obvious to us because we are already trained to respond, and we have already gathered enough present moment awareness to do so. From this moment of The Presence Process, the rate at which the negative charge in our emotional body diminishes is literally in our hands.

The unconscious unintegrated memories, the roots of our negative emotional charge that are now surfacing for us to clear, can be easily identified by the virtue that they will on some level appear as specific circumstances or people's behaviors that upset us. Generally, when we are upset, our behavior follows a particular pathway that leads us into a predictable state of "doing" that we call *reaction*. We master this reactionary state as children by witnessing how our parents interact with us and how they interact with their perceived obstacles and issues. Reactive behavior is passed on to us automatically as part of the emotional imprinting process. If we do not at some stage consciously choose to unlearn it and instead replace it with responsible behavior, then this reactionary behavior is automatically passed onto our children. The difference between reactive and responsive behavior is that reactive behavior always adds fuel to the fire while responsive behavior throws water on the fire. Again, it is all about "heat".

So how do we behave when we are in unconscious reaction to our life experience?

Firstly, when something happens that does not go our way or seemingly insults our sensibilities, we automatically become upset. We have then reacted. What makes a reaction a reaction is that it is any physical, mental, or emotional behavior that confirms that we automatically attribute the cause and therefore the responsibility for our upsetting experience to outside factors. This is clarified in that the reactive behavior in some manner, directly or indirectly, resorts to blame. In the final analysis, the only outcome of blame, whether we admit it or not, is guilt, regret, and shame. We have all had the experience of becoming upset, resorting to blame and then when we eventually come to our senses, feeling ashamed of how we behaved. This is all wasted energy and *is* avoidable. The trinity of the structure of reactive behavior is therefore:

Getting upset — blaming — feeling guilt, regret, or shame.

Let us examine the trinity of this reactive behavior pattern in more depth because we now have enough present moment awareness to see exactly what it is really unfolding:

1 **To begin with, let us examine this notion of becoming "upset".** Maybe we are not being upset as much as we are being set up. This will not have been the first time either. It is evident that the event that upsets us has been repeated over and over in our life *because* we are re-acting. Examine the word "reaction" visually. A re-action is by its visual definition a repetition of a particular action; it is a repeated-action. The structure of this word tells us that the event that sets us up has not led to any new behavior pattern on our part. It has evoked a habitual and predictable

behavior pattern that keeps surfacing over and over again every time a similar type of triggering situation occurs in our experience. The first stage in the trinity of reactive behavior is therefore to behave as if we are upset. This entails automatically acting out a calculated, habitual and therefore predictable physical, mental, or emotional drama. This particular drama was imprinted into our emotional body during childhood by witnessing how our parents dealt with a similar upsetting event.

1   The second stage in the trinity of reactive behavior is that whenever we are set up like this, we resort to a very specific type of drama that always has the same objective: blame. In other words, the drama that we bring out of our tried and tested repertoire is one that we use to attribute responsibility for what is happening to us elsewhere. Blame is one of those unique circumstances in which our drama is not only used to gain attention (usually sympathy) but also for the purpose of taking the attention off us and placing it on someone or something else. In life, we will resort to blame as long as we are not ready to take responsibility for the quality of all our experiences. In other words, blame is the act of accusing the mirror for the content of its reflection. But blame has consequences. Studying this word visually also reveals the authentic nature of our behavior when we resort to this tactic: to "b lame". By resorting to blame we automatically disempower ourselves because we are unconsciously declaring that we prefer to perceive ourselves as a victim and therefore as the powerless prey of others.

3   It is out of this sense of disempowerment that we then arrive at the third stage of the trinity of reactive behavior: guilt, regret, and shame. Consciously, we may feel guilty, regretful, or shameful because of the behavior we displayed when we reacted to being upset, but this is not all that is transpiring. Unconsciously, we feel guilt, regret, and shame when we blame another for the quality of our experience because by doing so we have betrayed ourselves. We have betrayed ourselves because when we blame another, we disempower our own Soul by declaring it to be enslaved by circumstances that are seemingly beyond its control. To do so is to metaphorically turn our back on the existence of the Law of

Cause and Effect and to do this is to ignore all that makes us equal and free.

Obviously, our reactive behavior pattern does not serve us on any level. It was learned through emotional imprinting and can just as easily be unlearned. Let us intend to consciously chart a new course for our behavior. Instead of bowing to this ancient reactive trinity, let us be confident that we have now already gathered enough present moment awareness to catch ourselves and to realize that whenever we become upset we are actually being "set up". We can reinforce this awareness by remembering that the universe is intentionally putting on a play so that we can see externally what we have hidden internally from ourselves. Keeping this in our awareness, let us intend to apply the four simple steps of The Emotional Cleansing Process whenever we are emotionally triggered.

Step One: Dismiss the Messenger. The first step is to acknowledge that the person or the event setting us up has nothing to do with what is actually happening; they are just "the messenger" (mess-ender). They are reflecting a memory that is surfacing from our unintegrated past. It is pointless to "shoot the messenger" because the universe has an unlimited supply of them! So the first step in The Emotional Cleansing Process is to *dismiss the messenger*. Internally, we can thank them for their great service and let them be on their way. In other words, instead of reacting to and venting at them we can say, "I could use a little time alone right now." In the beginning, this step of gracefully side-stepping our urge to react may require courage and powerful self-control because it requires breaking our lifelong habit of knee-jerking into drama. We have already been preparing ourselves to accomplish this.

Step Two: Get the Message. The second step is to not automatically resort to our predictable yet unconscious physical, mental, or emotional drama, but instead to *get the message*. We have practiced this too. To accomplish this, we turn our attention inward by describing to ourselves the nature of the emotional reaction we experienced from being set up. We find one word that captures our emotional reaction. We say out loud to ourselves:

"I feel angry. I feel sad. I feel hurt. I feel alone. I feel...." We keep searching in this way until we find the word that resonates physically with our emotional reaction. If we are angry, our face may flush, or our hands may buzz, or we may feel a downward movement in our solar plexus. Once we have accessed the word that describes the emotional reaction that the set up has triggered within us, then we have completed step two.

Step Three: Feel It. Instead of externalizing what is occurring to us by resorting to blame, we must now consciously internalize the experience. We must feel it. We have practiced this step as well. This particular step is a remarkable part of this whole procedure because instead of projecting our emotions out into the world as we normally did when we got set up in the past, we are now choosing to internalize and thus contain the experience. This is not to be confused with the act of suppressing our experiences. Our conscious choice to internalize the setup so that we can learn from it is not suppression: it is discovery. It is also called "containment". Suppression is the act of pretending it did not happen. Our choice to now be present with whatever upsets us enables us to realize that we can physically feel within our body what we initially thought was happening "out there". So whatever the emotion is that we have successfully named is what we must allow ourselves to feel without censorship or judgment. In essence, what the messenger (mess-ender) has done, or has been attempting to do, depending on how many times we have been triggered by this same event, is to bring to our attention the fact that we have an internal emotional blockage that we resist feeling our way through.

Step Four: Come Pass On. Once we can feel this emotional blockage as a physical sensation within our own body, we are ready to transmute it with "divine alchemy" by moving it out of our body by applying the power of our compassionate Presence. We have already prepared ourselves for this step as well. Take a careful look at the word "compassion". Phonetically and visually it reveals itself as "come pass on". Compassion throughout The Presence Process means: You can come to me and I will let you pass on without interference (entering fear) or judgment (agenda).

At this point in the procedure we might justifiably exclaim, "Oh, come on! Here we are feeling angry, our hands buzzing, and our solar plexus all tightened up, and now we are suddenly expected to switch to compassion? Get real!"

Getting "real" is exactly what we must intend. Activating compassion when we are in the midst of an emotional reaction involves the inclusion of our child self. To accomplish this, it is important to remind ourselves that the emotional reaction that was triggered within us by the messenger has nothing to do with our present adult life. It is a cry from our child self. It is an echo from the past calling for our attention because only *our* attention can restore *real* balance to the quality of all our experiences. We choose to respond to what we are experiencing emotionally therefore by closing our eyes and picturing our child self feeling exactly the same way we are as a consequence of being set up by the messenger. We have already practiced this too. By metaphorically embracing our child self, we automatically activate compassion. We are saying, "You can come to me, and I will love you unconditionally until what is frightening you, making you angry, or making you sad passes."

When we become sincere in approaching our child self, our chest will automatically start to well up with the emotion that we have resisted feeling for so long. This suppressed emotion will surface in waves and dissolve into tears. We will feel the energy moving up from our solar plexus, through our chest area, into and through our throat and eventually out of our body. Often we may even have the sensation of heat literally peeling off our body.

Once this experience of release subsides, we will enter a sense of relief and peace. Through consistent application of The Emotional Cleansing Process, we will discover that the messenger that had repeatedly triggered us over and over again will not return. Why should it when we have consciously received the message? Sometimes, it will take going through this emotional cleansing procedure two or three times over a couple of days or weeks to restore balance to a particular experience. With devotion and commitment, balance will be restored. The more diligently we apply The Emotional Cleansing Process, the more proficient we become at wielding it and subsequently the more efficient it becomes. So the new pathway of learned responsible behavior is:

Dismiss the messenger—get the message—feel it—come pass on.

We can apply this technique to solve disagreements, to heal physical ailments, and to integrate any situation of conflict and confusion arising in our life. Every time we apply it, we will be equally astounded by the realization that we can transform the quality of any experience "out there" by moving consciously into ourselves and compassionately making the internal adjustment. This technique confirms, without a doubt, that the quality of everything we experience outside of us is merely a reflection of our internal emotional condition. It proves that making peace has nothing to do with the other party. It shows us that an unbalanced adult is an unattended child. It also reveals that tears detoxify the Soul and that compassion is the key to reopening the doorway of our heart.

INTO THE WATER

THE SPECIFIC PURPOSE of the following section is to prepare us for the water sessions that we will be experiencing in the next three Sessions. If we have a condition or are experiencing a circumstance that precludes us from fully entering water, then we must simply continue as we have done with our regular 15-minute breathing sessions from Session Seven through to Session Nine. It is still beneficial to read all information about the water sessions, as this may be useful to us at a later stage.

We will be activating the next three Sessions by submerging ourselves in a bath of warm (not hot) water for 20 minutes. While in the water, we are not to consciously connect our breathing. We are to be *as still as possible* in the water and to place our attention on any emotional experience that surfaces in our awareness as a consequence of being in the water.

As soon as we exit our water session, we are to immediately attend to our 15-minute Breathing Exercise. We may discover that as a consequence of being in the water, our Breathing Exercise subsequently activates deeper physical, mental, or emotional experiences. Remember that if we perceive an experience as being uncomfortable, we must keep our breathing connected and remain relaxed until it passes. This will take as long as it takes. Aside from the three water sessions that we must do to activate

Sessions Seven, Eight and Nine, we are welcome and even encouraged to do added water sessions on the days between.

As we enter this phase of The Presence Process, let us do so with the knowing that everything that we have experienced to this point has served to prepare us for these water sessions. Let us therefore enter this part of our journey with confidence. The following information is intended to ensure that our water sessions are as gentle as possible:

1   **It is important that we drink plenty of pure water during the 24-hour period before our water sessions.** We should stop our water intake two hours before the session so that breathing is not done on a full bladder. By then our body will be thoroughly hydrated.

2   **We must ensure that the bath water is warm when commencing our session.** The water must not feel uncomfortable on entry, but it must feel warm to the skin. The ideal temperature for this procedure is our body temperature. For a gentle and comfortable experience, it is recommended that we purchase a thermometer that will assist us to test the water before entry.

3   **Throughout the water session, we are encouraged to lay back in the water so that our entire torso is submerged and that only our face is out of the water.** It is important that the water is over our heart area (chest) for as much of the session as possible.

4   **If someone is sitting with us during our water session, it is advisable to make sure that a specific signal is agreed upon (like tapping on the tub) so that they may alert us if our attention strays into time.** When this occurs, we will appear to fall asleep. We are not actually asleep: we are simply not present.

5   **If, for any reason, the water session becomes challenging, we must relax by reminding ourselves that whatever we experience during the water session is supposed to happen.** Any surfacing discomfort is the sign that a negative emotional charge is surfacing. It is only doing so because it is finally coming to pass. By remaining as relaxed and as calm as possible, this charge will be dispelled. Remember that we are feeling the discomfort

because it is passing through and out of our field of awareness. The only way out is through.

6   It is beneficial to mentally repeat our Presence Activating Statement during the experience.

Medical Advisory: For those who are elderly or whose health is fragile, for safety reasons, it is strongly advised that they have someone sit with them through the water sessions. If there is *any doubt* about the safety of our engaging in the water sessions, we must first consult our medical doctor. If we feel that we have a medical condition that for any reason may be compromised by this procedure, we must consult our healthcare practitioner before commencing.

⸺⸺⸺ ∞ ⸺⸺⸺

FOR THE NEXT SEVEN DAYS WE ARE REQUIRED TO:

1   Attend to our 15-minute Breathing Exercise twice each day.

2   Repeat our given Presence Activating Statement for the Session whenever we are not mentally engaged.

3   Review our reading materials. SPECIFICS: We are encouraged to apply The Emotional Cleansing Process whenever we are given the opportunity—that would be whenever we are emotionally triggered in any way. Eventually, we will integrate this technique completely, and it will become us. But until we reach that point, we must wield it consciously and consistently. Also, reread the section entitled Into The Water prior to the first water session.

THIS ENDS SESSION SIX.

⸺⸺⸺ ∞ ⸺⸺⸺

SESSION SEVEN
(OUR 1ST WATER SESSION)

————————

————

Our Presence Activating Statement for the next seven days is:

I feel safe in this body.

TO ACTIVATE THIS SESSION:

We memorize the given Presence Activating Statement.
We then read through all the written materials.
We submerge our body in warm (not hot) water and soak for
at least 20 minutes and then immediately attend to our
15-minute Breathing Exercise.

FEELING OUR WAY THROUGH

WE HAVE NOW REACHED a very powerful transition point in The Presence Process, so we are going to take a moment to review some of the information we covered in the first part of this book. This will assist us to integrate the nature of the journey we have made thus far and to prepare for the terrain that we are now about to enter.

In Part I of this book, we were introduced to The Pathway of Awareness. This is the pathway that our awareness moves along as we enter our experience of this emotional, mental, and physical world. Briefly reviewing the insights inherent in being aware of this pathway will enable us to better understand the relevance of the experience The Presence Process now opens to us: namely our entry into deeper emotional awareness.

As explained to us in Part I of this book, this Pathway of Awareness is easy to identify by observing the normal development of a newborn child. Even though our emotional, mental, and physical bodies are already evident and developing simultaneously alongside each other from the moment of our birth, there is a specific pathway that our individual awareness uses to move consciously into them. As a newborn child, we first cry and laugh (emotional), then we learn to talk (mental), and only then do we learn to walk (physical). Therefore the pathway our awareness moves through as it enters this world is:

From the emotional to the mental to the physical.

In Part I of this book, we were further familiarized with this Pathway of Awareness by being introduced to the existence of our Seven-Year Cycle and how it unfolds as we make our way from our moment of birth towards the experience we call adulthood. Our attention was brought to the way the emotional experience that was initiated for us the moment we left the womb began tapering off and in many cases ceased its development when we reached the age of seven. The end of our first Seven-Year Cycle marked the end of what we call our childhood. We were then declared to be young boys and girls. This marked our entry into a period in our life when we focused more intensely on our mental development. This is why we started our schooling around the age of seven. This second Seven-Year Cycle continued until we were about fourteen years old. We were then declared "teenagers". Then, our development started to become increasingly focused upon taking up a meaningful physical role in society. The closing of this third Seven-Year Cycle was then acknowledged by an event such as the celebrating of our 21st birthday. We were then declared to be "young adults". These three Seven-Year Cycles again underlined the pathway our awareness took as we moved through our emotional, mental, and physical development. From the perspective we have just reviewed, our Pathway of Awareness unfolded here as a means to equip us to successfully enter into and to establish our place in society.

We have also been shown how this Pathway and its movement through our first three Seven-Year Cycles serves as a means to imprint our destiny into our experience on an emotional, mental, and physical level. This Pathway of Awareness is indeed a fractal and therefore can be observed flowing systematically through many aspects of our life experience.

In Part I of this book, we were also introduced to the way this pathway is automatically reversed whenever we participate in activities with an intention to reconnect our awareness with our Source. In other words, when we metaphorically seek to reconnect with our vibrational "home", we reverse it. This is clearly illustrated to us when we observe a child in prayer: first they kneel and put their hands together (physical), then they speak to God (mental), and as they pray their words touch our heart (emotional). The practice of meditation is also another example of how we retrace our steps by reversing this pathway: first we adopt a posture (physical), then we repeat a mantra (mental), and only then do we evoke an experience of inner love and devotion (emotional). Thus the reverse of The Pathway of Awareness that we use to enter this world is:

From the physical to the mental to the emotional.

What The Presence Process accomplishes so magnificently is that it activates a journey within us that enables us to efficiently begin retracing our steps along this Pathway so that we may reestablish a connection with our Inner Presence. Without our even realizing it, this Process equips us to first reactivate physical presence, then mental clarity, and then emotional balance. Because of The Pathway of Awareness established by our entry into this world, there is no random procedure for reconnecting with our Source. Without deliberately reversing it, we cannot retrace our steps along it. Without first achieving physical presence, then mental clarity, then emotional balance, in that order, any attempt we make to reconnect with our Inner Presence is plagued with inauthenticity.

We can clearly observe the success of The Presence Process in its intent to correctly guide us along our pathway of return to ourselves by re-examining the structure of The Emotional Cleansing Process. This procedural tool systematically reverses The Pathway of Awareness that we used to enter our experience of this world, and that is why we are encouraged to wield it as often as the opportunity arises. The Emotional Cleansing Process first teaches us how to "dismiss the messenger" (physical), then to "get the message" (mental), then to "feel it to heal it" (emotional), and finally to enter a frequency of compassion for ourselves (the "vibrational" shift in our behavior that is a prerequisite for reconnecting with our Inner Presence).

When we entered The Presence Process, we were deliberately "set up" to step upon and begin traversing the path that returns us to our inner awareness. Our Breathing Exercise immediately began assisting us to reactivate physical presence. The Presence Activating Statements, reading materials, and the Perceptual Tools then teamed up together to gradually begin reactivating our mental clarity. Now, as we move through our next three Sessions, we are consciously initiating the task of reactivating our emotional awareness by adding the procedure of submerging our body in warm water. How and why this particular procedure facilitates increased emotional awareness will be explained to us after this review.

By entering Session Seven, we are now consciously entering the emotional leg of our reversed journey along The Pathway of Awareness. For many of us, this part of the journey, our entry, and movement through the emotional realm, may be very challenging. It may be challenging because we cannot *think* our way through the emotional realm: we must *feel* our way through it. It is during this phase of our Process that we are therefore reminded of the following:

We do not have to know "why?" to accept that what we are feeling or what our Inner Facilitator is communicating to us is real and true for us.

Feeling, as opposed to thinking, is what is required of us now so that we may be able to enter a deeper relationship with our Inner Presence. To integrate why feeling instead of thinking assists us in establishing a deeper relationship with Presence, we can visually examine the word "presence" and also listen carefully to its audible vibration.

PRESENCE = PRE-SENSE.

To activate an authentic relationship with our Inner Presence requires that we stop trying to make sense of everything. Trying to make sense of everything causes us to become too mentally preoccupied. When we are too mentally preoccupied, we struggle to accept an experience as being real and true for us unless we "understand" it first. This puts us at a disadvantage because our Inner Presence "knows" as opposed to "understands". It does not think or ponder or reflect. As we move through our water sessions, for example, it is not necessary for us to "understand" what is happening to us for the experience to be valid. The experience is valid because we are having it, and because we are feeling it, not because of what we think about it.

To begin restoring our emotional balance, we must now enhance the physical and mental experiences we have attended to thus far throughout The Presence Process by now opening ourselves to being guided by our heart. Emotional balance is purely about matters of the heart. Matters of the heart are not always easy for us in a world that does not yet perceive the condition of our emotional body to be of great importance in our evolution as human beings. Yet it is our heart, not our mind, that enables us to experience the depths of our humanity.

It will be natural and quite expected, therefore, that as we move through this next stage of our journey into present moment awareness, we will continue to *try* and think our way through what is happening to us. We will try to "understand". Our habitual and conditioned need to try to understand what is happening to us will cause us to experience varying degrees of mental confusion. Therefore, it is important as we move from Session Seven towards Session Ten that we hold the following "knowing" in the forefront of our awareness:

Right now, as we move through our emotional body, experiencing a sense of mental confusion is beneficial. It is a sign of progress.

Why? Because mental confusion serves us. It prevents us from attempting to barge our way into the emotional realm on the back of our ego. By giving ourselves permission "not to have to understand to know", we will ensure a gentler and less frustrating ride through this part of our experience. By being at ease with our inner mental confusion and accepting it as a temporary necessity and as a sign of progress, we will not indulge in unnecessary drama or slip into reactive behavior. There is nothing wrong if we feel somewhat confused every now and then between what unfolds from this point onward until our arrival at Session Ten.

As we commence Session Seven with our first water session, we are now being called upon to feel our way through to Session Ten. By feeling our way through the emotional realm, we are bringing added awareness and dexterity to our emotional body. We are awakening it and we are awakening to it. This added awareness automatically decreases our negative emotional charge. It does so because it empowers us to bring the focus of our Presence to emotional blockages that appear not to exist while we favor and exclusively frequent a time-based mentality.

We have been training specifically for this emotional aspect of our journey and are therefore well prepared. We are encouraged to consciously assist ourselves through this challenging transition point of our adventure into present moment awareness by recommitting to our entire Process.

We must attend to our Breathing Exercises daily no matter what.

We must endeavor to repeat our Presence Activating Statements with newfound determination.

We must diligently explore the new Perceptual Tools that are about to be shared with us.

We must continue to wield The Emotional Cleansing Process like a sword.

Whenever we perceive discomfort, we must "feel it to heal it".

We are now well on our way to reestablishing an open channel with our Inner Presence. This is no ordinary accomplishment. The Pathway of Awareness that we moved through as we entered this world enabled us to arrive and to anchor our consciousness here. But that was only half the journey. The Presence Process activates the other half of the journey so that we can achieve wholeness and thus restore a conscious awareness of our Holiness. The Presence Process enables us to consciously stand in this outer world and to simultaneously retrace our steps and reestablish a conscious connection with our Inner Presence—the state of Being from which we emerged.

The consequence of accomplishing this is that we established an open line of communication that enables us to consciously be both in this conditional world and simultaneously connected to the unconditional Source that brought every aspect of this experience into being. The possibilities of achieving this are unlimited. It elevates us into a state of Being in which we are in the world but not of it. It enables us to stand in a place in which we touch this world deeply through our shared Presence but remain untouched by it. It transforms us from victims and victors into vehicles of the highest service.

Accomplishing this task enables us to step into the ultimate unexplored frontier: our Self. In the realms of human exploration, this journey transforms us into heroes of consciousness. We have come a long way and have overcome many obstacles to enter this state of Grace.

Let us take a moment therefore to acknowledge ourselves for having come this far.

Let us know that what lies ahead is made easier and gentler by everything we have ever experienced. All that has ever happened to us, no matter what form it has taken, is what has deliberately brought us to this moment.

Let us therefore be grateful for the magnificence of the journey we have embarked upon, from being an unconscious molecule to embracing the limitlessness of present moment awareness.

Let us take our awesome accomplishment consciously into ourselves and allow it to fuel the unknown road that leads ever onward, inward, and upward.

COOLING OFF THE EGO

DURING THE FIRST SIX SESSIONS of The Presence Process, we focused on activating the procedures of "undoing" and on learning the procedures required to apply The Emotional Cleansing Process to our daily life experience. The act of "undoing" is our intent to allow the suppressed memories of our past to begin surfacing so that they can be consciously integrated. This intent is established and activated the moment we first consciously connected our breathing in Session One. The Presence Process facilitates this intent to "undo the past"—or concept of it—in such a way that we can gain experiential insight from what we have been through. The consequence is that by now we have started becoming aware of inherited behaviors and belief systems that do not serve us.

The setups that we have been through in the past weeks will have shown us by now that beneath each suppressed memory, limiting belief system, and unproductive behavior pattern is a negative emotional charge. It is this negative emotional charge that our breathing sessions have been bringing to the surface because it is this negative emotional charge that is responsible for the physical, mental, and emotional states of imbalance that have reoccurred in our life experience since we departed childhood. It is also this negative emotional charge that is responsible for all our dramas and our self-medication behaviors in which we consciously and unconsciously sedate and control our life experience. It is this negative emotional charge that has kept us unconsciously attached to and distracted by the past and/or projecting our attention into some future.

During the next three Sessions, we will be breathing. We may also be submerging our body in warm water. This is not a punishment; this is a profound tool and a safety net designed to short circuit the deviousness of our own egos. Let us take a look at the deviousness of the ego.

Remember that the trinity that makes up the structure of our ego consists of our behavior, our appearance, and the unfolding circumstances of our life experience. In other words, until we integrate our childhood traumas, our behavior, appearance, and life circumstances are to a great extent consciously and unconsciously fueled by the negative charge in our emotional body. However, to the ego, our appearance, our behavior, and the circumstances of our life constitute the sum total of who and what it believes us to be—or all that it would have us believe we are. Therefore, our negative emotional charge is the sand upon which our ego has built its illusionary identity.

To defend its illusionary identity and to prevent us from realizing the true nature of our authentic Inner Presence, the ego can and does use any of these three outer attributes as a means to fool us into thinking we have successfully dealt with our negative emotional charge. It can lead us to behave and appear as if we are feeling completely balanced, especially when we are approaching our core issues. It can also arrange the conditions of our life circumstances to appear as if, by all accounts, we are successful and thriving when in fact we are hurting and suffering in quiet desperation. The ego knows how to make it appear as if everything is okay, alright, and fine.

Why would the ego do this? Why would the ego make it appear as if everything is okay? It does this so that we will not question the unconscious arrangement we have of letting it run our life. It does this because it relies totally on our negative emotional charge as fuel for its existence. The negative emotional charge is the fuel that feeds all our drama and all our drama is the drunken dance of the ego. Remember that the ego is what we constructed as children to replace our authentic self. The ego is the inauthentic pretence that veils our authentic Presence. That is why, until our unconscious negative emotional charge is neutralized, the ego automatically shapes our appearance, behavior, and unfolding life circumstances. It does this in a manner that projects an inauthenticity that is manufactured from childhood fear, anger, and grief. Our inauthenticity is a coat of armor that prevents us from being vulnerable to the awareness and power of our Inner Presence. The ego encourages us to wear this armor proudly. It leads us to believe that this armor, or inauthenticity, is necessary to protect us from "the unpredictable outside world". That is why the ego so strongly encourages and supports the role of victim or victor. By keeping our attention focused on the potential enemy "out there", by keeping us transfixed by the mirror and our reflection in it, we remain unaware of the living Presence that is standing in front of the mirror.

This is one of the reasons why, at this point of The Presence Process, we use a tool that, though familiar to us, is applied in a manner that is foreign to the arrangement we have with the ego. Our arrangement with the ego is that bathing is for cleaning our precious body, for enjoying ourselves, for relaxing. It is a tool for cleaning and pampering our appearance, for calming our behavior, and for enhancing our present life circumstances.

Yet we are not going to be using the bathing experience for any of the above reasons; we are going to be using it to discharge the negative energy buildup from our emotional body by activating increased emotional body awareness.

So how and why is submerging our body in warm water effective in activating our awareness of and then decreasing our negative emotional charge? To explain this a brief recap is beneficial.

As we leave our childhood and enter the adult world, we are required to become inauthentic to some extent. In simplistic terms, this means we learn to say "no" when we mean "yes" and "yes" when we mean "no". An adult is, to put it in very simple terms, *a child in resistance*. To pass ourselves off as adults requires that we continually resist being authentic. We are by nature spontaneously joyful and creative beings, so any other state of Being that we portray is inauthentic. It is drama and most definitely resistance. By the time we are well into our adult experience, we are so proficient at being inauthentic that we identify the state of pretence as normal behavior. We have all heard children say, "Let's pretend we are..." or "Let's play pretend." What they are really saying is "Let's be like adults."

Our authentic nature can become so unfamiliar to us that if people become spontaneously joyful and creative around us we might even find ourselves becoming uncomfortable, annoyed, irritable, or even embarrassed in their company. However, we are secretly attracted to people who display their authenticity. We call them "free spirits", or flamboyant, artistic, or eccentric. We label them as if they are somehow faulty, damaged, and in need of repair. Yet they are secretly our heroes, and we always mourn the loss of their presence when they are gone. Such beings are the beautiful mirrors that enter our life to remind us of the child that died within us.

Our ongoing resistance to being emotionally authentic creates heat within our emotional body because all resistance causes friction and friction causes heat. Our continual resistance to being authentic generates a constant build up of this heat, and in The Presence Process, we call this heat build-up "a charge". It is this charge that becomes the core of all our physical, mental, and emotional discomfort. This inner heat becomes emotionally externalized and defined by us as fear, anger, or grief. This is "the negative emotional charge" that will be brought to our awareness and decreased during the water sessions and through our conscious application of The Emotional Cleansing Process.

As we journey further into adulthood, we unconsciously develop behaviors of sedation and control in an attempt to cope with the discomfort of our negative emotional charge. All our uncomfortable emotional, mental, and physical symptoms are a direct link to this hidden negative emotional charge. Instead of realizing this, we automatically and unconsciously resort to sedation and control which merely throw our experiences into more acute states of imbalance. This automatic and unconscious reaction to our symptoms of imbalance is also imprinted on us by how our parents reacted to their negative emotional charges. Despite our attempts to suppress this discomfort, our negative emotional charge inevitably overflows into our life and manifests as fear, anger, and grief. Fear, anger, and grief are the emotional trinity of discomfort that causes all the dis-ease we see in the world today.

When we enter The Presence Process, we first work on becoming physically present. Consequently, we become aware of uncomfortable physical sensations in our body, unproductive aspects of our everyday behavior, and negative interactions with our outer world that may have not been evident to us before. We then gain some semblance of mental clarity and start to make a connection between our belief systems and the overall quality of the life experience we are having. However, many of the core events that imprinted our emotional body with the states of imbalance that we intend to neutralize occurred before we had any real grasp of language and/or mental concepts. So we cannot reliably think or talk our way back into those places. This is where traditional therapy fails and becomes as outdated as shock treatment. This is also where and why we climb into the bathtub of warm water and submerge our body for 20 minutes prior to our Breathing Exercise.

There are many explanations for why the presence of water activates the emotional content of our experience. It is accepted universally that the element of water has a strong association with our emotions. Tears are liquid. We talk of the sea as being "an ocean of emotion" and in that way it represents the emotional body of the planet. We have already suggested that the word "emotion" is an abbreviation for "energy in motion", and if ever there was a self-evident energy in motion on this planet, it is the liquids that constantly move above, upon, and beneath its surface. Like the planet, our human body is more liquid than solid. The moon is also universally associated with the feminine principle and therefore with emotion. We know that the full moon has an impact on our emotional content just as it has an impact on the tidal activity of any large body of water. Emotions themselves can be metaphorically thought of as tides that rise and fall within us. When someone is being over-emotional we say they are being "a drip".

We can go on and on citing the associations and metaphors that relate water to emotion. What is clear through this simple observation is that water and emotions are and have always been intimately connected. Water is energy in motion that we can visibly observe despite having our attention *trans*fixed by the physical world. It is an energy flow that "matters" to us. Observing the behavior of water in our life enables us to use expressions like, "Do not get so upset; learn to go with the flow."

What is so profound about introducing warm water sessions to this Process is that it empowers us to make real adjustments to the negative emotional charge that we carry by activating emotional body awareness. It is our awareness of this negative charge that causes the internal rebalancing. This becomes evident when we submerge our body in it for an extended time. By doing so, we activate the realm of pure feeling: the place that we were in before we learned language. We also activate our vibrational memory of having been in the womb, as well as our birth moment, and our first few emotional years of life. These places may have been some of the last experiences we had of being completely present.

When we submerge our body in warm water as a tool for gaining present moment awareness, we are activating emotional body awareness. Everything that makes the experience uncomfortable is everything that stands between who and what we "think" we are now and our original core of authenticity. In other words, all the discomfort that comes to our attention is our drama, our pretence, and thus the dynamics of our ego.

This is why those of us who are very uncomfortable with our own emotions generally do not like to take long hot baths. Any surfacing discomfort during the water session and in the breathing session that follows is the negative emotional charge that must be integrated to restore balance to the quality of all our life experiences. It is integrated by our conscious awareness of it.

By submerging in warm water, we are deliberately bringing the heat created by our resistance to being present head to head with the warmth of the water in the bathtub. The one is real (the water) and the other is pretence (our emotional resistance). These two states of heat combine, and unless one of them gives way, we may feel a growing state of disease, or we may feel claustrophobic, or that something terrible is going to happen. What we are feeling is our accumulated fear, anger, and grief coming to the surface to be integrated by our conscious attention. We are also feeling the desperate desire of the ego to hold onto its inauthenticity.

Of course the warmth of the water in the bathtub is not going to give way just because we don't like it, so the only way through this experience is for the negative emotional charge we are carrying to be released. In other words, part of the ego dies a death. This ego death can occur physically through bodily sensations, mentally through thought processes, and emotionally by an outer expression of our fear, anger, or grief. As the ego's hold on our life experience dies, a charge is simultaneously released from our emotional body. This release occurs in a moment of surrender or "letting go". In this moment, an aspect of our outer drama also peels away from our awareness. Consequently, we lose a piece of pretence and regain a portion of Presence.

This is also occurring during our daily Breathing Exercises. We may at times experience rising waves of heat that suddenly subside leaving us feeling a little cooler than normal. This is the surfacing and releasing of the negative emotional charge.

Metaphorically, doing a session in warm water is akin to having the opportunity to allow some of the weight of our past emotional baggage to pour down the drain. It is our unconscious reaction to this weight that has caused us to adopt the many unproductive behaviors and negative beliefs that do not serve us. The moment that we consciously release a portion of this negative charge from our emotional body is quite possibly the first moment in our life that we literally start making room for ourselves to breathe. Once this load is lessened, we are metaphorically able to stand up straighter, to take a deeper breath, and to scan the horizons of our life—right here, right now. This new perception is what we might call "seeing our life in the present moment", as opposed to seeing it through the distorted lenses of the past or the projected future.

With the completion of each additional water/breathing session, our negative emotional charge continues to be lessened and the evidence that we are being liberated from the past continues to manifest in many ways. After our first water session and the 15-minute breathing session that follows, we may feel a sense of emptiness. This is natural. Something from our past that we have carried unconsciously (because we do not always have to know what it is) and mistakenly presumed to be part of who and what we think we are will be gone. After our session, our body may also radiate heat. This is heat that is literally peeling off our emotional body. This is the discharge of the negative charge. Often this is followed, over the next day or so, by the sensation that our overall body temperature is somewhat cooler than we are accustomed to. This is because we have released something that we have been resisting and therefore our overall body heat will have decreased. Our body will quickly adjust and find a new equilibrium. All of these sensations may initially feel unfamiliar, but we will automatically pass through and acclimatize to them. They are physical confirmations of the adjustments that we have made to the overall condition of our emotional body. They are occurring automatically because the suppressed memories that were activated and brought to the surface as a consequence of the first six Sessions are now being effectively cleared away like oil from the surface of water.

However, there is no vacuum in space. This is why we must simultaneously, from this point in the Process, start metaphorically filling ourselves up with positive behavior patterns and concepts that will serve us. In other words, we must now make it a priority to replace our diminishing unconscious negative emotional charge with an increasingly conscious positive emotional charge. That is why we must now begin to focus on physical presence, mental clarity, emotional balance, and making a connection with our life purpose. Our life purpose is our conscious connection to life itself. When we are in charge of our life, we automatically live on purpose. We live deliberately. We live to liberate ourselves.

As we journey through the next three Sessions, it is important to keep the following in the forefront of our mind: With each water/breathing session, we are gathering increasing emotional body awareness. By submerging our body in water for 20 minutes and then attending to our breathing immediately afterwards, we are activating accelerated present moment awareness. This means that the distance between our thoughts, words, and deeds and their consequent manifestations (the quality of our life experience) will appear to be getting increasingly shorter. What is actually occurring is that we are now seeing the connection between the instances of cause and effect in our life. This improved perception makes it seem or feel as if time is speeding up. In order that our experience is enjoyable and not threatening, we must commit here and now to becoming responsible for all our thoughts, words, and deeds. We must only sow what we intend to reap. We must endeavor not to entertain old patterns of "'stinking thinking". We must commit to using The Emotional Cleansing Process whenever we feel emotionally triggered. We must continue to breathe for 15 minutes twice a day, no matter what.

From this point in the Process, we are also welcome to submerge our body in warm water, immediately followed by our Breathing Exercise, as often as we feel inclined. The more we submerge our body in warm water with an intention to activate emotional body awareness, the quicker our negative charge will surface to be cleared. However, we must not force anything.

Cautionary Note: Consciously connecting our breathing while we are in warm water, as opposed to simply submerging and being still in the water, intensifies emotional body awareness. This should not be attempted by individuals going through this Process for the first time and/or individuals entering water sessions without the presence of a facilitator. Consciously connecting our breathing while in warm water accelerates processing and may cause sudden surfacing of past fear, anger and grief. It requires guidance, experience, and the presence of a companion to serve as a witness. It is therefore not recommended that we attempt this. For the purposes of The Presence Process, as it is laid out in this book, we are simply to submerge our body in warm water for 20 minutes, then immediately exit the bathtub, dry off, and attend to our 15-minute breathing session without delay. If we experience emotional, mental or physical discomfort during our 15-minute breathing session, we are to keep our breathing connected until this discomfort passes. Following these simple instructions ensures gradual and gentle processing.

TAKING CHARGE OF THE NEGATIVE

THE PRESENCE PROCESS has discussed the negative emotional charge in great detail. The existence of the negative emotional charge almost gives us an opportunity to "blame" our present circumstances on the past. Unfortunately, this line of thought will not wash, especially since we are now consciously and consistently diminishing the effect our negative emotional charge has on our present circumstances. It is likely that we have initiated more emotional rebalancing in the last six Sessions than in our entire previous life experience. The next few Sessions accelerate the procedure. Soon we will not have any excuses for not enjoying our life experience, no matter how it unfolds. Or will we?

During our preprocess reading, we were encouraged to approach questions in a new light. We were asked to focus on the process of asking the question and not on attempting to force the answer in any way. Just for this brief moment, we can forget that instruction because here come some questions to which we will be given the answer. As we read what follows, we must remember that the truth will always set us free, especially if we can admit it to ourselves.

There is no way that we can deny that where our attention is focused is exactly where our life experience occurs. Or that the quality of all our experiences is determined by the quality of our intentions. If we think about it for a moment, we will know that this is true. Just as the Law of Cause and Effect renders us all equally responsible for every thought, word, and deed we initiate, the quality of our experience = attention + intention. This universal arrangement places us all on a level playing field. Who else can be responsible for the consequences of the thoughts, words, and deeds that we consciously choose to generate? If we can accept this to be true, then:

> *Why, if we can consciously choose to love, do we hate?*

> *Why, if we can consciously choose harmony, do we fight?*

> *Why, if we can consciously choose peace, do we choose conflict?*

> *Why, if we can consciously choose to be supportive,*
> *do we choose to be cynical?*

> *Why, if we can consciously choose laughter, do we choose sadness?*

> *Why, if we can consciously choose to smile, do we choose to frown?*

> *Why, if we can consciously choose gratitude,*
> *do we choose to complain?*

> *Why, if we can consciously choose to encourage,*
> *do we choose to compete?*

> *Why, if we can consciously choose to feel confident,*
> *do we engage in doubt?*

> *Why, if we can consciously choose to be comfortable,*
> *do we choose to suffer?*

> *Why, if we can consciously choose to be optimistic,*
> *do we engage in negativity?*

The answer to all these questions and to any others that we can ask related to why we continue to choose radiating negativity instead of the uplifting radiance of our Inner Presence is the same. It is because:

> *Instead of choosing to develop the emotional maturity*
> *required to "give" ourselves the attention that we seek, we*
> *prefer to manifest outer drama so that we can "get"*

this attention from others.

When we commit to giving ourselves the attention we seek, we commit to our freedom. NOW is a perfect moment to choose to grow up emotionally. It may not be the easiest choice, but it is the most responsible.

EMBRACING PHYSICAL PRESENCE

EMBRACING PHYSICAL PRESENCE is the first step that we must take in our life to accomplish a permanent shift from reactive to responsive behavior. Unless we are physically present in our life, we cannot make responsible choices that will serve us. Responsive behavior is causal and will therefore automatically lead to an experience of increasing inner peace and outer harmony, but we must show up in our life to activate this state of Being.

When we are not present in our physical body, we are adrift in the mental plane. This means that our awareness is floating in some conceptual place that we call "the past" or "the future". We are then making our life decisions based on the perceptions that we are gathering from these illusionary places. How can this possibly benefit us in any way? Decisions made based on what happened in the past and what may happen in the future are usually reactive and therefore always self-destructive. They are usually based on effects and are therefore ineffectual. This is why such a big emphasis is placed on attending to our daily Breathing Exercise. Consciously connected breathing is the most accelerated procedure for extracting our awareness from this mental condition of "living in time" so that we can begin to accumulate and maintain the awareness of physical presence.

It was during our childhood that we began our habit of mentally evacuating our physical body and entering the illusionary mental experience we now call "time". We did this because we were afraid of what was happening to us in the present moment. It is really that simple; we lost our sense of Presence because we became afraid. Fear causes evacuation of the physical body. We traded our authentic Presence for the armor of pretence. We had experiences that caused us fear, and because we did not understand what was happening to us or what to do about it, we mentally escaped into the illusionary corridors of time. In this unreal place, we could pretend that everything was or would at some point be all right.

This is no longer our predicament.

In the past six Sessions, we have gained a deeper insight into the causes of our physical, mental, and emotional imbalance. We have also been training ourselves in perceptual procedures that will assist us to lay the foundations for returning to present moment awareness. Through our application of The Emotional Cleansing Process, we have already begun changing our perspective towards our life experience from one that is reactive to one that is responsive. The fact that we have made it to this point in The Presence Process is evidence that we are sincerely choosing to take responsibility for the quality of our life experience.

It is not hard for us to now begin making the perceptual leap of faith that empowers us to accept that all the challenging (fearful) experiences that have shadowed us from the past have always been disguised opportunities for growth and gain. We could not see this in "time", but it becomes blatantly obvious as we enter present moment awareness. On a conscious level, once we have made this perceptual leap of faith, once we see that all of life is a growth opportunity, then we no longer have any reason to be afraid. Why be afraid when we know that *our life only happens so that we may grow?* Especially when we are now being empowered with the Perceptual Tools that enable us to consciously participate in and integrate all our growth experiences. We can now begin to feel safe in this state of knowing.

As we continue to become proficient at responding to all our surfacing unintegrated life experiences, our sense of safety will also gradually seep into our unconscious. What this means is that as we step consciously into the role of taking responsibility for the quality of all our experiences, our child self will also begin to feel safe again. And a safe child is a spontaneously joyful and creative child.

It is safe therefore for us to begin departing this illusionary experience called "living in time" and return to and reenter the only real home that we have while we are journeying through our present life experience—our physical body. By choosing to return to our physical body, we are also choosing to become physically present in every aspect of our life experience. Our newfound physical presence is a gift because it empowers us to redirect our energy towards consciously navigating ourselves into experiences that we know will serve us. Therefore, this is the moment in The Presence Process when we must consciously embrace the task of navigating our experiences.

We only have two tools that we use to navigate towards, through, and out of all our life experiences; they are our attention and intention. Our attention is the tool of our mental body and is the "what" of our focus. Our intention is the tool of our emotional body and is the "why" of our focus. The quality of our life experience in any given moment is determined by how consciously we wield our attention and intention. It is that simple, but we have to be physically present to consciously wield these two Perceptual Tools in a way that will serve us.

In every moment of our life, we are automatically wielding both our attention and intention. Mostly, we have been wielding them unconsciously based on what we believed happened to us in the past and what we suspected may happen to us in the future. In other words, until recently, we have been designing the quality of our life experience based on childhood interpretations and future "guesstimations". It would be more accurate to say that we have allowed our misinformed child self to be in charge of determining what is best for us based on its interpretations of the world. These interpretations are the stories we told ourselves as children that we have since established as our unconscious library of core belief systems. None of these stories are true; therefore, it is hazardous to continue allowing these unconscious core belief systems to be the parameters by which the quality of our present life experience is determined. It is imperative that we now become conscious navigators.

Focusing our attention and intention twice a day on the simple navigational tool that is now going to be shared with us will train us to begin accomplishing this task. For the next three Sessions, we are encouraged to use this tool to navigate our experience towards one of increasing physical presence, mental clarity, and emotional balance. Applying this tool consistently will give us a taste of the consequences of consciously wielding our attention and intention.

This simple but extremely powerful navigational tool operates on the premise that the different attributes of our means of perception must be tuned to a particular frequency in order for us to have a particular quality of experience. This can be best understood by bringing to mind the image of an orchestra. All the musicians of an orchestra must be playing from the same composition in order for them to achieve harmony with each other. In the same way, the different attributes of our means of perception must be consciously tuned to a common frequency if we are going to achieve a particular quality in our experience. We may think of our personal frequency as being what we most frequently think about. During the course of the next three Sessions, this navigational tool is designed to tune our personal frequency to physical presence, then to mental clarity, and then to emotional balance.

To make best use of this tool, we ask our mind the listed questions twice every day (morning and evening) after our 15-minute Breathing Exercise. We have already discussed the approach we are encouraged to take during The Presence Process regarding the process of asking questions in The Consciousness of Questions. A brief recap here may be beneficial.

Normally in our life, when a question is asked of us, we immediately apply our attention to finding the answer. If we cannot access the answer, we consciously end our mental search with a limiting self-judgment about our mental abilities. The Presence Process—and especially this particular navigational tool within it—asks us to take a different approach; for the purpose of this exercise, it is the asking of the question that is of importance, not the finding of the "correct" answer.

It is therefore not necessary to mentally hunt for or to force the answers to come into our awareness. We sincerely ask ourselves the list of questions and observe the first answer to each that surfaces in our mind. We do this without placing any weight on the answering process. If no answer surfaces in our mind, we move on to the next question. We then allow the answer to be given to us when we least expect it. If an answer does surface, we take note of it, and then move on to the next question.

The efficiency of this tool is based on asking the questions consistently, not finding the correct answer. The mind will automatically take care of the answers. The nature of this tool is that these answers will not necessarily manifest to us as mental concepts or thoughts or even images, but as a favorable adjustment in the quality of our experiences. In other words, friendly "messengers".

Using this navigational tool immediately after we have completed our

Breathing Exercise is most beneficial, as this is when we have the most present moment awareness to fuel our conscious intentions. Our present moment awareness magnifies whatever we consciously focus it on.

By asking these questions after our breathing sessions,
we navigate our experience towards physical presence.

What is the purpose of physical presence?

What sound do I associate with physical presence?

What color do I associate with physical presence?

What smell do I associate with physical presence?

What taste do I associate with physical presence?

What emotion do I associate with physical presence?

What texture do I associate with physical presence?

What physical form does physical presence take for me?

What movement do I associate with physical presence?

What visual symbol do I associate with physical presence?

*Where am I experiencing effortless physical presence
in my life right now?*

FOR THE NEXT SEVEN DAYS WE ARE REQUIRED TO:

1 **Attend to our 15-minute Breathing Exercise twice each day.** We are also welcome to do more than just the one water session that is required to activate this Session.

2 Repeat our given Presence Activating Statement for the Session whenever we are not mentally engaged.

3 Review our reading materials and apply the navigational tool as instructed.

THIS ENDS SESSION SEVEN.

SESSION EIGHT
(OUR 2ND WATER SESSION)

Our Presence Activating Statement for the next seven days is:

I am responsible for my own peace of mind.

TO ACTIVATE THIS SESSION:

We memorize the given Presence Activating Statement.
We then read through all the written materials.
We submerge our body in warm water and soak for at least
20 minutes and then immediately attend to our 15-minute
Breathing Exercise.

ACTIVATING PEACE OF MIND THROUGH FORGIVENESS

ON SOME LEVEL WE ARE ALL angry because we were not loved unconditionally as children. We were all conditionally loved. This is not an accusation; it is the predicament of being born into a world of constantly changing conditions. Since childhood, we have unconsciously spent our whole life and all our energy attempting to live up to the conditions that we thought would earn us unconditional love. This has manifested as the endless physical, mental, and emotional "doings" or dramas that we have performed in an attempt to gain attention and acceptance. Unfortunately, unconditional love is not an experience that we can force others to channel in our direction through the manifestation of drama. All attention that we attract through drama is by its very nature conditional. The truth is that we have failed at every turn to get the attention we have sought. We have failed because unconditional love is not money; it is not something we have to or can earn. Love is not something we have to achieve through merit. We do not have to qualify to be loved. Love is our birthright. Love just is. Love is who and what we are.

During our childhood, the example of love set for us through our parents' interaction with us and with each other became our primary definition of love. This is the automatic outcome of emotional imprinting. Consequently, as adults, whenever we seek to manifest an experience of love for ourselves, we unconsciously manufacture a physical, mental, or emotional scenario that will recreate the emotional resonance we experienced during our initial childhood interactions with our parents. This resonance does not have to be comfortable or in any way pleasant. It only has to be similar.

For example, if we received abuse when we asked for love, then abuse would have become part of our childhood definition of love. Consequently, as adults, whenever we feel a need for love in our life, we would then automatically manifest an experience that would include the emotional resonance of abuse. We do this unconsciously. We do this automatically. Why? Because this is the only way we know how to get what we think love is. But the love we end up getting always hurts. It always hurts because of its conditions. On a conscious level, we might then say, "Why does this always keep happening to me?" The reason why we keep manifesting the same hurtful experiences is simple. It is because we do not know any better. This is the predicament we are all in. This is the open wound in the heart of humanity. This is why many of us automatically assume that love hurts. Yet "hurting" is a condition, love is not.

Throughout The Presence Process, we are gradually being taught how to see beyond the limitations of our own childhood interpretations. We are being taught how to grow up emotionally. The consequence of this emotional growth is that we are gently beginning to lift the illusionary veils set in place by our childhood experiences. As these veils of fear, anger, and grief gradually lift, we begin entering a very different world experience. It is not a world experience that is made up of the past or the projected future, but a world experience that is accessed through present moment awareness. Confirmation that we are awakening to this world of present moment awareness is that we begin to have profound realizations and insights about the real nature of our shared human condition. One of these insights is:

> *Without exception, everyone we encounter, no matter how his or her behavior may appear to us on the surface, is looking for the experience of unconditional love.*

Initially, this is not apparent to us because the behavior we all use in an attempt to manifest the experience of unconditional love for ourselves seldom reflects the unconditional love that we seek. This is because we are all attempting to "get" this love from others, so in our individual experience, it appears, through the process of reflection, that everyone in this world is attempting to "get" something from us. The feeling that this world is constantly attempting to get something from us is the automatic reflection of our own behavior. We assumed this behavior from childhood by parroting our parents. They assumed it by parroting their parents, and so on.

When we gain enough present moment awareness to truly see that we have unconsciously manifested a life experience based purely on our childhood definition of what we think love is, then we can accept the comic tragedy of our predicament. We have blindly followed the example set for us by our parents. How could things have turned out differently based on the initial input? In fact, it is true to say that *we are our parents until we unlearn and overcome the belief systems they imprinted upon us.* It is a case of the blind leading the blind.

Understanding and accepting this predicament empowers us to forgive ourselves for all our misguided behaviors of the past. We were looking for love in all the wrong places and in all the wrong ways. This insight enables us to understand why we have manifested the quality of the life experience that we have gone through up to now. We can enter a state of authenticity by accepting and admitting that we do not know what unconditional love is. Not having a clue what unconditional love is has nothing to do with our level of intelligence or the nature of our personality. In a world of constantly changing conditions, the experience of unconditional love is metaphorically the rarest of all gems. Awakening to unconditional love in this world is like attempting to find a breath of fresh air in the depths of the ocean. And therein lies the clue to awakening to unconditional love in this world: if we want to experience a breath of fresh air in the depths of the ocean, we had better make sure we place it down there ourselves.

By understanding our own predicament, we can begin to laugh at ourselves for all the drama we have manifested. This laughter is the medicine we are really after because being able to laugh about our own dramas is the evidence that forgiveness has actually taken place.

Once we can truly accept this about ourselves, we can then begin accepting this about everyone we encounter. No matter how anyone's behavior might appear to us, they are looking for the experience of unconditional love based upon the example that was initially set for them. In other words, no matter how we perceive the quality of their behavior, the appearance they project, or the life circumstances they manifest, everyone really is doing the best they can with the example that was demonstrated to them. We really are all doing our best.

However, even though we mentally understand this predicament we all share, we may still find it very challenging to forgive others for the hurt we perceive them to have caused us. Initially, we may be able to accept this seemingly tragic and misguided state of affairs as far as our own predicament is concerned; we may be able to accept that because we did not know what unconditional love is, we ended up hurting ourselves and others. Yet we may be unwilling to see and accept this as being the plight of others—especially when it comes to our parents and anyone in our life who has hurt us. Why? Because there is an aspect of our experience that is still clouded with anger. There is an aspect of our experience that still feels the need and the right to blame. There is an aspect of our experience that still seeks revenge for not having received what we believe we deserved. This is our needy and wanting child self. We know we are regressing into our needy and wanting child self when we hear ourselves say:

> "They were our parents; therefore, they should have known better."
> "They brought us into this world, and it was their responsibility
> to keep us safe."

This is our drama. This is the voice of a child who does not yet understand the predicament we are all in. Overcoming our anger, our need to blame, and our insidious desire to take revenge requires that we overcome one of the greatest obstacles set before us on the path of our own emotional evolution:

Arrogance.

It is only our arrogance that prevents us from being able to recognize our plight flowing through the life experiences of others. Once we clearly understand the mechanics and consequences of emotional imprinting, then it is only our arrogance that stifles our ability to forgive others. The consequence of our arrogance is that we may easily be able to accept that we did not know any better. Yet our anger, unless we choose to release it, will make sure that we will not easily accept that others, especially our parents, did the best they could with the hand that they were dealt by their parents. Neutralizing our arrogance requires the following simple understanding:

> *All behaviors that we witness during our interactions with
> others that are not acts of unconditional love are cries for
> unconditional love.*

On the surface, this may not initially appear to be apparent because we adults are masters at hiding the true nature of our internal condition. As adults, we have become professionals at pretending that everything is alright. As adults, we know how to act like we want one thing when we actually want something else completely. In the adult world, everything is always fine, nice, okay, and not too bad. But the emotional condition hidden beneath the surface of the adult world is that all the people we meet who are not spontaneously joyful and creative have children within them that are afraid, angry, and heartbroken because they did not receive unconditional love. This insight is the key to our own liberation. This insight is the doorway to our own peace of mind. This insight is the foundation of all forgiveness.

Our negative judgments about the behavior of people around us are the act of interpreting a cry for love as something else. Our negative judgments are the consequence of looking at the world that is in front of us right now and seeing our past and our projected future reflected in it. As we begin approaching present moment awareness, we will begin seeing clearly that the world that is in front of us right now is always asking, in the only way it knows how, for our unconditional love. This is because we are as well. It mirrors our plight.

At this point in our journey through The Presence Process, it is beneficial to honestly ask ourselves how we have treated those in our world who have asked for our unconditional love. Let us remind ourselves that they have used the only means at their disposal: the misguided examples that were emotionally imprinted into them as children. Does our arrogance lead us to assume that they should have behaved differently, that they should have known better, even though there was no one to set a better example for them? Did *we* know better?

It is crucial that we now intend to consciously bring to mind all those people in our life whom we cannot forgive. These people are the focus of our childish revenge. They are the victims of our arrogance. These are also the people who are waiting to help us unlock our own peace of mind. Until we release them from the incarceration of our judgments, we will remain imprisoned by our confusion. Our anger towards them *is* our lack of clarity. It is the cause of our lack of peace.

Let us ask our Inner Presence for the strength, the compassion, and the emotional maturity to be able to forgive them. Let us ask our Inner Presence to reveal to us the opposite of arrogance. The people in our life experience that we have chosen to punish and to condemn by withholding our forgiveness are our saviors in disguise. Forgiveness cannot be forced, nor can it be mechanically accomplished because it is "the right thing to do"'. This is why we must humbly ask for assistance. By asking our Inner Presence for assistance in this matter, we begin to dismantle the fortress of our arrogance. Humility extinguishes arrogance.

We must remember that all parents were children once too. When we look at a parent through the eyes of present moment awareness, we will see a child who was also plunged fearfully into this conditional world. This child, like the child self that is within us, seeks only to be loved unconditionally. Can our parents be held responsible for copying the behaviors taught to them by their parents? How does holding on to our anger benefit us more than making the compassionate choice to recognize the errors in our perception? Judgment is a lack of understanding, a lack of clarity, and a virus that has infected our perception. Judgment on all levels is arrogance. It is a double standard. We are blaming others for a predicament we share with them. Therefore, let us now forgive our parents by blessing them with the unconditional love we wished we had received from them when we were children. By this one act of love, we shatter a tragic cycle that has devastated countless generations before us. By setting ourselves free in this manner, we sow peace into the experiences of all who are to come well after we have stepped beyond the borders of our present experience.

Authentic forgiveness is initiated within our behavior towards our child self. We must love this aspect of our experience unconditionally; otherwise, we will never be in a position to place the resonance of unconditional love into our outer world. This is because our outer world is and always will be our mirror. It reflects us.

Unconditional love must be given to be experienced, for it is only through the act of giving it that it is *experienced.*

Our journey into the arms of unconditional love must start with the act of giving to ourselves that which we have been seeking from others. If we do not know how to give love unconditionally to our child self *and* the adult self that we made as a reaction to our childhood experience, then we must intend to learn. We must ask our Inner Presence to show us how to accomplish this. We must intend to love ourselves, no matter what. We must intend to be compassionate with ourselves, no matter what. It is that simple and that challenging. Only by accomplishing this for ourselves, will we fully understand the following revelation:

Unconditional love is for giving.
Unconditional love is forgiving.

Until our child self has been shown by the example of the compassionate behavior of our adult self that unconditional love is only experienced through the act of giving, it will continue to believe and act as if love is something we need to go out into this world and "get". Unless we place the example of unconditional love into our own life experience, the unconscious activity of our misguided child self will continue to frustrate us. It will frustrate us because whenever we consciously seek to experience unconditional love, it will unconsciously sabotage our own good intentions with its misguided approach to what love is.

There is no reason, excuse, or justification for treating ourselves with anything less than unconditional love. We deserve to give and receive it. It is our utmost responsibility in this life to discover what unconditional love really is so that we can be in the position to place it into our experience of our outer world. This is the greatest service we can render to humanity. This is how we place a breath of fresh air into the depths of the ocean.

Our journey into uncovering the nature of this great mystery starts with having compassion towards ourselves. Compassion founded on personal understanding is the root of all forgiveness. Forgiveness is the soothing balm that heals the hurt caused by the misunderstandings that breed judgment. By forgiving ourselves for the learned errors in our own behavior, we automatically forgive the world.

Beyond the experience of forgiveness is our return to peace of mind.
Peace of mind is the eternal wellspring of spontaneous
joy and creativity.
Spontaneous joy and creativity are the resonance of
present moment awareness.

THIS IS OUR NAVIGATIONAL TOOL FOR SESSION EIGHT:

By asking these questions after our breathing sessions,
we navigate our experience towards mental clarity.
Apply this tool as instructed in Session Seven.

What is the purpose of mental clarity?

What sound do I associate with mental clarity?

What color do I associate with mental clarity?

What smell do I associate with mental clarity?

What taste do I associate with mental clarity?

What emotion do I associate with mental clarity?

What texture do I associate with mental clarity?

What physical form does mental clarity take for me?

What movement do I associate with mental clarity?

What visual symbol do I associate with mental clarity?

*Where am I experiencing effortless mental clarity
in my life right now?*

FOR THE NEXT SEVEN DAYS WE ARE REQUIRED TO:

1   Attend to our 15-minute Breathing Exercise twice each day. Aside from the water session we do to activate Session Eight, we are welcome to do added water sessions if we feel so inclined.

2   Repeat our given Presence Activating Statement for the Session whenever we are not mentally engaged.

3   Review our reading materials and apply the navigational tool for achieving increased mental clarity.

THIS ENDS SESSION EIGHT.

SESSION NINE
(OUR 3RD WATER SESSION)

Our Presence Activating Statement for the next seven days is:

I invite myself to be spontaneously joyful.

TO ACTIVATE THIS SESSION:

We memorize the given Presence Activating Statement.
We then read through all the written materials.
We submerge our body in warm water and soak for at least
20 minutes and then immediately attend to our 15-minute
breathing session.

RESTORING EMOTIONAL BALANCE

BY THIS POINT IN THE PROCESS, we have accumulated enough present moment awareness to gain insight into and begin making conscious adjustments to what we shall call "our personal negative pattern". This negative pattern results in the unpleasant circumstances that we inevitably manifest every time we want to initiate the experience of unconditional love in our life. This pattern invariably manifests as the very "conditions" in our life that make the experience of unconditional love impossible for us. This negative pattern can also be thought of as the theme that underlies all our personal physical, mental, and emotional drama.

All of us have one primary dramatic theme in our life that has been repeating since we departed our childhood. Generally, this theme remains hidden from us until we have enough present moment awareness to see it and to do something about it. This theme involves our unconscious definition of love, a definition of love that was imprinted into our emotional body through our relationship with our parents and our observation of our parents' relationship with each other. This is not our adult definition of love; it is the dysfunctional definition of love that our child self learned, one that it relentlessly imposes on our adult life seemingly against our best intentions.

Our unconscious definition of love seeps into every aspect of our adult life, but it reveals itself most clearly when it comes to our intimate relationships. Examining the outcome of all our failed intimate relationships effectively reveals our unconscious definition of love. We can specifically use the occurrences around our intimate relationships to discover what our unconscious definition of love is, because in this world our desire for love and our desire for intimacy are joined at the hip, so to speak. If our primary intimate relationships (being those we had with our parents) were dysfunctional, then this will be clearly reflected in our intimate relationships with our lovers.

For each of us, this unconscious definition of love will take on a different face, yet the mechanism of its manifestation will be identical. Our unconscious definition of love is the emotional signature we experienced as children when we asked for love. Therefore, it is the emotional signature that we unconsciously recreate in our life experience whenever we feel the need to be loved or whenever we attempt to show our love to a specific "other".

Initially, before we gain enough present moment awareness to see this pattern within ourselves, we will see it clearly in others. Whenever we attempt to have a loving relationship, it will appear as if the "other" keeps doing "this unloving thing" to us. Our personal negative pattern will reveal itself in the "conditions" the "other" lays down for us. What is also important to hold in our awareness is that our unconscious definition of love reveals itself not in the way our intimate relationships begin, but in the way they end. This pattern is always evident in *the outcome* of our attempts at experiencing love. If our relationships do not end, then this pattern is revealed in the way they sour. Initially, we will always see this outcome as the other person's fault.

Fortunately, we now have an understanding of how this works; this is the mirror-effect at play. The person who metaphorically breaks our heart is "the messenger". How we emotionally react to this experience contains the details of "the message". By now we have the tools to begin decreasing the negative emotional charge carried by this message. However, at this point in the Process, we are also ready to take another massive step towards deactivating our unconscious definition of love from consistently sabotaging our intimate relationships. We accomplish this by bringing awareness to it.

From past experiences, we can see that it is so much easier for us to see our unconscious definition of love as something that is happening *to* us, as something that appears to be propagated by someone else's behavior. This is because our fear does not allow us to look at ourselves and because our anger causes us to react to our own reflections in the world with blame and revenge. Yet underneath it all is our deep sense of loss. This is our grief.

For a child, there is no greater cause for grief than to have opened itself to the experience of unconditional love and instead to have received hurt (or rejection or even humiliation). This grief is increased when the child enters adulthood and consistently has this unpleasant experience repeat over and over again. So how do we end this unconscious hurtful cycle? It is as easy as asking a question. In this case, however, it involves a series of questions. By asking the following questions sincerely and allowing our Inner Presence to reveal the answers to us, we make a perceptual shift that begins deactivating this reoccurring negative pattern. There are five steps for initiating this perceptual shift:

Step One: How Does It Always Turn Out?

The first step is to identify what our personal unconscious definition of love is. This is very easy to accomplish. We ask ourselves how all our intimate relationships have ended or soured. There are three ways to approach this:

1   By describing what happens when our intimate relationships end or sour by starting with the word "we": "We always end up...."

2   By describing what happens when our intimate relationships end or sour by starting with the word "I": "I always end up...."

3   By describing what happens when our intimate relationships end or sour by starting with the word "They": "They always end up...."

The object of Step One is to access a word or a phrase that describes the common denominator to the way all our intimate relationships have generally ended or soured. Initially, it may appear that the circumstances of each instance are different. This is where Step Two comes in to assist us in clarifying what is really occurring.

Step Two: How Am I Feeling?

Step Two requires that we shift our attention away from the physical circumstances surrounding the way our intimate relationships have ended or soured. We must take our attention off the physical behavior of both our partners and ourselves. Up until recently, the physical circumstances of the relationship would have been the focus of our attention, and this may well be the reason why our various relationships appear to us to have different outcomes. What we must now do is to place our attention on how we were left *feeling* after each relationship ended. In other words, what was the nature of the emotional content? What was the emotional aftertaste left in our mouth? To accomplish this, we complete the following sentence:

"Whenever my intimate relationships end, I am left feeling...."

We must do our best to find a word or a phrase that is more meaningful than "sad". Do we feel abandoned, abused, betrayed, taken for granted or...? If we struggle to find this word or phrase that resonates, we can again look at how our partner treated us which caused us not to want to be with them anymore. Or how we behaved that caused our partner to leave or to stop behaving lovingly towards us. Then we must look beyond the physical behavior and into the emotional content of the outcome. We must seek the emotional signature underlying the uncomfortable experience.

The object of Step Two is to find a word or a phrase that describes the common negative emotional outcome of our failed attempts at intimate relationships. This common emotional signature is the key to uncovering the theme of the way all our intimate relationships end. This theme will be "our negative pattern", and this pattern will be our unconscious definition of love. It will also be the unconscious motivation behind the drama we manifest in many other aspects of our life experience.

For example, we may realize that when our intimate relationships end we feel abandoned. This tells us that from early childhood we have equated being abandoned with being loved. In other words, during our early childhood, we had a very powerful experience of being abandoned in a moment when we really needed to feel loved. We will know this to be true if our intimate relationships start with romance and flowers yet end with us being and/or feeling abandoned. This is, of course, if our particular pattern is abandonment. Our pattern or theme may well be abuse or betrayal or deception, and so on. We may also have numerous subdefinitions of what we unconsciously think love is, but there will always be one primary theme. We will know if we have accurately identified our unconscious definition of love by taking the next step.

Step Three: How Do I Share This With My Family?

We now observe the outcome of attempts at intimate relationships within our immediate family. First we look at our parents. Does the one word or phrase that we have chosen to describe the way we feel when our intimate relationships end or sour fit in with how we recall our parents relating to each other when we were children? Does it fit in with the way they behaved towards us? Does this one word or phrase describe the emotional outcome of any of the intimate relationships that have been manifested by our siblings?

If we can see our negative emotional pattern manifesting in some form in the life experiences of our immediate family, then we know that we are on the right track. The reason for this is that our unconscious definition of love is not something that is exclusive to us. It is something we inherited from our parents and that they inherited from theirs. If it was passed onto us, it was also passed onto our siblings. It is an unconscious belief system about the nature of love that we share with the rest of our immediate family. It will appear within our family's relationships in some form or another because families usually share the same unconscious definition of love. We may not initially see it in their physical interactions, but it will show its face in the negative emotional reactions that occur if their intimate relationships end or sour.

Step Four: What Is the Opposite of My Unconscious Definition?

Step four is simple but often challenging. It requires that we now take that one word or phrase that describes our unconscious definition of love and ask ourselves what its opposite is. This task may not be as easy at it initially appears, and the reason for this is that *we do not value the opposite to our unconscious definition of love*. Because we do not value it, accessing it mentally or emotionally may initially be challenging. We may therefore draw a mental blank to this question or select the word "love" as an opposite. However, it is unlikely that the word "love" will be the opposite of our unconscious definition of love. So if we initially mentally choose it, it is because we are seeking the easy way out!

We must also not just settle for the first answer that comes to mind. Like our approach to the navigational tool that we have been using in Sessions Seven and Eight, we must ask the question but not force the answer to come. We must sincerely ask it and then allow our Inner Presence to effortlessly reveal it to us. We will know when we have accessed the right answer because it will resonate with us on many levels. It will be an "Aha!" moment, like discovering something that was lost yet right in front of us all along. It is often an "Aha!" moment for us because the opposite to our unconscious definition of love is something we have been seeking all our life.

Once we have accessed our unconscious definition of love and then discovered its polar opposite, we are then ready to activate the procedure of restoring emotional balance to our life experience. But before we take Step Five in this emotional balancing procedure, it is necessary that we take a closer look at another aspect of our inherited behavior. We have already touched on this topic in Session Eight.

From childhood, we are taught by example that to receive something we must go out and "get" it. So the rule that is adopted by us without question is that "getting is receiving". However, if we look at this behavior from a Oneness perspective, then it does not make sense. Embracing a Oneness perspective requires our ability to metaphorically see ourselves as a single cell in the body of all that is. This visualization assists us in comprehending how we are simultaneously individual and interdependent. From a point of Oneness, the act of receiving through getting does not make sense because it always entails the process of taking away from another. One cell taking from another initiates imbalance in the body as a whole. In other words, the consequence of the consciousness of "getting" is that someone or something in the totality of our experience is invariably losing out. When we attempt to "get" anything from this world, we always initiate a reflection of lack in our experience of it. How can the act of "getting" ever restore balance to anything?

The act of "getting" always initiates a reflection of lack.

Please get up, go to the mirror, and do the following exercise: To see and understand this clearly, all we need do is stand in front of a mirror and behave as if we are taking something from the reflection that we see. We will notice immediately that as we take, so the reflection takes from us. Taking or getting is the cause of all our experiences of lack. When we feel lack in any aspect of our life, it is only because somewhere and somehow we have been attempting to get this very thing from others. If instead of attempting to get what we felt was missing in our life, we first found a way to give it to ourselves and then to our world, we would feel our sense of lack noticeably begin to decrease. Using the mirror again, we can easily see for ourselves how this works. When we hand something to the reflection in the mirror, we will see that it automatically hands the same thing to us. This demonstrates that "giving is receiving". Even though this above exercise can be visualized mentally without a mirror, it is important to actually get up and go demonstrate it to ourselves in front of a mirror so that this teaching will be grasped emotionally by our child self. It will only take a moment, a moment that could change the quality of our entire life experience.

"Giving is receiving" is the energetic frequency upon which our universe is aligned. All other approaches to energy exchange immediately cause dissonance and disharmony in our life experience. This again is purely in line with the Law of Cause and Effect. This is also the key to the door that enables us to enter the experience of unlimited abundance. However, the fruits of living at this frequency only become evident in our life experience when we align ourselves with the Oneness consciousness of present moment awareness instead of the separated or disintegrated consciousness of the ego. Present moment awareness connects us with every other cell in the body of life while our ego believes that our single cell identity is the whole body and is therefore separated from all other life forms. Our Inner Presence knows only to give while the ego's concern is only "to get". Realizing this, or at least being prepared to test it out in our life, brings us a step closer to the point where we can begin to restore emotional balance to our life experience. Let us now return to our perceptual steps.

Once we have identified our unconscious childhood definition of love, as well as uncovered its polar opposite, we are then ready to take the next step. This step can only be initiated sincerely when we do so from a point of Oneness consciousness.

Step Five: Giving Is Receiving.

This fifth step calls upon us to give the very thing that we seek to receive. There are two phases in taking this final step to begin restoring balance to the quality of our life experience:

1   **We must begin by unconditionally giving to ourselves what we seek to receive from others.** There is no way around this. If, for example, we have discovered that our unconscious definition of love is "abandonment" and that its opposite is "commitment", then we must sincerely choose to commit to ourselves, no matter what. We must commit to loving ourselves unconditionally, no matter what. Whenever physical, mental, or emotional symptoms of imbalance surface in our experience, we must commit to responding to them instead of reacting to them. We can accomplish this best by applying The Emotional Cleansing Process because by doing so we are decreasing the charge that fuels the manifestations of our symptoms of imbalance. We must commit to guiding, nurturing, healing, and teaching ourselves. We must commit to rescuing our child self from its feelings of being abandoned in some concept of the past. We must commit to saying "yes" when we mean "yes" and "no" when we mean "no". We must commit to our own emotional growth. We must commit to activating our awareness of and our relationship with our Inner Presence. We must commit to entering present moment awareness.

2   **We must then unconditionally give what we have been attempting to get from others to all the people who enter our life experience.** If for example, the opposite to our unconscious definition of love is "commitment", then we must, through our own example, show all the people in our life experience that we are committed to them. We must place commitment into all our outer experiences. The most important part of this step is that *we must do this without conditions*. Our behavior must not be determined by what we desire the outcome to be. It must be applied with a "no matter what" clause. This is not about getting; it is about *giving*. This is not about what others may think or how they may or should respond to our intentions. This is purely about doing whatever it takes to restore balance to the quality of our life experience.

Instead of wallowing in the dramas manifested by our unconscious definition of love, we must now choose to take immediate steps to stimulate the opposite of this experience within us and in our interactions with everyone around us. By initiating this course of action, we will instantly feel a shift. Why? Because the world is and always will be a mirror. This adjustment in our interaction with our world and ourselves will instantly show us:

That giving is receiving.
That we are not separated from anyone or anything around us.
That when we give unconditionally, we have an unlimited
amount of whatever the opposite is of our unconscious definition
of love to give this world.

The realization we must awaken to as soon as possible is that:

There is nothing to "get" from this world.

There is no love to "get" in the world. The world is as neutral as a mirror; all we see in it is what we place before it. If we attempt to "get" love from this world, we will always navigate our experience deeper and deeper into one of lack. When we truly integrate that there is nothing for us to get in this world and that instead we are the ones who have come to place unconditional love into our experience of this world, then we will have crossed the bridge to a new and profound life experience. Then, we will have learned the secret of experiencing unconditional love, which is that we must give love unconditionally. Why? Because in our experience we are the only ones who can. We are 100% responsible for the quality of all our experiences.

This is "the message" that our parents, our family members, and all those who brought any form of intimacy into our life experience have been attempting to get through to us since we entered this world. It was never their responsibility, and it never will be their responsibility to place unconditional love into our experience. It was their responsibility to reflect back to us the imbalances that we brought with us into this life from our previous life's experiences. These imbalances that were deliberately imprinted into our emotional body during our childhood are the very "conditions" that we have come into this life to overcome because they are the very conditions that have prevented us from experiencing unconditional love.

The moment we sincerely take these five procedural steps to restore emotional balance into the quality of our life experience will be the moment we begin to see our parents, our family, and all our loved ones of the past in a new light. The veil that our unconscious beliefs have projected upon them will begin to lift, and we will then begin to see them all "in the light" of who and what they really are. They are the ones who loved us enough to take on the painful roles of reflecting our own hidden pain back to us so that we had the opportunity to see it, feel it, and integrate it.

It was we who pushed this pain so deep that the only way we could see that it was there was if it was acted out for us as an outer drama. The moment we sincerely take the responsible action required to heal our imbalances is the moment this tragic play that has been performed in front of us all through "time" will no longer be necessary. Then, we can take our fear and our anger, our blame, and our thoughts of revenge, and even the seemingly bottomless pit of our grief, and trade them in for compassion, forgiveness, and gratitude.

All along it was us who could not see. The actors (the "messengers"), whether they are consciously aware of it or not, have always had our best interest at heart. For behind the surface of their roles has been the unconditionally loving energy of our shared Inner Presence doing everything in its power to awaken us as gently as possible to our own power without robbing us of our inherent responsibility. Our Inner Presence knows that freedom without responsibility is not freedom at all. For if we are not truly able to respond consciously to each moment, how can we possibly be free? This is all we really have "to get" to receive everything.

When we struggle to let go of our past imbalances, then the angels that come to free us will appear as demons. But the moment we surrender and take up our magnificent roles in the present moment, all these demons will once again transform into the angels they always were. They are our brothers and sisters working with us to establish a conscious balance within the whole. This conscious balance is born of responsible awareness. The moment we really "get this", our fear, anger, and grief will subside and our experiences will be washed clean with gratitude. This is one of the reasons why we have been given a life to live: so that we can learn what it means to give unconditionally of ourselves.

What we really are and therefore all we really have to give is love.

Anything else that we give is not real and lasting; it is an illusion. Yet love, when given unconditionally, is eternal. Once we integrate this lesson and begin acting on it, peace and harmony will automatically begin soaking into all aspects of our life experience.

The consequence of this will be that we will begin experiencing wonderful unexpected moments of present moment awareness. This present moment awareness will begin seeping into our life experience for no reason at all. Present moment awareness requires no reason to be. Present moment awareness "just is". Experiencing present moment awareness effortlessly is the proof that we are finally achieving real "justice" in our life, that we are finally taking responsibility for the quality of all our experiences, and that we are finally grasping the courage to embrace our freedom. Nurturing our experience of freedom through the activation of our present moment awareness is our only real responsibility. It is our birthright. To accomplish this is to accomplish everything.

THIS IS OUR NAVIGATIONAL TOOL FOR SESSION NINE:

By asking these questions after our breathing sessions,
we navigate ourexperience towards emotional balance.
Apply this tool as instructed in Session Seven.

What is the purpose of emotional balance?

What sound do I associate with emotional balance?

What color do I associate with emotional balance?

What smell do I associate with emotional balance?

What taste do I associate with emotional balance?

What emotion do I associate with emotional balance?

What texture do I associate with emotional balance?

What physical form does emotional balance take for me?

What movement do I associate with emotional balance?

When last did I experience effortless emotional balance?

What visual symbol do I associate with emotional balance?

*Where am I experiencing effortless emotional balance
in my life right now?*

FOR THE NEXT SEVEN DAYS WE ARE REQUIRED TO:

1   Attend to our 15-minute Breathing Exercise twice each day.

2   Repeat our given Presence Activating Statement for the Session whenever we
    are not mentally engaged.

3   Review our reading materials and apply the five perceptual steps that restore
    emotional balance to the quality of our life experience. We are also encour-
    aged to continue wielding our navigational tool after each breathing
    session.

THIS ENDS SESSION NINE.

SESSION TEN

(NO WATER SESSIONS ARE TO BE DONE FROM NOW
THROUGH TO OUR POINT OF COMPLETION.)

Our Presence Activating Statement for the next seven days is:

I appreciate myself.

TO ACTIVATE THIS SESSION:

We memorize the given Presence Activating Statement.
We then read through all the written materials.
We sit still and connect our breathing for at least 15 minutes.

FROM THE MOMENT THAT WE ENTER Session Ten, we still have seven full days left of The Presence Process. To reach a full sense of completion, we must continue to attend to our 15-minute Breathing Exercise twice daily for the next seven days. Only then should we activate conscious completion by connecting our breathing for at least 15 to 30 minutes. Then we can continue and read Part IV: Consequence and Part V: Completion.

LIVING ON PURPOSE:
OR, RELEASING OUR DRAMA IN EXCHANGE FOR OUR DHARMA

THE UNIVERSAL LAW OF CAUSE AND EFFECT states that "what we seek, we shall find" and "what we ask for, we shall receive". Therefore, the automatic and unfaltering consequence of this Law is that we will always see only what we are looking for, and all the experiences that we have in our life will always be exactly what we have been asking for. In other words, our life and the way we experience it *is* the ongoing answer to questions that we have been and continue to ask. The reason why this may not immediately be apparent to us is that most of our looking and asking is taking place unconsciously based on a whole range of belief systems (misinterpretations) that we adopted as children. Therefore, if we do not like what we see or the quality of what we are experiencing, it is our responsibility to go within to access and then change our unconscious causal beliefs. No one can do this for us. Having the ability to do this for ourselves is exactly what free will is. This is exactly what freedom is. This is what true responsibility is. This is what The Presence Process has given us the opportunity to accomplish.

To Live On Pupose

There is a gap between every other human being and us. This gap is the space between us. This gap appears real because of our physical body. In the gap between everyone else and us is where the world manifests. What we call "our world" is this gap.

Because our physical body leads us to believe that this gap is real, we automatically believe that we can be separated from others. We believe that our body is separate from the bodies of others and that we therefore have our own physical sensations. We believe that we have our own mind and therefore our own thoughts. We believe that we have our own heart and therefore our own emotions. We believe that we have our own spirit and therefore our own spiritual experiences. This perception leads us to believe that when we are not in the company of another human being, we are therefore on our own. Having a physical body allows us to believe that we can be alone.

Yet we all have experiences that prove this is not true. Let us call these "Oneness experiences".

We have seen others physically hurt themselves and then felt their pain within our own physical body. We have thought of someone and then bumped into him or her or received a phone call from them within minutes. We have felt something behind us and turned around to see someone watching us. We have found that as we are about to utter a thought, someone standing next to us has expressed it for us. We have been about to confide in someone as to how we feel emotionally when they have pre-empted us by telling us that they are having the same emotional experience. We have also had spiritual or philosophical insights, experiences or realizations that we thought were unique to our experience, only to hear others verbalizing that they had just recently had the same experience, insight, or realization.

We can call these "Oneness Experiences" being psychic, transference, intuition, empathy, telepathy, or the outcome of being sensitive. It does not matter what name we give them; what matters is that we adjust our beliefs about the nature of our paradigm according to the ongoing proof that is being laid before us by these "Oneness Experiences". The proof inherent in these Oneness experiences reveals to us:

That our physical bodies, though appearing separate, are not; they are connected energetically somehow to every other body.

That our mind is not the physical brain in our head; its capacities extend beyond the confines of our physical body to any distance that we care to think about.

That our emotional experiences are not confined to us alone; they are shared by the world around us.

That our ongoing and unfolding spiritual awareness is not personal or exclusive; it is universal and inclusive.

Aside from these obvious Oneness experiences, which our mind dismisses as quickly as possible, what keeps us believing that we are generally having a separate experience from others is our inability to clearly communicate what is actually happening to us. We do not realize when we explain ourselves to others that we are constantly verbalizing the same experience to each other. We do not realize this because we are focused on our personal interpretation of the experience that we are having and not on the experience itself. The moment we interpret any experience, we personalize it and in doing so turn it into an individual and therefore separate incident. When others cannot understand or relate to what we are attempting to communicate, we then automatically feel a sense of separation or alienation. This then reinforces the illusion that we are separated from others and can therefore have "our own experiences".

The obstacle that we place before us when we are attempting to communicate our physical, mental, and emotional experiences to each other is that we are too focused on what our experiences *mean* to us and not on what is really happening to us. Because of our differing belief systems about the nature of experience, a specific occurrence will mean different things to different people. In accordance with our beliefs, we will always see what we are looking for. Or we will always bend the interpretation of what we experience to confirm that what we believe is true.

Another problem that will and does occur is that if what appears before us does not fit into our personal belief system, then we will find a way to explain it away. This is the same as not seeing it at all. This is the very reason why our mind continually explains away all our Oneness experiences—because they do not fit in with our present planetary belief that our physical bodies separate us from each other.

Therefore, there is no point in entering a debate or discussion on whether we are One or not. Because, according to our personal belief systems, what Oneness means to one person will differ from what it means to another. It is more productive therefore to ignore what we think about Oneness and focus rather on what our Oneness experiences are actually revealing to us. Let our experiences be the proof.

If we think of someone and then they immediately phone, why do we continue to act as if we are separated from them? What is overriding the proof within these blatant experiences?

As we approach the experience of Oneness, which is the intimate connectedness of our Inner Presence with each other and all life, we must keep in mind that we are all still unconsciously enslaved by ancient limited belief systems that have been diligently passed down through the generations. From the moment we entered our present life experience, we automatically inherited these ancient beliefs from our parents. Let us begin, therefore, by acknowledging that by their very nature, these ancient beliefs about "how the world is" are completely out of date. Even though they are familiar and therefore comfortable to the mind, they are ineffectual. We can acknowledge that they may at one point in our evolution have served us, but now they no longer do. Now they limit us and maintain the mistaken illusion that we are separate from one another, that we can be alone, and that we must "go out and get ours" or else we will go without.

These outdated belief systems are the foundations of all our present experiences of lack. They are also the foundations of all fear, anger, and grief. With the proof that our present day Oneness experiences have placed and continue placing before us, maintaining the belief that we are separate from each other on any level is madness. It is delusional. It is denial. It is the same as believing that the earth is flat when we can clearly see the curve of the open horizon before us.

The best way to approach this massive updating of our perception so that we can accommodate the experience of Oneness is to consciously invite the experience of this Oneness paradigm to come flooding into our awareness. We can begin this process effortlessly by choosing from this moment onward to believe that we are One with all life around us. In the same breath, we can invite our daily occurrences to confirm this for us through personal experience.

Ask and you will receive.

In other words, we can activate The Law of Cause and Effect; we can consciously look for evidence that we are one body, one mind, one heart, and one spirit. By looking for it, we will see it because The Law of Cause and Effect states that we will always see what we are looking for.

Seek and you will find.

However, we must make a promise to ourselves that when these experiences are placed before us, we will not explain them away. The best way to ensure that this does not happen is to apply the procedure of *containment*; when these experiences occur in our daily life, we must not attempt to explain them to others. By attempting to explain them to others, we are just seeking acknowledgement that what is happening to us is real. Yet, no one can ever really confirm that our personal experience of Oneness is real.

In fact, the act of explaining Oneness to someone else is an acknowledgement of separation. The moment we explain Oneness, we go from being one to two! We have to "separate" to explain. A person's agreement or disagreement with us has no bearing on the validity of our experience. If we do not attempt to explain these Oneness experiences to others, they will not be explained away. Then every time we have a Oneness experience and contain it, we will digest it. The nutritional benefit of holding these experiences within will be that our faith in the Oneness paradigm will grow into a "knowing" that will permeate our consciousness and daily experience in spite of what the world may believe is so.

"Faith" does not require outside support: only "belief" does.

After agreeing to contain and digest what we experience, we can then accelerate the process of inviting this Oneness paradigm to flood our awareness. We can accomplish this by taking an active step towards having this paradigm confirmed for us; we can choose to live this way on purpose. Accomplishing this is simple. Accomplishing this is what The Presence Process has been leading us towards. This is the invitation inherent in experiencing our own Inner Presence. Oneness is the terrain of present moment awareness.

Let us now place our attention back into the gap that we perceive to exist between us, the gap in which the world exists. In this gap between us, there is stuff—and plenty of it. We have given names to all this stuff. We know what the stuff is in the gap between us because we have agreed on the names we have given to the individual components that make up this seemingly endless array of stuff. For example, if we place a pen between us, we both know what it is because we have an agreement about what we have called this particular item and what its purpose is. Because of our agreement, we can then say, "Could you pass me the pen?" or "Could you refill the pen with ink for me?", and we will understand each other without debate and discussion. We understand each other because we are not debating or discussing what the pen is or what it means. We are referring to it according to the name and purpose we have agreed upon.

This is the nature of all the stuff that is to be found in the gap between us; it has a name and it has a purpose. The names of the different items that occur in the gap are usually all agreed upon. The names may at times change because the person using the item may speak a different language, but beyond making the translation, we will generally all agree that a pen is a pen, a car is a car, a house is a house.

Where differences of opinion begin to occur, where the meaning of the stuff becomes relevant in the experience of the user, where debate and discussion and inevitable misunderstanding may occur about any particular item is in the nature of its purpose. The pen itself, like all items that occur in the gap between us, is neutral. Of itself it has no purpose and therefore has no meaning. The user always provides its meaning and purpose, and so it is at this point that the experience becomes shared or separated. For example, a pen may be used to write a love letter or to sign a declaration of war. The pen itself is not fueled with love or hate; it is wielded by it. Whether we support love or hate determines whether we share the experience of the person using the pen or not. The pen is there to facilitate the experience.

To continue this train of thought, we are now invited to suspend our ancient beliefs about separation to consider the predicament this idea of separation has placed us in. We can easily accept that there is a gap between all other human beings and ourselves. We can also accept that it is in this gap that the world as we know it exists.

What The Presence Process invites us to consider now is that this gap between us, which is the world that we have named and given a purpose, is the very thing that stands between us and our experience of what God is. What The Presence Process invites us to consider is that the distance that we perceive between any other human being (or living creature) and ourselves is the distance that lies between our experience of God and ourselves. In the same breath, we are being asked to consider that in any given moment, the importance we have placed on this gap is what prevents us from realizing that it is always The Presence of God that is looking directly back at us from the other side of the gap.

It is beneficial to reread the above paragraph again slowly with the intent of allowing our heart to feel this idea for a moment.

The Presence Process is inviting us to see that this gap between us, that this world that we have made, is a veil, a veil that is thinner than a butterfly's wing and more transparent than a breath of air. Yet because of the importance we have placed on the stuff in the gap and on its meaning and its purpose, we have forgotten how to see what is "real". We have forgotten how to see across the gap.

That which is real is that which never changes.

All the stuff in the gap keeps changing; therefore, it cannot be defined as real. If we could remember how to see what is real, what we would realize (real eyes) is that Presence (not the ego) which is looking back at us from the other side of the gap is always the same. By looking at what is unreal, we are focusing on the *expression* of Presence and not Presence itself.

To be able to look beyond the ego on the other side of the gap, we have to remember how to see beyond the trinity that makes up the structure of the ego. In other words, we have to train ourselves to place no importance on the behavior, the appearance, and the life circumstances of the form of Presence in front of us in any given moment. Why? Because these aspects of Presence in front of us are also always changing and therefore not real. They are all part of the veil of illusion that stands between us and what is unchanging. When we can look across the gap and see beyond these aspects of any life form that appears before us, we will realize that it is always the same Presence.

There is only ONE Presence.
Our Presence is ONE.

Being able to "see" this takes some practice and inner work because it requires that we first open ourselves to the idea that our own identity is something beyond the trinity of our own ego. While we believe our own behavior, appearance, and life circumstances to be our real identity, we will automatically identify others in this way. While we cannot connect with our own Inner Presence, we will struggle to connect with the Inner Presence of others.

Our predicament is that we believe in separation because we have forgotten how to recognize the Presence on the other side of the gap. We have forgotten how to recognize that we are all one body, one mind, one heart, and one spirit. We have forgotten how to recognize our own Presence reflected back at us from within all life. Because the conditional belief systems passed down through the generations have only honored the significance of the gap and the attributes of the ego, we have as a consequence lost our awareness of the continual, endless, and eternal connection between us.

Fortunately, choosing to begin dismantling this illusion is easy and only requires the wielding of our intent. We intend to adopt an agreement between us. We can agree that there are only two options before us in any given moment: we are either opening the gap between us by living according to these outdated belief systems, or we are closing it by opening ourselves to the unlimited possibilities of Oneness. We are either valuing the gap and all that is to be found in it, or we are valuing the Presence on the other side of the gap. It is this simple. It is this obvious. It is this easy.

For example, when we are paying for our groceries, we are either focusing on the stuff that we are purchasing or we are focusing on the cashier who is ringing up the items for us. We are either fretting about the prices of the products in front of us or we are greeting the cashier warmly. We are either worrying about whether we have got all the right things for the dinner we need to prepare or we are asking the cashier how his or her weekend was. We are either opening the gap by focusing on the stuff in it, or closing the gap by acknowledging the Presence on the other side of it. It is this simple. It is this obvious. It is this easy.

When we focus on the stuff of life, on the world that we have built between us, the gap widens. When we focus on the Presence on the other side of the gap, the gap closes. Every experience we have is one in which we are either opening or closing this gap. Opening the gap is a reaction to life, while closing the gap is a response to life. Every moment that we live through is one in which we either support the veil of separation or consciously part it in the name of remembering our Oneness, our shared Presence.

Opening or closing the gap is not a "doing"; it is a state of Being. There is no specific time or place or job description that makes opening the gap possible or impossible. It is a state of mind. It is a place in the heart. It is an intent. It is a choice. It is a consciously chosen level of awareness. It simply requires our Presence.

Our interaction and relationship with the stuff in the gap also determines whether we are opening or closing the gap. We can use the stuff of this world to serve either purpose because stuff has no inherent purpose of its own. We can agree that everything in the gap that we call the world is neutral, because it is. A bomb is a lump of stuff until we assign its purpose. A rose is just another life form until we give it to someone. So we can agree that all stuff is neutral because the user always supplies the meaning and purpose of all the items that are found in the gap. The user decides whether a pen will write love letters or hate mail. If we write love letters, we are closing the gap; if we write hate mail, we are opening the gap. The choice is ours, and our experience of life is always a consequence of the choices we make, of the intentions we set. This is the inevitable consequence of The Law of Cause and Effect.

When many of us enter The Presence Process, we want to know what our life purpose is. We believe it must be something that we must *do*. We believe that if we can just figure out what it is we are meant to be doing—what our special calling or gift is—we will then find balance, harmony, and fulfillment. We believe that finding our purpose will bring us peace. This idea that we entertain, that our purpose in being alive will be found in the specifics of something we are meant to be doing, is a misunderstanding that was initiated during our childhood. It is a misunderstanding that was passed on to us as part of the ancient belief systems that have been imprinted on us from the generations that came before. The root cause of this misconception is very simple:

Because we were not unconditionally loved for who we are, we
began attempting to figure out what we had "to do" to be
deserving of this unconditional love.

Because we were not unconditionally loved as children, we became uncomfortable within ourselves. This set off a chain of events in which we began to seek that which would restore our inner peace. Because we were not accepted for who we are, we turned away from our authentic Presence and went in search of who we were supposed to be. Our parents asked us, "What do you want to be when you grow up?" We believed that if we could live a life that would supply the correct answer to this question, we would then receive the unconditional love that we did not receive as children. This search set in motion the endless "doings" that became our adult life. We tried to prove that we were worthy of being alive by succeeding or by not succeeding. Even though we were already alive, we went in search of our purpose so that we could "earn a living". The truth behind it all is that what we have really been trying to accomplish is attempting to "earn a loving".

The consequence has been imbalance, confusion, separation, lack, and all that stems from the trinity of fear, anger, and grief. The consequence has been a poisonous quest to find meaning and purpose in all that we "do". Because we have seen no importance in our Being, our Inner Presence, we have sought to realize this importance in all our outer "doings". More than that, we have sought to place great importance on all "the stuff" that we do things with. By believing that all our doings and all the stuff we have enlisted to serve our doings could be the source of our liberation, we have inadvertently used them to build a brick wall between us and what is real. We have used it all to manufacture an illusionary gap between our sense of wholeness and ourselves. This gap is the source of all our fear, anger, and grief. This gap is not our purpose, and our purpose can never be found in it. This gap is something we did. This gap is something we made because we could not, were not, and have not been shown how to recognize and appreciate the value of our own Inner Presence.

If The Presence Process has set out to accomplish anything, it has been this: to facilitate us in rescuing ourselves from our endless unconscious array of doings and to instead invite us to return to our authentic state of Being. From the beginning, this Process has asked us to stop. To stop and breathe. To stop and watch. To stop and respond. To stop and feel. To stop and pay attention. To stop reacting.

> *JUST STOP FOR A MOMENT AND BREATHE.*
> *WE ARE ALREADY ALL WE CAN "BE".*
> *WE ARE PERFECT AS WE ARE.*
> *THERE IS NOTHING TO "DO"*
> *BUT TO BE PRESENT*
> *IN THIS MOMENT,*
> *HERE AND*
> *NOW.*

The Presence Process has invited us to stop so that we can have the opportunity to discover that our purpose is not a "doing"; it is a state of Being. We are human beings, not human doings. Until we realize this, which we can only accomplish by bringing our life to a point of stillness, we will forever be lost in a world of unconscious reaction. Until we learn how to stop and take a breath, we will forever be adrift in a world in which we mistakenly believe that if we uncover what we are supposed to *do* that everything will be all right.

Now, as we approach completion of this particular journey, The Presence Process places one more task before us, a task that we are being invited to take beyond this Ten Session journey into the entirety of the life that unfolds before us. Again, this is not a task that involves "a doing", but one that is in line with the entire journey that we have been through. It is a task of Being. We are asked to make a simple choice, to set a firm intent:

> *We are being asked to appreciate ourselves for who and what we are—right now, without judgment or concern, without conditions or expectations. We are being asked to appreciate ourselves because, in our experience, we are the only one who really can.*

What does the word "appreciate" really mean to us? On the surface, it means to admire, to value, to be grateful for, and so on. But there is another application for this word. If we have stocks and shares and they start increasing in value, we say that they are "appreciating". In other words, when something is appreciating, it is increasing in value. To therefore appreciate something is to make it more valuable, to make it more. One of our creative abilities that we do not make full conscious use of is that *whatever we give our attention to increases.* Whatever we have most of in our life experience is what we are giving most attention to. If we meditate on this for a moment, we will know it to be true. Our life experience in any given moment is the evidence of this truth. Within this truth also awaits the liberation from any experience we presently find uncomfortable.

In The Presence Process, the word "appreciation" therefore means "*to lovingly make more of something by seeing and acknowledging the value of it.*" This sheds a new light on the Presence Activating Statement we were given for this final session. We are being asked to appreciate and value our own Inner Presence so that we can lovingly increase our awareness of it, so that we can call our own Inner Presence forth to fill our whole life experience with all its natural and therefore effortless attributes:

PEACE,
INNOCENCE,
CREATIVITY,
SPONTANEOUS JOY,
UNCONDITIONAL LOVE,
ONENESS WITH ALL LIFE,
KNOWING NO ORDER OF DIFFICULTY.

At first we may find it hard to truly appreciate ourselves. We may at times find it hard to see the value of our own precious Presence. Our Session Ten Presence Activating Statement is to remind us and encourage us. By setting the intent to appreciate ourselves, we will be well on our way. It is something that no other human can do for us. Until we can do this for ourselves, we will not have the capacity to see beyond the illusion of the gap and therefore to recognize and appreciate the familiar Presence that is always looking back at us from and through all life.

When we choose to appreciate our Inner Presence unconditionally, in order that we may remember how to appreciate the Presence on the other side of the gap, then we have chosen to live on purpose. By intending this, we are committing to closing the gap with every breath that is given to us. We are committing to using every item in this world for the purpose of closing the gap. The consequence, according to the Law of Cause and Effect, is that we will automatically and effortlessly begin to have a most extraordinary experience:

We will realize that we are not and never were alone: we only "thought" we were.

We will realize that we are indeed a cell within the body of everything: therefore, we are intimately connected to all life.

We will realize the power of our thoughts: that if we believe in separation and act on these beliefs, our experience will adjust itself to confirm that what we believe is true. Yet if we choose instead to believe in the intimate Oneness of all life, then so be it.

We will realize that living as if we believe in Oneness leads to a life of greater possibilities: such an experience is far more extraordinary than a life built on a belief in separation.

By choosing to close the gap with the tool of appreciation, we will discover something that will propel our life experience into unending awe. We will discover that the natural propensity of the universe is to close the gap. We will discover that the moment we sincerely commit to using all our experiences and "the stuff" of this world for the purpose of closing the gap, the entire resources of the universe will rally behind and support our every move. We will then realize that all our discomfort, all our imbalance, all our confusion, all our experiences of lack and loneliness, all our fear, anger, and grief, stem from the fact that we have thought, spoken, and acted as if we are separated from everyone else. The universe could never support such thoughts, words, and deeds because the universe cannot support what is not real or true. We have had to support this illusion with our own blood, sweat, and tears. Living as if we believe in separation is like attempting to push a river back to its source.

If we have accomplished anything under the misconception that we are separated, we have done so with great effort. What's more, whatever we have accomplished in this manner will not be real and therefore lasting. However, when we sincerely commit to being One with all life—no matter what—we will discover a whole new way of Being—we will discover ease, clarity, spontaneous joy, comfort, safety, and unlimited unconditional love. We will discover peace and harmony. We will discover what is real and what has been present before our eyes all along. We will discover the power of our Inner Presence, a Presence that we all share, that is everywhere, in every moment, able to accomplish anything.

It is a simple task that lies before us. We are being invited to metaphorically take our attention off the groceries of this world and instead to choose to look into the eyes of the cashiers on the other side of the gap with an inner intent to acknowledge and so contact their Inner Presence.

"Hello," we may say. "How are you today?"

It is that simple. It is that obvious. It is that easy. Then when our encounter is complete, we may say, with appreciation:

"Thank you for taking care of me today."

It is this simple. It is this obvious. It is this easy.

In this moment of acknowledgement, recognition, remembrance, and most of all, *appreciation*, we will be inviting their Inner Presence to consciously look back at us. Before our eyes, we will witness them become more present. This, in turn, will cause us to feel more present. When we intend to look beyond the trinity of the ego, beyond the behavior, the appearance, and the life circumstances of those across the gap, we invite into our life an experience of that which is real and therefore lasting.

By setting our intention to appreciate the Inner Presence of another, we simultaneously make a choice to give ourselves an opportunity to look directly into the eyes of God. We simultaneously give God the opportunity to look back and give us a wink. We give ourselves an opportunity to remember that we are all connected cells in One body that has One mind, that feels from One heart and that dances with One spirit.

As we practice "calling out the Presence" without explaining to anyone what we are up to, we will witness the miracle of life. We will recognize present moment awareness awaken in seemingly total strangers and in an unlimited array of unexpected ways. In the moments when we least suspect it, we will witness the power of Presence return our appreciation with playful and loving gestures.

As we allow ourselves to have more and more of these Oneness experiences, we will know without any shadow of doubt that we can never be alone—that we never were and never could be. We will also treasure the company of all life. And when, through personal experience, we truly accept that we are all One, then in this moment, the veil will lift and we will see that everything is on purpose—that it always has been and that it always will be.

LOVE IS OUR PURPOSE.

As these experiences of Oneness begin to wash into and flood the awareness of our life, we must remind ourselves to hold the joy of these moments within and to contain and digest them rather than to attempt and explain them away to some "body". Oneness is not something we need explain to God. It is an experience only "we" can appreciate.

GRATITUDE

IT IS RECOMMENDED that we take time after each breathing session (morning and evening) to mentally bring into our awareness five aspects about our life as it is right now that we feel grateful about. What do we *appreciate* about our life experience?

In other words, we are encouraged to think of and mentally take note of ten different aspects a day. We must ensure that each time we attend to this task our daily mental list contains new items. We must also make sure that none of the items on our mental list are founded on comparison. In other words, we should not place items on our mental appreciation list that we are grateful for *because* others do not have these things or experiences. Gratitude by comparison separates.

The items we place on our list may include any physical, mental, emotional, or spiritual aspect of our life experience. Remember that whatever we appreciate increases. This is the power of the focus of our Presence. This is the gift of gratitude. Gratitude is appreciation.

It is no coincidence that the word gratitude suggests the words
"great attitude".

FOR THE NEXT SEVEN DAYS WE ARE REQUIRED TO:

1   Attend to our 15-minute Breathing Exercise twice each day.

2   Repeat our given Presence Activating Statement for the Session whenever we are not mentally engaged.

3   Review our reading materials and apply the Perceptual Tool that empowers us to begin closing the gap. Let us wield the sword of appreciation to call out the Presence in every life form we encounter. After seven days, we must activate completion by consciously connecting our breathing for 15 to 30 minutes. Only then do we continue and read the parts Consequence and Completion.

CONGRATULATIONS!

THIS ENDS SESSION TEN AND OUR EXPERIENTIAL
JOURNEY THROUGH THE PRESENCE PROCESS.

PART IV

CONSEQUENCES

Where there is a gardener, there is a garden.

THE LIFE OF A GARDENER is possibly the most appropriate metaphor with which to communicate the nature of the Presence that we have named God. When we metaphorically roll up our sleeves and bury our hands in the earth with a clear intent to fully participate in all that is life, we automatically bring present moment awareness to the quality of all our experiences upon this planet. We automatically become causal and to become causal is to become God-like. We are then the conscious gardeners of life. This elevates us to a level of service that empowers us, through our own example, to open the gates that lead into the cooling shade of present moment awareness for everyone we encounter.

"By their fruits they shall be known." (Matthew 7:16)

This next part of this book brings to our awareness some of the wonderful consequences of choosing to be responsible with the garden of our unfolding life experience. It reveals to us the fruits and flowers of our intent to bring the radiance of Presence into all our experiences. These fruits and flowers are the blessings that we have opened the door to by consciously choosing to show up here and now.

Yes, there are many other intriguing places and experiences in the universe, within and without. But right now we are here because this is where we are supposed to be. Only by truly being here, now, can we gain the wisdom and momentum required to jettison our spirit consciously beyond the limitations of our present human condition. We cannot evolve through denial and distraction. We cannot evolve by wishing we were somewhere else. We can only evolve through responsibly facing and embracing the circumstances and opportunities before us—here and now.

The Presence Process began by inviting us to take a consciously connected breath and then to take another and then another until our journey of awakening into present moment awareness was fully activated. It extended this simple invitation to us because it is only by nurturing the life that we are experiencing right here and now that the ladder to anything else is constructed. Whether we completed this Process experientially or whether we simply absorbed the text, we have set in motion an energetic intention that will forever change the course of our life experience. Every aspect of The Presence Process is causal, and so the effects are already spoken for.

Let us now bring greater awareness to just some of the consequences of consciously having initiated this journey into present moment awareness.

Fruits and Flowers

FRUITS AND FLOWERS TAKES A LOOK at some of the wonderful possibilities that we awaken to as a consequence of choosing to embrace present moment awareness. We may already recognize some of these shifts in our life experience. As we do, let us consciously acknowledge and "appreciate" them by saying a silent "thank you" to our Inner Presence.

1   **We automatically respond in situations where we used to react.** This is purely a consequence of functioning more consciously. When we truly integrate that we are responsible for the quality of all our experiences, then we are less likely to react to our life circumstances, no matter how they may unfold. On a very deep level, we know that our life experience is always the sum of our past thoughts, words, and deeds and that reacting to anything that happens to us with blame is a blatant denial of this truth. We will also discover that as a consequence of having neu-

tralized a substantial amount of the negative charge in our emotional body, we are less likely to move through our life carrying a charge. We are therefore less likely to "blow our top" or explode over nothing. We are less likely to manifest experiences tinged with fear, anger, and grief. Reactive behavior is unconscious behavior. The more conscious we become, the less likely we are to entertain this state of denial.

2   **We have more energy.** Before we had an opportunity to begin decreasing our negative emotional charge, we invested a large amount of energy in sedating and controlling the discomfort emanating from our emotional body. Also, before we realize that the world functions as a mirror that serves us by reflecting what we cannot see about our inner condition, we tend to use a large amount of energy dueling with our reflections. To add to this, investing in fear, anger, and grief on any level is exhausting. Holding grudges and unconsciously plotting revenge for what happened to us in the past is draining. Attempting to control the future so that the past will not reoccur tires us out. The moment we let go of all our investments in these sorts of reactive behaviors, we immediately have increased energy and vitality.

3   **We accomplish those tasks we've been meaning to get to for years.** Aside from having increased energy, this occurs because anything worth doing can only be done Now. In a time-based paradigm, we always have lots of plans about what we will do when the time is right. However, the time is never right when we spend it reflecting on the past and longing for the future. As we accumulate present moment awareness, we discover that *the right time is right now*. Without giving it much thought, we become occupied with the activity of the present moment rather than reminiscing about the past or daydreaming about the future. Consequently, we accomplish tasks that we had planned and planned and planned but had never initiated.

4   **We finish tasks quickly, effortlessly, and feel as if we have more time to do them in.** Before we learn how to integrate our negative unconscious activity, it is ongoing in our life experience 24 hours a day. Under such circumstances, when we are at work, we may think that our full attention is

on the task at hand, but it seldom is. Much of our attention is involved in the unconscious conflicts taking place within us. Once we begin integrating this unproductive unconscious activity, our focus on our present moment activities increases dramatically. The consequence is that tasks that used to be hard and draining become effortless and come to completion in much shorter time periods. Consequently, we have the sense that we have more time and that everything we are doing is happening faster. Also, because we have less unconscious activity distracting us from our present moment activities, we discover that we begin enjoying and feel energized by the tasks that previously used to drain us. Our increasing present moment awareness automatically transforms the mundane chores we resisted into meaningful and joyful activities.

5   **We no longer hurry through our day or our tasks.** Aside from the explanation given above, one of the consequences of accumulating present moment awareness is that we realize that there really is a time and place for everything in the unfolding adventure of life. We realize that it is pointless to force into motion that which will not move or to attempt to stop that which is inclined to motion. We do the best we can, therefore, in any given moment, but if we do not finish, we are at peace with that. We do our best, but we do not hurry madly. We realize that to hurry is to unconsciously manifest experiences of lateness in our life. As we start to tap into our eternal consciousness, we realize that there is no end to life and therefore no point in hurrying to finish it. We trade destination-consciousness for journey-consciousness. Not hurrying through life has the automatic consequence of increasing the quality of our attention, and this inevitably increases the quantity of our accomplishments.

6   **Our working conditions become more enjoyable.** This is related to the previous explanation. Often, before entering The Presence Process, the idea of leaving our place of work and finding another job is rustling around in the back of our mind. A consequence of "living in time" is that we do not enjoy our means of earning our income or our place of work. However, as we complete this Process and continue onward with our

life journey, we discover that our place of work becomes more enjoyable. We discover that our work colleagues are more enjoyable to be around, that our work appears to become more interesting and effortless, and that the idea of leaving dissipates. We realize that we are where we are supposed to be and that we will be there until our point of completion in that particular environment. We know that if and when we leave, the doors of change will open up effortlessly and automatically. We realize that being in that particular space in this particular moment of our life is part of the fulfillment of our life's purpose. We enjoy our working environment more, not because it has changed at all but because by resolving our inner conflicts, we have changed our experience of it.

7 **We are less resistant to the currents of life.** This is also a natural occurrence of the "knowing" that everything in our life has a time and a place. Accumulating present moment awareness enables us to understand that everything that occurred in our past, especially the challenging experiences, were all raw materials for our emotional growth and the evolution of our humanity. We realize that happiness comes and goes and is a transient state, and that during these "happy moments", we enjoy ourselves but that we do not really grow emotionally. They are more like rest periods in our emotional evolution. This is why we opt for authentic joy. Authentic joy is not an emotional state; it is a state of Being in which we accept all that life has to offer, especially the challenging moments. Authentic joy knows that as happiness is a time for laughter and rest and play, our moments of seeming unhappiness are a time for growth and introspection and gaining strength for our endless journey. In this light, what we think of as happiness and unhappiness begin to blur into one. We are joyful in both states because we accept both as essential ingredients for accomplishing a life of balance and harmony. Embracing both brings our experience to wholeness, and this is how we tap into our Holiness. Therefore, we are less resistant to life's currents. We eventually learn how to surrender completely and go with the flow. We allow life to carry us in its ever-changing arms, knowing that no matter how it may appear in any given moment, all of our experiences are unfolding for our highest and most beautiful intent.

8 **We experience spontaneous creativity.** What we think of as God is not "a healer". What God created cannot be broken because it is always perfect, and what is created perfect by definition cannot experience imperfection. However, what our egoic self made of it becomes imperfect because of our interpretations. Our interpretations of what is are often deluded because they are based on what we think happened in the past and what we think may happen in the future, as opposed to what is happening right now. This is why we become so involved in the idea that we must heal ourselves. However, when we realize that all we need heal is our experiences (our interpretations) and then accomplish this—there is no more need for the idea that healing ourselves is required. Then our energy can begin to enter authenticity. Healing is not an authentic use of our energy. Healing is transitional; it is a temporary realignment process. If we remain in the healing phase of our life experience, then we are just like a dog chasing its tail (without having as much fun). What we think of as God is not a healer; God is a creator. So the moment we accomplish the task of healing our experience, we automatically begin to enter an experience of wholeness, of Holiness. Subsequently, our experience aligns with God's Will. The result is that we become creatively inspired. To be God-like is to be creative. To be continually concerned with the idea of healing is to limit ourselves to being a broken human "doing" instead of evolving into a creative human being. When we choose healing as "a profession", we are in danger of unconsciously choosing to remain broken as a way of life.

9 **We feel more comfortable amidst out immediate family.** Until we resolve our suppressed emotions and go through the procedure of decreasing our negative emotional charge, our immediate family is the clearest mirror of the inner work that awaits us. Until we realize how this mirroring works, and until we consciously choose to look into these reflections as a means to grow up emotionally, we can find it quite challenging to be in the company of our immediate family. This is because they will constantly be showing us aspects about ourselves that we do not really want to see. This will translate into them seemingly annoying us and pushing our buttons. However, the moment we begin to do the inner work required to grow emotionally, we will

no longer see our issues being reflected back by our various family members. Instead, we will experience signs of our progress through a sense of increased comfort and joy from their presence. We will feel more at peace around them. Consciously attending to our emotional growth is what enables us to feel at home around our family.

10 **Circumstances and people that once annoyed us no longer take up our attention.** The same explanation applies as is in the previous point; when we consciously choose to respond to what the reflection in the mirror is showing us, instead of reacting to it, things that annoyed and irritated us about our world seem to miraculously disappear. In actuality, they do not disappear. If we look carefully, we will see that they are still there, unchanged. It is us who have changed our inner condition and, as a consequence, our interpretations of our outer experiences have adjusted. The Presence Process stops us cleaning the mirror in an attempt to heal the blemishes in our life experiences.

11 **Our intimate relationships improve.** This again is a consequence of accepting responsibility for our emotional growth. Just like our family, our intimate companions are powerful mirrors in our life. Before we consciously attend to our emotional growth, we are always attracted to someone because they reflect our unresolved issues. Initially, this reflection pleases us because we feel that now we have a chance to be happy. The idea that *this* person can make us happy is an unconscious knowing that if we deal with the issue that this particular person is reflecting back to us that the quality of our life experience will improve. Unconsciously, what we are really seeking is to bring to completion our unresolved childhood issues that originated with mom and dad. However, we must keep in mind that this is all unfolding unconsciously.

Consciously, we believe that we are in love and that we have finally found the person we are looking for. They are the person of our dreams. Yes, they are the person that we are looking for, but not because they are coming into our life to make us happy; it is because they are coming into our life because we have a sacred agreement with them that they will reflect to us exactly what it is that we have to work on to regain our Presence. When it becomes apparent that our romantic notions are just that, romantic notions, as opposed to realistic notions, we then become embittered.

Because we do not embrace the opportunity to consciously work with what they are reflecting back to us, the attributes that initially attracted us to them begin to annoy and irritate us. We then dress in armor and take on defensive and attacking postures. However, the moment we agree to consciously resolve our emotional baggage, this entire scenario transforms. We then start to discover that whatever it was that initially attracted us to our companion was the superficial stuff; it was our sense of incompletion with our parents that we were seeking to resolve.

Once we accomplish emotional resolution within ourselves, our partner then transforms before our eyes. Remarkably, we discover someone standing in front of us who we appear to be meeting for the very first time. We begin to see them for who and what they really are as opposed to who and what of our past they had reflected back at us. This change in our experience can go in one of two directions: our love blossoms into an authentic intimacy, or we come to terms with the insight that we are not meant to be intimate with each other at all. Either way, our relationship improves and becomes closer because it becomes more authentic.

12 **We stop interfering in other people's lives.** When we understand that our own life is flowing exactly as it is supposed to, and that if it does not feel comfortable, it is because of the nature of our past thoughts, words, and deeds, then we are unlikely to give other people unwarranted advice. We understand that like us, they too are flowing according to the unfaltering Law of Cause and Effect. They too are doing the best they can with what they know and understand. They too will awaken to their inherent responsibility when they are ready, and not a moment before. To interfere in someone else's life by giving them unsolicited advice on how they should be moving through their experiences is unconsciously acting on the belief that their appearance, behavior, or unfolding circumstances can affect us negatively. Other-

wise, why would we bother? To interfere is to enter fear. To interfere in anyone's life is to blatantly deny that we are all 100% responsible for the quality of our own experiences. Embracing present moment awareness empowers us to see that everyone is where they are on their path because of the past thoughts, words, and deeds they initiated. And so are we. Therefore, we need to have no fear that another's behavior can have any real affect on the quality of our experience. If they do have an affect on the quality of our life experience, it is only because they are reflecting our unresolved issues. We already know by now that we cannot come to any authentic resolution by including "the messenger" in our drama. We can only achieve resolution by listening to, watching, and gaining insight from the reflection they cast. Thus, as we accumulate present moment awareness, the Law of Non-interference is automatically awoken within us. When we resolve our own fears, we cease to enter fear because of others.

13 **Our sleep is more restful.** Until we agree to consciously process our emotional baggage, we will attempt to process it unconsciously. This has two consequences. Firstly, throughout our day, our conscious awareness will resort to as many sedation and control tactics as possible in order not to deal with our "stuff". Secondly, at night when our conscious mind dissolves into sleep and our unconscious mind gains the upper hand, it begins doing its best to sort through and process our unintegrated experiences. This unconscious activity requires energy, and so it robs us of restful sleep. The moment we choose to consciously take responsibility for the quality of our life experience, we will discover that our sleep pattern will go through a transitional period. Initially we may want to sleep a lot more. Then, we may discover that we are not able to sleep at all when we really want to. Finally, our sleep pattern will settle down, and we will begin to enjoy a more restful sleep experience. Then we will only remember dreams that are relevant to our conscious life. This overall adjustment to our sleep pattern occurs mainly because we are now attending to our inner work while we are awake instead of having to attend to it unconsciously during our period of rest.

14 Nagging symptoms that we may have experienced for years are resolved. This is a natural effect of cleaning up the debris in our emotional body. Often we come to an experience like The Presence Process because of the major issues in our life experience. Yet if we have major issues, then we predictably also have many minor issues that we live with and accept as part of our life experience. It is wonderful to witness how these little nagging symptoms automatically begin dissolving. They automatically dissipate when we take care of the larger issues.

15 Long-term habits cease. The above explanation also applies here. We may discover that without realizing it, a life-long habit of biting our nails or scratching or picking at our body stops. It may stop so suddenly that it may be weeks before we realize that it has gone. These types of habits, these nervous itches, are all caused by anxiety, and all anxiety is a desire to exit the present moment. The moment we become comfortable within the present moment and thus within our physical body, these nagging behaviors automatically dissipate.

16 We gradually begin losing weight without dieting. No matter what physical symptomatic disorder a doctor tells us that our overweight condition stems from, being overweight is an indication that we are carrying excess emotional baggage. That is why diets do not and never will work. Dieting without resolving the underlying emotional baggage is like placing band-aids on a shark bite. We may find many ways to temporarily smother our restless internal condition by forcibly sedating or controlling the outer manifestations of our inner misery; however, until we make a change at the causal point of our condition, we will never really be able to eat in peace. Sooner or later we will drop our guard and the weight that we forcibly adjusted through dieting will return. The moment we resolve to integrate our emotional baggage and take the required steps to do so, our weight automatically adjusts. Being overweight is an "effect", not a "cause". Within every big person is a big emotional issue begging for attention and resolution.

17 We enjoy being around children. This is a natural consequence of resolving our own childhood issues. There is a saying, "It is never too late for a joyous childhood." The child within us never dies; the insecure adult that we become simply smothers it. When we remove the insecurities of our adulthood, our inner child self automatically wants to come out and play. Often other adults around us cannot satisfy this impulse because they are too busy pretending to be grown up. Consequently, we find ourselves naturally gravitating to the children in our presence, and they naturally find themselves enjoying our company too. We are all children of God. Heaven is a state of Being that excludes the pretences cultivated by adulthood.

18 **We laugh more and are more playful.** Again, it is never too late to have a joyful childhood! In the present moment, we come to the realization that an adult is a human concoction while a child is a creation of God. Adults are very, very serious (and boring) and are too busy to play. Because adults kill God, they then have to run the whole world, and we know what an important and exhausting job that is! On the other hand, children are light and full of laughter. In the present moment, we discover that there are no adults in this world: there are children that are alive, present, and playful; and children that are dead, serious, and working very hard to keep up their very important adult pretences. Once we let go of our past grievances and our future fears, what is there to bring us down? We are alive and within life anything is possible. It is a misconception that spiritually aware beings are serious, pious, and in deep contemplation of the heaviness of Godliness. The more awake we become, the more we laugh. When we learn to laugh at ourselves and at our seemingly endless dramas, we then have access to seemingly endless laughter. We must never forget, whether we have the courage and insight to admit it to ourselves or not, that in the end, laughter is the medicine that we are all after. True and pure laughter dissolves all ignorance, all discomfort, all sorrow, and all sense of separation. Laugher is truly God's orgasm.

19 **Our diet changes automatically and effortlessly.** This is a natural consequence of being more present in our physical body. When we "live in time", we eat but we do not feel the effect of the food that we eat because we do not spend long enough in the body to consciously

digest this aspect of our life experience. However, as we accumulate present moment awareness, especially on a physical level, we start to become increasingly aware of what different types of food feel like within our body. We first perceive this physically; then we start to integrate the mental and emotional impact our diet is having on our life experience. Foods that do not sit well with us automatically become less appealing. Foods that are alive and vital become attractive. We do not have to force this transformation in our diet; we need only activate present moment awareness. The way we eat is an "effect" not a "cause" of anything. Often we eat as a means to sedate and control our emotional discomfort. We use food to stuff down surfacing emotions or as a distraction from the present circumstances of our uncomfortable life experience. Once we resolve our emotional discomfort, eating as a form of self-medication ceases. Then we start to eat not for achieving false pleasure and fake happiness, but for the purpose of nutrition, health, and well-being. Many think that eating driven by nutritional concerns as opposed to pleasure-seeking leads to a boring diet. Yet the foods that are alive and therefore nutritional always taste and look better. They also feel better in our physical body, and give rise to lighter mental states and calmer emotional activity. However, we have to accumulate present moment awareness to realize this.

20 **We take an active interest in our health.** This is for the same reasons as above. Only when we really become present in our physical body do we feel the condition of our body and the boomerang effect that our physical state has on our mental and emotional well-being. The body is in itself purely an effect of our emotional and therefore mental states until we become present within it. The moment we become present within it, we can begin wielding it as a causal instrument. We can accomplish this through exercise, yoga, and meditation. When we activate physical presence, it will dawn on us just how privileged we are to have a human body. It is a remarkable organic mechanism that has more functions than could ever be counted. However, its most superior function is to serve as a point of focus for the grounding of our full consciousness into our present life experience. This we accomplish

by accumulating present moment awareness. It is very challenging to be present in an uncomfortable body. Learning to nurture our own physical well-being is an intimate part of the road towards accepting 100% responsibility for the quality of our life experience. Without a body, we cannot dance. Without dancing, we are not alive. Without a body, we cannot be present, here and now. It *is* our temple, for within it is the altar upon which we lay our prayers of gratitude to the Source of all that is. Naturally, as we accumulate present moment awareness, we begin to tend gently, lovingly, and responsibly to this attribute of our life experience.

21 **People are attracted to us and enjoy out company.** This is mainly because we are becoming more authentic—more real. Whether we realize it or not, we are all looking for something real. Unfortunately, we look for it in very unreal ways, and that is why we do not find it. Also, many of us seek authenticity because it is in our nature to do so, but at the same time, we are not yet quite ready or prepared to do what it takes to achieve such an experience. Whenever many people are attracted to one particular individual, we may think it is because of his or her appearance, behavior, or life circumstances. However, it is seldom because of these outer attributes. It is because of their Presence. The suppressed present moment awareness in everyone is seeking to awaken and be liberated, so it is automatically attracted to anyone who is awakened to his or hers. Like attracts like. Presence, even when it is suppressed, is attracted to Presence. Therefore, the more present we become in our life experiences, the more attractive we appear to people. We appear to have what they seek even if they do not consciously realize they are seeking it. We often hear people describe this experience of magnetism when they meet someone who is "larger than life". They say that that person has such a powerful presence.

22 **We enjoy solitude.** This is a natural consequence of activating present moment awareness. When we find being present challenging, we often use the company of others to distract ourselves from the issues that are bubbling beneath the surface of our emotional armor. The

moment we resolve these issues, we no longer seek out the company of others for the purpose of self-distraction. We start enjoying the peace and quiet of our own company. We trade in loneliness for aloneness. To enjoy our solitude is a clear sign of emotional maturity.

23 **We appear to know or sense events before they occur.** This occurs because Presence functions from beyond what we think of as "time". It really does know everything that has ever happened and everything that is about to unfold in each given moment. It really is intimately connected with the flow of all life. By listening to our Inner Voice, it appears as if we are hearing what is happening in the future; in actuality, we are hearing the consequences of what is happening right now. What is happening right now has consequences. We cannot appreciate this when we "live in time". The more present we become, the more we intuitively tune into the consequences of life as it unfolds. To us, it appears as if we know things before they happen. In one respect, this appears true. But a consequence is something that has happened already, even if it has not yet manifested in our field of present moment awareness. Every cause necessitates an effect. When we live in the causal point of life, the present moment, the inevitable effects, even if they are not yet physically, mentally, or emotionally manifest, are already apparent to us. This is because a cause and its effect are not two separate occurrences; they happen simultaneously. In time, they appear to happen with delay. This is the trick of time. Everything is actually happening simultaneously. Our mind cannot hold this simultaneous experience when we are invested in time-consciousness. However, this paradigm begins to leak into our awareness the more present moment awareness we accumulate.

24 **We experience synchronicity in the events of our lives.** This occurs for the same reasons as explained in the previous point. Synchronicity is an experience that occurs when we enter present moment awareness and are able to perceive the energetic connection between cause and effect. *Déjà vu* is also a consequence of present moment awareness. This occurs when our awareness touches upon the effect before it becomes conscious of the causal point. When it does eventually become con-

scious of the causal point, we feel as if what is happening in that moment appears to have happened already, or before. Again this is a consequence of entering the consciousness of simultaneity.

25 We experience greater abundance financially. Money is an outer reflection of an inner energetic flow. When our emotional body experiences severe blockages, this is manifest outwardly as a lack of money-flow in our life. However, it is incorrect to assume that as we become increasingly present through activating emotional growth in our life experience that we suddenly accumulate large amounts of money. More than not, the *accumulation* of large amounts of money is a sign of fear and insecurity towards life, especially if this "wealth" is accumulated through blood, sweat, tears, and the control and manipulation of others and our outer world circumstances. As we enter present moment awareness, money becomes like bread; we manifest exactly what is required to sustain us in any given moment. We do not hoard it but instead allow it to flow freely, but responsibly, *through* us. If out of fear of hunger we were to buy enough bread to last years, it would all become moldy and useless to us before we had even eaten our way through two loaves. Money in the present moment is a flow of energy that arrives in our experience in the quantity that we require in the moment we require it, or a few moments before we require it. We have no fear about the flow of money when we are present because we know that we are the ones regulating its flow. The more present we become, the less likely it becomes that we are going to cause ourselves discomfort, and so the less likely it is we are going to manifest experiences of lack. In each moment we manifest enough, and because we live in the moment, we always have enough. We know that it is only by having enough *right now* that we can have enough in all our future Nows. Financial abundance in the present moment does not mean having a lot; it means having exactly what we require when we require it. We may think of this as living in tune with God's Economy. God's Economy does not require large vaults built out of fear to store immense wealth just in case tomorrow does something unexpected. God's Economy is founded on faith, and this faith is initiated in having confidence in our ability to be responsible for the quality of our experiences. There is no greater waste of energy than to accumulate for the sake of accumulation. To be rich for the sake of being rich is an illness born of fear and propagated by an addiction to time-based perceptions.

26 **We feel less inclined to plan the future.** This point is largely covered by the previous explanation and by the acceptance that if we take care of what is happening right now, which is the only moment we can truly attend to, then all our future Nows will be taken care of. Planning is a bit like floating down a river and simultaneously deciding what course the river will take to reach the ocean. This is obviously a sign of arrogance and delusion. There is only one course that the river called life takes, and that is what is called God's Will. Of course the idea of not planning and of there being such a notion as God's Will is threatening to the ego. The ego desperately believes in free will. However, the ego believes that free will is being able to do "exactly what I want to do when I want to do it". The ego believes that free will is the ability to function completely separately from the whole. This is, of course, as deluded as thinking one can determine the course of a river by floating in it. In the human body, if a cell involves itself in this sort of deluded behavior, we call it cancer. In the world, if a human behaves this way we call it ambition. Once we set off on our journey into present moment awareness, we begin to understand how entrained we actually are by our childhood experiences. We begin to understand that while "living in time" what we think of as free will is an unconscious reaction to our life—an unconscious reaction energetically implanted within us during childhood through our initial emotional interactions with our parents and family. We begin to see that even our mannerisms are photocopies. How then can we call our life *free* when we have become duplicates of our parents? There is only One Being in all creation that is free, and that Being is what we call God. God is free. We can connect very quickly with what we call God through our Inner Presence. In other words, our connection to God is not determined by how we move about in the outer world but by how we enter the silence and stillness within ourselves. The more we go within and align ourselves with God, the freer we really become. Free will is only a valid concept in the present moment. There is no free will in a time-based paradigm

because all time-based activity is an emotional photocopy of what has gone before. There is no free will in reactive behavior. It is only by aligning ourselves with what God is for us that we restore our freedom. Freedom is essentially responsibility. When we surrender to the present moment, we are freed from time. When we consciously choose to be responsible for the quality of all our experiences, as God is, then we are free—free to respond to whatever is happening in any given moment. In such a state of Being, what need is there to plan ahead? Planning means that we believe that there is a possibility that a wrench may be put into the spinning wheel of our unfolding intentions. If we really believe that we are 100% responsible for the quality of our experiences, then who is there to ambush our progress?

27 **We spring-clean our house and let go of "stuff" that we have hoarded for years.** Just like excess body weight, our propensity to hoard or to clutter our life with excess "stuff" is an effect of unresolved emotional issues. It is a desire to hold onto the past and barricade ourselves from the future. Once we resolve our emotional baggage, we see our accumulated stuff for what it is: clutter. Giving or throwing it all away is liberating. It causes a lightness of Being. Often thin people with emotional issues carry their "weight" in the amount of stuff that clutters their outer life experience.

28 **We manifest less drama in our life experiences.** What is drama but an unconscious cry for attention? The moment we learn how to become our own parents, and thus to guide, teach, nurture, and heal our own experiences, is the moment when we are ready to let go of our tendency towards the manifestation of drama. It is also in this moment that we begin naturally parting company with those who wave their drama as flags of accomplishment. The moment we relinquish our desire for the drama is the moment we begin to awaken our thirst for our Dharma. Behaving reactively prevents us from doing anything "on purpose".

29 **Certain people automatically move out of our sphere of activity.** Aside from our decrease in attraction towards drama, one of the reasons for this is

that not everyone seeks to consciously process their past. Not everyone seeks to embrace present moment awareness. Not everyone seeks to live consciously. Those wishing to hold onto what happened yesterday and to make fearful preparations for all the terrible things that are to come tomorrow do not enjoy the company of those who choose to consciously awaken themselves from such dramatic illusions. People who choose to sleep on in a time-based consciousness of fear do so because they still need their rest. For this reason, they will gradually move out of our sphere of activity when we choose to accumulate present moment awareness. This is more comfortable for them because if they stay in the radiance of our increasing Presence, we begin to become very clear mirrors of their suppressed emotional issues. Present moment awareness does not entertain blame or regret; it does not use life's unfair wounds as topics of conversation. Therefore, those who are not ready to overcome victim and victor mentality get blown like dust from the body of anyone accelerating into the consciousness of responsibility.

30 **Our outlook naturally becomes optimistic.** And why should it not? When we are responsible for the quality of all our experiences, why not enjoy every moment along the pathways of life? Life is awesome! When we truly know that all unexpected or challenging experiences are only thrown upon our path for our highest good, then we remain positive and optimistic even in the most challenging circumstances. It is easy to be optimistic when life is easy, but it takes present moment awareness to be optimistic—no matter what. Present moment awareness does not embrace a *forced* positive attitude. A forced positive attitude is usually a form of denial. In the present, our optimistic approach to life is not annoying or contrived; it is automatic and infectious. Negativity is a form of drama. Negativity is a state of denial. Negative people believe they are victims or victors—that their experiences are happening to them and so must be overcome or controlled.

31 **We become interested in our spiritual well-being.** Through increased present moment awareness, we automatically start to touch an aspect of our

Being that remains unchanged, no matter what. Immortality as an experience therefore begins to dawn as a real "knowing" in our consciousness. We begin to remember something that has never changed. We gain increasing awareness of that which always is. Naturally, we seek to develop our relationship with this aspect of our Being because it becomes clearer as we accumulate present moment awareness that it is from our Immortal Self that all that is authentic flows. We become inclined, therefore, towards outer and inner practices that stimulate awareness of our spirituality. God ceases to be a personality, limited by our past needs and future wants. God becomes a faceless, timeless energy that is simultaneously nothingness as well as the harbor of all that life has to offer. It is natural that we become curious about this—whatever It is. However, unlike our ventures into spirituality when we lived in a time-based consciousness, our way of approaching what God is for us in the present moment is fueled with authenticity. It is usually devoid of pretentious outer rites, rituals, and ceremonies because we know that this God-experience is only accessible through the silence and stillness that is to be found within the peace of our body-temples. It is therefore *within* that we turn our attention, and we do so without outer pretence or performance.

32 **We cease seeking distractions.** When we are unconsciously nursing our negative emotional charge, we do so by finding endless ways to distract ourselves from it. Whether it is loud music, food, sport, the company of others, or work, we are constantly seeking to be busy and on the move. Our inability to be still is evidence that we are constantly seeking to cover something up. Stillness is the only way to activate Beingness. Nothing we *do* can assist us to *be*. Only in stillness and silence can our Beingness, our authenticity, be celebrated, acknowledged, experienced, and explored. When we keep ourselves busy, it is because we are unable to *be*, just to *be*, and thus unable to enjoy the treasure of our beautiful Being. By decreasing our negative emotional charge, we diminish being frantic. We begin to come to rest. When we live in a time-based consciousness, the hardest thing to do is nothing when there is nothing to do!

33 **We are more gentle and compassionate towards ourselves.** When we do not receive unconditional love as children, we assume that it is because we are not deserving of it. This leads to unconscious behaviors of self-punishment and self-belittlement. Not only this, but when our parents have marital or behavioral problems, we as their children, often assume that it is because of our presence. When we are children, we automatically blame ourselves for everything that goes wrong. This is because we know unconsciously that we are responsible for the quality of our experiences. However, in our innocence, we assume that we are also responsible for the quality of our parents' and siblings' experiences. This can lead to a life of trying too hard, of making unnecessary sacrifices, and of becoming "the helper". Becoming "the helper" is something that often occurs to children of parents who are afflicted with addictions. In this world, it is normal to grow up not knowing how to nurture ourselves and even to believe that such behavior is a sign of weakness or selfishness. All this changes when we move through The Presence Process. We then realize that only we can really nurture ourselves because unconditional love is not something we can "get"; it is something we must first learn to give to ourselves, and only then are we able to give to others authentically. Thus we become more gentle and compassionate with ourselves. We realize that our essence, our Presence, will only come forward in gentleness. We realize that whatever we have sought from others is what we must first learn to give ourselves, and only then do we develop the capacity to unconditionally give it to everyone who enters our experience. When we give ourselves gentleness and compassion, then the world mirrors this, and then our immediate experience is of a gentle and compassionate world.

34 **We experience less and less anxiety.** The word "anxiety" contains the two words that make up the phrase "any exit". Anxiety is a state in which we seek to escape the awareness of the present moment in favor of the illusions of elsewhere. One of the powerful attributes of The Presence Process is that it teaches us a Perceptual Tool called The Emotional Cleansing Process. Mastering this tool literally enables us to integrate any life experience no matter how challenging. When, through our

consistent application of this tool we truly realize that we can integrate any life experience—no matter how challenging—our level of anxiety automatically begins decreasing. It decreases because the uncertainties of life no longer hold fear for us. We know we can process any event, and can grow from our challenges by gaining insight and therefore wisdom from them. Our uncertainty then turns to acceptance and finally to embrace. Where is the anxiety in a life that we lovingly embrace?

35 **We are more compassionate and have more patience with others.** We become more compassionate and patient with others because we know that we are all in the same boat. Life is not easy, especially when we do not know the mechanics behind the manifestation of our unfolding experiences. This is how The Presence Process empowers us; it reveals to us the mechanics behind the manifestation of the quality of our experiences. It shows us how we all learn from the examples set for us during childhood and how we are then faced with a choice to make the best of that or to unlearn what does not serve us and replace it with teachings that do. It is arrogant to be judgmental about another's life experiences when we see this predicament reflected in everyone's path. Everyone in this world is taught and shaped by example and then does the best with what they are given—whether it appears that way on the surface or not. Everyone's life is a manifestation of how they believe they can attain unconditional love. The Presence Process assists us to naturally develop more compassion and patience for what others are faced with by empowering us to see the truth of this predicament in our own life experience.

36 **Our life becomes a journey and not an intended destination.** While "living in time", our desire to *finish* whatever we have been doing is unconsciously motivated by our seeking of approval, acknowledgement, and unconditional love. We unconsciously believe that through our accomplishments and through the things we get done that we will finally receive the unconditional love that we have sought. Of course, this is an error in our thinking. Once we realize that nothing we do can assist us to *be* and that nothing we do can "get" the unconditional love we

seek, then we automatically begin to relax and reassess the situation. While "living in time", our focus is always on the beginning and end of things and on everything being a means to an end. However, as we enter present moment awareness, we realize that nothing really begins or ends: it continues forever. Also, it becomes clearer to us that nothing ever stops: it changes into something else. Present moment awareness empowers us to tune into the eternal essence of our Being that exists beyond all that we might ever do. Consequently, we slow down and metaphorically begin to smell the roses. There is no rush because in actuality we are going nowhere (now here). We then automatically trade in quantity for quality. We enjoy the moment and take our attention off the outcome. Also, our understanding of the Law of Cause and Effect helps us to see that we need only be concerned with the causal point of anything, as the effects are automatic. "The journey" is a causal place to be; whereas, "the destination"' is always an effect. Accumulating present moment awareness, as we will continue to discover, is a journey. If God is infinite, then so is the journey towards God-realization. So what is the hurry? Smell the roses, enjoy the afternoon, take a deep breath, smile and be at peace. In this light we continue.

37 **We experience wonderful waves of spontaneus gratitude.** Gratitude is a good barometer of knowing just how present we are. The more we enter present moment awareness, the more grateful we feel for absolutely everything. Life seeps with abundance even if we hardly have a cent. It flows with joy even if things appear not to be going our way. It oozes with health even if we have aches and pains. This quality of gratitude is hard to describe to someone who has not yet experienced it. This is gratitude that is not founded on comparison. This is gratitude that requires no reason, no justification, and no explanation. The gratitude we feel as we enter present moment awareness is not just for stuff, for appearances, or for circumstances: it is for everything that life is and the endless honor of being part of it. As we embrace present moment awareness, we perceive what flows beneath the changing surface of the world. Consequently, we feel the invisible force of what God is for us — embracing us, holding us, and moving us mysteriously towards a blessed destiny. In this light, we are grateful for all of our past experiences, whether they were harsh or

glamorous. We are also grateful for all that is to come, even though it has not yet manifested because we know that whatever it may be flows towards us upon a river of grace. Our gratitude at times feels as if it is pouring out of the very pores of our skin and completely saturating our experience. This is an experience that cannot be forced; it is not something that we can demand or go out and get. It occurs spontaneously *because* we have chosen authenticity. It causes us to gasp in awe at life because we are in it and because we are it.

38 **What we require comes to us instead of our seeking it out.** Before we entered The Presence Process, we most likely behaved as all do who "live in time". If we wanted something, we went out and got it. We sweated blood and tears to make it happen. There is nothing wrong with this approach. Hard work is warranted as long as it is joyful work. However, after having activated our present moment awareness, we will discover that this sort of behavior starts diminishing in our life experience. We then become more like The Medicine Buddha who sits still, eyes closed, with palms opened upwards. All that The Medicine Buddha requires effortlessly appears in those beautiful hands. We all have the same ability. This ability starts to unfold automatically as we gain more and more present moment awareness. We discover that when we effortlessly think of something, it just as effortlessly appears in our experience. It is as if we become magnets. We notice that the more effortlessly we place our attention on what we require, the more effortlessly it manifests. This is because our Inner Presence is also in everything and everyone. It is the director behind all of life's movements. If we choose the blood, sweat, and tears path that is paved with fear, doubt, and lack of faith in the connectedness of all life, then our Inner Presence will stand back and let us walk this way through our experiences until it exhausts us. This is because our Inner Presence adheres strictly to the Law of Noninterference. But when we release our control and allow Presence to bring to us what we require through our faith and trust that God is paying personal attention to us, then so be it. This is one of the teachings of the Presence of The Medicine Buddha. The Medicine Buddha frequency waits patiently within us all. It too is activated through present moment awareness.

39 **We feel a deeper sense of connection with nature.** All life upon this planet, whether it is manifest as a rock, a tree, or a cloud, contains present moment awareness. It contains the same present moment awareness that we activate through The Presence Process. This is because there is only One Presence, and it resides within everything. Everything is Its manifestation, Its expression. The more we tune into It within ourselves, the more this inner relationship is reflected in our outer world experiences. We then naturally find ourselves starting to resonate with all life. As we enter present moment awareness, we will have moments when it appears as if the birds and butterflies are completely aware of us. This is because *they are*. It is only when we "live in time" that we believe that nature is unconscious and oblivious. However, this is not and never has been true. Nature only appears oblivious when we are. Each plant that we pass and each breeze that ruffles our hair is aware of our Presence. Initially, this is hard for us to accept or comprehend because we think nature is ignorant and unaware. We think only humans have intelligence beyond what we call instinct. We behave as if nature is inanimate. We think that the birds sing just to make a noise. Yet nature is as alive and as conscious and as aware as we choose to be. Just like all other humans, nature reflects us. The more present we become, the more connected with it we automatically feel. Only a person who is not present can harm nature. Only a person "living in time" can kill for sport. In "time", our heart-center is closed, and we cannot feel the impact of our Presence on the life around us. The more present moment awareness we accumulate, the more conscious we become of the effect we are having on our natural surroundings and of how intimately we are connected. As we accumulate present moment awareness, we begin to walk gently through this world; consequently, the natural world starts to walk gently alongside us. We are One with it.

40 **We become more aware of natural cycles, such as the occurance of the full moon.** The more emotionally present we become, the more aware we become of the energetic cycles that roll through our universe. In fact, it is quite accurate to say that our entire universe is an energetic cycle. When we "live in time", we do rituals and ceremonies because it is

Full Moon or Winter or Summer Solstice. However, as we enter present moment awareness, we operate very differently. We do not consciously attend to these ceremonies, yet we discover that we still acknowledge the movements of these cycles. For example, we may decide on the spur of the moment to have a nighttime picnic, and as we lay out our picnic blanket beneath the stars, we look up and notice the Full Moon rising. Or we may decide in the moment to spring-clean our house, and when we have finished, someone tells us that some planet has gone retrograde and that this is supposedly a good time to clean out the clutter in our life. These synchronistic incidents happen because when we anchor ourselves in the present moment, we automatically acknowledge the cosmic cycles of our universe without having to make a show of it. We do not have to do anything special or extra or out of the ordinary because these cycles become part of our normal life experience. We automatically acknowledge them as a normal part of our life experience because we are present in the moment they unfold. We *become* the cycles and no longer function as separate entities that have to perform activities to acknowledge them. We become them and therefore no longer have to "observe" them.

41 **We see through the window-dressing of the world.** One of the most powerful consequences of The Presence Process is that it suffocates our pretentiousness. We therefore do not have to wear special clothes to know how special we are. We do not have to wave a banner to let people know that we are here. We do not have to give ourselves Native American names so that we feel the currents of our indigenous self flowing within our ordinary life. We do not have to put a sign up on the door that says "Healer". Once we really enter present moment awareness, we do not even have to advertise what we do. We strive to *be* it, and Presence automatically brings those Souls to us who require our services. This approach does not only apply to the metaphysical professions, but to sales and marketing and advertising and filmmaking. It applies to everything. Again, this is the teaching of the Presence of The Medicine Buddha. We will also discover that we do not have to go out and find those whose services we require; they will appear in front of us in the moment when we are ready to interact

with them. This works just like God's Economy. We let people around us know what we are doing *by being it* as opposed to talking about it. There are many of us living like this already. We do not advertise our Presence because we know Presence is omnipresent. We do not sell ourselves. We do not seek out clients. We get on and perfect our art and let Presence bring to us those who require our attention. And then thou "art" in heaven.

42 **We no longer seek the extraordinary.** When we are strangers to the present moment, we automatically seek out the extraordinary. We do so because we cannot appreciate the inherent magnificence and beauty of the present moment that we already occupy. This is one of the reasons why we resort to special clothing, Native American names, superficial working titles, and all other means of inauthenticity. However, as we begin to accumulate present moment awareness, we begin to see how silly we are, and we begin to enjoy a good laugh at our own pretentious behavior. This laughter transports our experience back into authenticity. It is our laughter at ourselves that frees us from this nonsense. As we begin to truly enter the present moment, we discontinue our search for the extraordinary. We begin to realize that if we are truly present with each ordinary moment of our life experience, whether it is showering, eating, washing the dishes, or chatting with our neighbor, then our entire life becomes extraordinary. We discover that it is not in seeking out the extraordinary that makes for a truly extraordinary life. It is in our ability to take each seemingly ordinary moment and to embrace the extraordinary energy of life that flows through it. And so we can relax and enjoy each moment as it is, for it is truly extraordinary, just as God orchestrates it.

43 **Our inner voice/intuition grows and becomes a real companion.** This is a very big one. This is the final step we must take to free ourselves from thinking, from planning, and from our attempts to control this world. Our attempts to control the world are our attempt to control God. God will play along and let us entertain all manner of dramas, but in the end, we will have accomplished nothing. To relieve ourselves of this pointless plight requires that we reconnect with our Inner Voice because our

Inner Voice is the voice of what God is for us. Our Inner Voice is silent and still. It will not shout above the arrogant voice of the ego. It will speak clearly, and it will tell us everything we need to know if we learn how to listen to it. This voice comes from beyond time, so it knows everything that has ever happened and everything that is about to happen. When we listen to and trust this voice, we will no longer need to plan our day; we will simply walk into it and pay attention to each moment as it unfolds. We will no longer need to make shopping lists; we will instead walk through the shop with a cart and be receptive. This Inner Voice will replace our alarm clock and even the watch on our arm if we allow it to. It can also talk to us through anyone and anything. But we must be prepared to listen to hear it. It can cause a window to blow shut to tell us a storm is coming or a neighbor's dog to bark to tell us that we must awaken from our afternoon nap. It can talk to us through our boss as easily as through our silent intuition. However, we have to train ourselves to listen, not just to hear with our physical ears, but to listen with our heart. The challenge is that this voice does not always make sense to us because it speaks from beyond the position we are on in our timeline. Yet when we obey it, we will see that it always has our best interest at heart. It will warn us about impending accidents and earthquakes, just as readily as it will tell us that we have left a tap running or are low on milk. Tuning into and trusting this voice is the greatest of accomplishments because to accomplish this is to open a line directly from God's mouth to our inner ear. Then we do not need intermediaries; we do not need priests or fortune tellers or even weather forecasters. Then we mainline God. Then where is the fear? Where is the anxiety? It all disperses, and we walk directly and intimately into the vision God has for us. Then we live in awe at the miracle called life. Learning to live *is* learning to listen.

44 **We feel blessed with a deep sense of purpose.** By going through The Presence Process, we begin to understand that there is nothing that we can do that can make us more or less than what we already are. We are perfect and unchangeable. Maybe our experience is out of balance, but we now know how to rectify this situation. That we are perfect as we are is the realization that we are encouraged to reach out and grasp in

this very life experience. Our real purpose is not a job that we are supposed to be doing; it is to really be here, now, where we have been placed. Through the vehicle of The Presence Process we are being asked to accept that there is no greater purpose than to show up in our life and to be available and useful purely through being fully present and paying attention. By accomplishing this, we truly become God's eyes, ears, hands, and feet. We walk for God and talk for God, live for God and love for God. Our Presence *is* God's Presence. When we allow this to be so, then we live life deliberately, and everything that we do is therefore on purpose. We just are. We have no agendas, no plans, and no interpretations. Life becomes an "as-need-to-know-experience": we know what we need to know in the moment that we need to know it. This is our relationship with our Source. We take nothing, interfere with nothing, interrupt nothing, and want for nothing. Our life and its contents become a box of tools used to stimulate our individual and shared evolution through love and understanding, compassion and faith. We live to love and love to live.

45 **We automatically seek to make a contribution to our world.** As we enter present moment awareness, it becomes obvious that our highest frequency of activity is to serve, to serve the whole by taking care of the part that is within our experience. As we accumulate present moment awareness, this enthusiasm to serve erupts automatically from within us, and when we follow its beckoning, it leads to a joyous and deeply satisfying life experience. There is no more blessed place to stand than in the center of a life that is dedicated to unconditional service. This is the source of the eternal fountain of unconditional love. This is the top of the highest mountain that we can climb. To have an opportunity to wear the wings of joyful service is the greatest gift that we can bring to our own hearts. The footprints of loving service always emerge from and lead into the center of God's heart. First we must serve ourselves by restoring our present moment awareness. Then we must serve our family by seeing them as perfect, whole, necessary, and a blessing to our every step. Then we must serve our community by walking wide-awake through it without judgment or concern. Then we must serve our city by holding a vision for liberation from the fog

of time for all that occupy it. Then we must serve our planet by standing at the center of our experience and allowing what God is for us to be as present as possible in our every breath. Then, as deeply as we are able to look within ourselves, we must also look out across the universe and smile at the stars and the moon and the sun. For the greatest service of all that we can render on earth is to stand awake and say in silent certainty:

I AM are here, now, awake and alive.
I AM a human being and yet so much more.
I AM spirit fully present and conscious in matter.
Through my Presence, God is looking at you with love.
Awaken from the spell of time, and sing with us the song of life.

RADIATING PRESENT MOMENT AWARENESS RESPONSIBLY

As we awake,
Let us gently get out of bed,
Quietly tiptoe out of the darkened room
And into the morning light.
Let us play here.
Let us not shake others in their beds,
For they are sleeping because they still require rest.
When they awake and hear us playing,
They will surely come and join us.

LET US REMIND OURSELVES that Jesus did not change anyone's experience. Nor did Buddha, Hazur Maharaj Charan Singh, Krishna, Mohammed, Osho, Bodhidharma, Lao Tzu, Ramana Maharshi, J. Krishnamurti, or any other of the Masters and Spiritual Teachers who have graced this earth and who will always continue to do so. The act of deliberately changing someone else's experience is interference and any evolved Soul knows better.

All Masters and Spiritual Teachers awaken themselves by actively changing their own experience of this world. Wherever they travel, they then radiate their present moment awareness responsibly into every cell of the creation that they encounter. Those blessed enough to step into the radiation of their present moment awareness are automatically infected by it. Present moment awareness is highly contagious. Anyone exposed to the radiance of Presence automatically activates changes in their own experiences.

On the surface of life, it appears as if these awakened Masters and Spiritual Teachers are "doing something" to others. But this is not so. Whatever they do, they do only unto themselves. Their acts of spiritual alchemy occur within; then, we see the consequences reflected outside in the world that they walk through. This is how we can tell a real Master or Spiritual Teacher: they never interfere with the path of another's evolution. Never. This is because real Masters and Spiritual Teachers know better than to take power from another. Their Soul purpose is not to interfere but to be an example of human potentiality. Their example is their compassion. This attitude of noninterference is an important lesson for us to digest:

> *If we pick up anyone and carry them, when the moment comes for us to put them down, their feet will land in the exact same spot from which we picked them up.*

Nobody in this world needs "help" because the unfaltering Law of Cause and Effect renders us all equal. Every single being on this planet *right now* is having an experience exactly equal to the consequences of his or her past thoughts, words, and deeds. This is hard for us to comprehend, especially when tragedy strikes. It is hard for us to comprehend because we live in a mental paradigm called "time": a state of distraction and disassociation in which the connection between cause and effect cannot easily be perceived. However, our lack of awareness of the universal Law of Cause and Effect does not render it inactive.

This is why Masters and Spiritual Teachers are always here and continue to walk consciously and compassionately among us. They know too well that the mental fog of "living in time" has caused us to forget that the mechanism that makes us equal when we are present also imprisons us when we are distracted. They therefore walk gently through this world in such a way as to rekindle the memory of our inherent responsibility. They know that reminding us of our responsibility is the only authentic way to awaken us to our freedom. Through their compassionate and patient example, they gently offer us our freedom without taking it from us. They do this by becoming responsible for their own experiences, by activating their own present moment awareness; through this simple procedure, they bring light to our life experiences without interference. In other words, they never go *into fear* (interfere) about the circumstances of another because they know that everyone, no matter how it appears, has placed themselves in the center of their circumstances. They also know that everyone has the ability to change the quality of their experience.

In this light, The Presence Process also invites us to rise up from our dreamtime and to walk through our experience of this world as examples of responsibility. It teaches us that we must primarily begin walking into the experience of present moment awareness for ourselves. We cannot do it for another, and no other can do it for us. The steps that we must take towards our liberation from a time-based consciousness into present moment awareness must be taken for and by ourselves in order for our journey to be authentic. Once we pick up the pace, our devotion to this quest will begin to radiate awareness into every cell of every life form that we bless with our Presence. It is at this point in our journey that we must consciously embrace the task of radiating our present moment awareness responsibly.

To wake others up just because we can see that they are asleep is foolishness. It is arrogance. It is interference. It is ignorance. Sleep is not a mistake; it has purpose. A seed sleeps until it sprouts. It sprouts not only because it is ready for life but because all life around it is also ready to intimately support its awakening. To force a seed to sprout is to see it in separation and to therefore dismiss and disregard the intimate participation of all life in the miracle of our awakening.

To discuss the task of radiating our present moment awareness responsibly, I am going to step back from describing our collective journey into present moment awareness and once again reenter my individual experience. Sharing my own experience of awakening to the resonance of noninterference is the most authentic way I know to pass this teaching on to you. This teaching is vital, for the more present we become, the more responsible we must intend to be. Knowledge calls forth integrity.

Our increasing level of presence awareness enables us to begin clearly seeing the plight of others as they sleepwalk their way through this world. If you have ever awoken a sleepwalker, you will know what a state of shock and disorientation they experience. The best course of action to take when encountering sleepwalkers is not to awaken them, but to gently guide them to the safety of their beds where they may rest in comfort and awaken naturally. To shake them awake is a very dangerous mistake. I had to learn this lesson. This is what I wish to share with you now so that your experiences may be gentler and infused with more responsibility than mine initially were.

As I have already explained to you in the introduction to this book, The Presence Process was uncovered by my intent that such a procedure should exist and that I should discover it by walking it myself. I did not want "enlightenment in a flash"! I still do not. In fact, I suspect that I am the only one in my world who is unenlightened. I have a strong feeling that once I consciously and completely reenter the eternal present moment, I will discover everyone already there waiting for me. The banner that they will be waving will say, "What took you so long?" It is at that point of my journey that I anticipate dropping to my knees and laughing hysterically at my own folly. This particular bout of laughter is the medicine that I am really after. However, because I love the concept of service (serve us) I have intended that my entry into everlasting 100% present moment awareness dawns on me gradually and methodically so that I can clearly map the terrain. I have chosen this approach so that my footprints may serve as an example for others interested in such a journey. This is my small contribution to the Dharma of humanity. I know there is a paradox interwoven here, but that is what life is: a paradox that is immune to the understanding of the mind but very clear to the intentions of the heart.

When I initially began to walk into my own experience of gathering present moment awareness, I did so unconsciously as a desperate means to rebalance my own life experience. I began this journey by entering the world of healing, not because I initially sought to be a healer, but because I was in such great pain. Yet, as I became exposed to the different modalities of the healing arts, I also simultaneously found myself carried away by the possibilities of being able to affect not only my condition, but also the conditions of others.

There is enormous ego nutrition in approaching healing as a so-called "profession". It sneaks up on one without any warning. It happened to me. Before I had restored any semblance of balance into the quality of my own life experience, I was already attempting to heal my world. I thought of myself as a healer, though I camouflaged my inflated ego by humbly admitting to be a self-healer. Secretly, I loved the idea of wielding some invisible, mystical, and magical power that would bring comfort to the suffering, rest to the weary, and hope to the desperate. Drunk from the notions of saving my world from its desperate plight, I soon forgot about attempting to heal my own experience and became almost power-hungry in search of perfecting my ability to heal the ailments I saw reflected at me everywhere. Of course my reflections in the world played along; the more I wanted to heal them, the more unbalanced they appeared to be.

Eventually this egotistical pathway, that by all accounts appeared to be "paved with good intentions", led to a dead end. After ambitiously opening my own healing practice, I soon became increasingly troubled, and the people I attempted to "heal" seemed to remain as stuck as I was. Eventually my own afflicted life experience overwhelmed and threatened to drown me, so I ran as fast as I could from anyone who appeared to want my help. I could not stand to hear another's complaint, moan, or groan because it was becoming painfully obvious that I could not do anything real about it.

For a period of about two years, I suffered from deep physical distraction, mental confusion, and emotional turmoil. I felt spiritually shipwrecked and stranded on an island of disappointment. This condition continued and became so acute that I became fearful of literally losing my body and mind. I had long since lost touch with my own heart. I had long since betrayed my spiritual integrity. I could not understand how the path of good intentions that I had stepped onto had led me into such desolate circumstances. It was only when I reached the point of absolute hopelessness and desperation that I was able to hear and listen to the wise words of another:

"When are you going to take your own advice?
When are you going to do for yourself what you have been attempting
to do for others?
When are you going to heal yourself, healer?"

This moment of realization and my willingness to end my foolish and arrogant rampage to heal the world was the moment I began to climb out from the pit of the wounded healer. I looked into the mirror and saw clearly that my life hung by a thread and that one more moment's arrogance or pride could manifest an experience of severing that thread completely. I realized that I could heal no one else, and I had to admit that none in my world needed a healing of their experience more than me.

The world had been my trusted and obedient mirror as always. As long as I had convinced myself that it needed *my* help, it reflected this deluded condition back to me. It beckoned for my help in every direction that I looked. It overwhelmed me with its pitiful cries. There was no end to its misery. But the moment I realized that it was I who needed assistance, and the moment I shelved my arrogance and pride long enough to ask for help, in that very moment real help came forward in all shapes and forms to lift me from my pit of delusion. Only then did my world bring forward the wise teachers who began to show me how to nurture, guide, heal, and teach myself. As each of these teachers imparted their lessons, they also departed as quickly as they had appeared so as not to allow me to become reliant on them. They revealed the task, but left me to carry it out. They did not carry me. They did not interfere. They lovingly placed their lessons before me and then quickly stepped away so that any choices made would be mine alone. They approached without pity or sympathy and departed without concern. They offered empowerment but asked for nothing in return.

This therefore became the foundation to my approach to and construction of The Presence Process. From the moment I began making myself available to facilitate this journey, I declared myself to be no more than a willing student of present moment awareness. I am no teacher; I am a willing but quite mediocre student. I know this now. It is the Presence that we all share that is responsible for any achievement that has graced my life experience.

In this light, I have done my best to keep the door of my heart and mind open so that others may continue to be my teachers. In essence, everyone who has come to me to be personally facilitated through this Process has been my teacher. Each one of these individuals came and placed their teachings at my feet. It was their commitment to activating their own experience of present moment awareness that solidified the integrity of this remarkable procedure. On the surface, it appeared that I was facilitating them and that I was constructing this Process. Yet this has never been true. I was willing to discover how to efficiently activate present moment awareness. They all came, sent by the Presence we all share, to show me how.

In that light, every single individual who entered this Process by allowing me to sit and act as a facilitator enabled this book to be written. They are the real heroes of this endeavor. In spirit, this book is a gift placed into your hands by each of them. I have not for a moment assumed that I was "healing" them of anything. At all times I have done my best to keep it clear in my heart and mind that I was healing my own experience and learning as much as I could about present moment awareness by watching and listening to anyone who arrived to show me how to further improve this procedure. In this respect, life has been my teacher and I its student.

This is therefore how the Process unfolded; from watching how others charted their course towards present moment awareness and from my own footprints through the lessons they placed before me. It came from asking big questions and then waiting patiently for the answers. Everything about The Presence Process is gathered from real present moment experiences. That is why this journey has such a powerful impact on everyone who enters it. In my heart, I know that all who consciously choose to read this book or to complete this procedure, take a profound leap into their emotional abyss and consequently activate the experience of "raising themselves from the dead". This is the pathway walked by the bravest of the brave. The Presence Process is indeed an act of faith created by an act of faith.

It is important to remember that The Presence Process as an experiential journey may not be appropriate for everybody right now. Those who are ready for it will need no convincing or persuasion *because* they will be

THE PRESENCE PROCESS

ready. Those who are not ready will outwardly show their lack of interest. This is not an experience others must be sold on just because it works for us. This is a journey that is only entered experientially by those who are ready and only completed by those really seeking authenticity. Some of us will get exactly what we need from it by reading it. No matter which level of entry we choose, we will all plant seeds in our garden of present moment awareness. And each and every seed is acceptable, welcome, and to be celebrated. We may only plant one single tiny seed, but it may turn out to be the seed of a Mustard Tree or a Baobab.

Remember that by completing this journey, by reading your way through or participating experientially in the Process, you automatically begin to transform your entire experience of the world. Your world only changes because you change your experience of it. As your life unfolds from this point, you will begin to realize that The Presence Process has profound consequences that have to be experienced to be comprehended. Through your ongoing experiences, you will begin to integrate how you literally radiate present moment awareness into the experiences of everyone that you encounter. This consequence will continue and grow for the rest of your life upon this planet and beyond. You will be able to share the bounty of what you have given to yourself through this experience with all in your world. Some will eat what you have grown with gratitude, and some will ask you how they too can plant their garden. Know the difference between the two groups, and you will not make the mistake of interfering.

I have not gone into any case studies in this book. However, as I bring closure to this part of our journey together, there is one case study that I would like to share. By looking deeply into it you will begin to comprehend the infinite impact of having activated your own present moment awareness. When the penny really drops, you will be in awe at who and what you are and at what is possible when you "do unto yourself as you would have others do".

The Story of Clive and Nadine

One day a man called Clive phoned me and asked if I facilitated children. He said that he had a 12-year-old daughter called Nadine who had recently been confined to a psychiatric institution. He said that she had been diagnosed as having a bipolar mental disorder and was being administered Lithium. He explained that he was recently divorced and that his daughter had consequently been living with his ex-wife. Apparently, after their divorce proceedings, Nadine, unbeknownst to him, had taken to very strange and unpredictable behavior. This behavior included violent outbursts and apparent acts of mental derangement. It had escalated so rapidly that his wife had agreed through the advice of a psychiatrist to have Nadine medicated and institutionalized. Clive told me angrily that when he had heard about this he had immediately rushed to the institution and removed his daughter despite the protest of the staff. Now he had a severely drugged and unpredictable 12-year-old in his house and wanted to know if I would work with her. My reply took him completely off guard:

> "No. But if *you* are willing to come and do this work with me, I promise you that she will fully recover from her condition."

I briefly explained to him that when we have children, unless we have already resolved our own childhood traumas, all our unconscious and unintegrated emotional issues are subsequently imprinted upon them. I told him that until our children are able to integrate what we unconsciously offload upon them, they cannot begin to live their own life experiences. I told him that all troubled children are reflections of their troubled parents. I asked him what his ex-wife's response was to their daughter's condition. He said that she was concerned, obviously, but that she was satisfied that the psychiatric institution would "deal with it", even if it meant her daughter lived an institutional life laced with lithium. In other words, she could not cope, and she did not want to. He said that although *she* was apparently unable and unwilling to take on Nadine that he had to because he could not cope with the idea of his daughter being in this predicament for another moment. He said he felt traumatized by her condition.

I told him that from our brief conversation, and because of his deep concern for his daughter, and because *he* had approached me with this predicament, that it was clearly evident to me that his daughter's predicament was in actuality to a larger extent reflecting his unresolved childhood issues. I explained to him that that was why he was "the deeply concerned one". I said: "There is nothing wrong with your daughter, Clive. She is just reflecting your unintegrated childhood stuff. If you deal with your suppressed emotional baggage, she will immediately regain balance in her life."

Understandably, he was startled. He said that he had never heard of such an approach. I then asked him what had happened to him when *he* was 12 years old. There was a silence on the phone; then, his voice came back weakly. "My father left us," he replied quietly. "How did you know something happened to me when I was 12?" I briefly explained the Seven-Year Cycle to him and then asked him if he could see his past circumstances repeating right now like clockwork in his daughter's life experience. He said that until that moment he had been completely unaware that his daughter's condition had anything at all to do with his own troubled youth.

To this day, I do not think that Clive completely digested what I had to say about "emotional imprinting" and the nature of our Seven-Year Cycle until he had completed the Process himself. I believe that he initially agreed to my approach of first healing his own experience before meddling with his daughter because he was desperate and because, like him, I did not approve of Nadine's medicated predicament. I think it was also profoundly insightful for him to make the connection I assisted him to make, namely the connection between his daughter's predicament and his own unresolved emotional traumas. He agreed to begin The Presence Process immediately. He also agreed to calculate how to gradually begin weaning Nadine off her lithium in such a way that she would be completely off the medication in the time it took him to complete his journey through the Process.

I will not tell you that what Clive went through with Nadine over the course of the following ten Sessions was easy. But it was real for both of them. Because of his commitment to completing The Presence Process, the intimacy of a father and daughter relationship was resuscitated, and the joy of it gradually seeped back into their home. For the first three Sessions, Clive continued to attend to the Process fueled purely by faith and the desperation of a concerned father. I personally had no doubt about the inevitable outcome of his quest because I have witnessed over and over again what The Presence Process accomplishes. He appeared to have no other alternatives but to persist, and I am sure that for the first few sessions he clung to my absolute certainty about the outcome. Then, as he touched and soothed his own emotional body, miraculous shifts began to manifest. He would go home from his sessions to discover sudden inexplicable changes in Nadine's behavior. He would arrive at his sessions shaking his head in disbelief. "She is not shouting at me anymore" became "She sat in the kitchen and spoke to me last night" became "She started doing the dishes with me last night without my even asking her to" became "She put her arms around me in the car today and told me she loved me."

When Clive's ten Sessions concluded, Nadine was back in school, off her medication completely, and doing whatever teenage girls do. His ex-wife was startled, especially when Clive dropped Nadine off to spend some time with her. Nadine's approach to her schoolwork also transformed to such an extent that her teacher phoned Clive with glowing reports. As Clive left after completing his final Session he asked, "Why does the world not know about this?" Of course I smiled because I know that there is a time and place for everything. He said he wanted to write a book about what had happened. I knew that was his way of saying how grateful he was for the fruits and flowers of present moment awareness. I sincerely hope he writes Nadine's story for all the Clives and Nadines of this world. If not, his voice has been heard through the sharing of this case study.

Clive and Nadine's story is just one of many. I have chosen to share their story with you because I want you to know in your heart that The Presence Process is not about going out and healing this world or anyone in it; it is about having the guts to heal our own experiences of this world. This procedure must never be used for interference. It must never be suggested to someone that they do it so that they will become the type of person you think they should be. Remember always that the road paved with good intentions often leads to a hellish outcome, especially if our conscious or unconscious intention is to change others so that they fit into our picture of life. If we do not like what we see in others, then we must change our own perceptions, not the outer circumstance that we look upon. The Presence Process is intended as a journey that we only take for and into ourselves, by ourselves. Yet, as we see through Clive and

Nadine's story, the miracle of it all is that when we sincerely activate our present moment awareness, *all* benefit.

Present moment awareness radiates like the smell of ripe peaches.

It was only after I had overcome my misplaced desire to heal the world that I truly started my journey towards wholeness. I began by looking at myself and working with the obvious issues that were causing discomfort within my life experience. Then I looked to my family as I would into a mirror and used them as reflections to see more of what I could heal within my own experience. Our immediate family members will always be the clearest of mirrors and the most honest reflections of our unresolved issues. Anything and everything that we find "wrong" with our immediate family members to the point that it emotionally upsets us is *our* stuff. This is hard medicine to swallow, but there is unfortunately no exception to this rule. Our family is always mirroring us; this is what makes them family. If we make the mistake of attempting to clean the mirror to deal with the unpleasant reflections, we will add to the debris of unhappy families that already scatter this planet. Yet, if we look upon our immediate family as those who love us enough to play the roles of our most honest reflections, then we can literally accomplish miracles.

Once upon a time I ran from my family. I chose any company but theirs. Today, because of the blessings and insights that are the inherent gifts of present moment awareness, I look at my own immediate family and see them to be as they really are. They are perfect. Everything that I would have changed about them in the past has become everything that I would miss about them if they were not in my life right now. Today I am blessed with a joyful family, not because I changed any of them, but because I adjusted my own experience of them through what they reflected back to me. They have always been perfect. It was my perceptions that were clouded.

Once we attain peace within our family, we then automatically begin radiating present moment awareness into our community, then our city, then our country, and finally over our continent and across our planet. I have embraced this as my journey. This book is not written to change my planet or the people that I share it with, for we are all created perfect.

However, I have sent it out as an invitation to anyone who is having an experience that they are finding uncomfortable. This book can assist anyone to change the quality of their experience by teaching them how to take responsibility for their predicament. To date, I have not been able to change anyone. I thank God for making it so, for I do not seek to interfere with His beautiful creation. I now know that if something is amiss in my experience of this world, it is because I am seeing it amiss. Therefore, this is how I know if I am present or not:

If I look at my world and see things from the past that should have been different, or if I start making plans to attempt and change the way things are right now, then I know that I am living in the illusionary and unforgiving place that we call "time".

Time is a place where nothing is right—Now.

Yet if I look at my world and see its beauty, its perfect imperfection, its fullness of life, and if I feel a deep gratitude for being in it, for every moment and particle of it, then I know I am right here, right now.

It has taken me a long "time" to embrace "the everything" that life is. I am now deeply in love with it all, for it is all an expression of what God is to me. There is not one freckle on the face of life that I seek to change. In sickness and health, in richness and poverty, in youth and old age, in sleepiness and in the waking, I love and cherish every moment of it. Life *is* my God and present moment awareness the altar upon which I lay my prayers of gratitude. Now, I want for nothing. Now, there is nothing that I do not want. Now, I have what I want and want what I have. How could it be any other way? In my own heart, I now feel the warmth and bubbling smile of my endless and eternal Presence. What greater gift and blessing could I have placed before my own feet? As long as this journey continues is as long as I will gladly take the ride.

I know that there are doors opened through the activation of present moment awareness that go beyond the borders of what can be written in a book. These are places and states of Being that can only be communicated through a personal experience of present moment awareness.

This is the abyss that I fling myself into as recklessly as I know how.

These are the adventures I invite you to navigate into.

These are the big questions I encourage you to ask.

My friend, listen:

Contrary to what the world may say, we are not meant to bring peace to this planet. Such a notion is delusional. It is a distraction. This planet is neutral. As such it is the perfect "setup" for any Soul ready to evolve through the lesson of responsibility. We are here because we have been "set up". We are here because we have asked to be. This earth school is the grandest of all halls of mirrors. Notice that earth and heart are the same word; the letters are rearranged. We are here, now, to discover that we can only find peace here and now when we authentically offer this experience to our own hearts. When we offer peace to ourselves, the mirror that is this world begins to laugh at the play of it all. Then peace comes cascading in from every direction.

PART V

COMPLETION

THROUGHOUT THE PRESENCE PROCESS, we have planted more seeds than it is possible to count. This journey represents the springtime of our awakening into present moment awareness. By completing this Process, we have ensured that the garden of our life experience will become full and bountiful—so much so that we will be able to invite others in to share our cool shade and to enjoy the beauty and bounty of our fruits and flowers. This is, of course, as long as we consciously take care of the seeds of awareness that we have planted.

"Completion" according to The Presence Process does not mean "finishing". Completion of this particular journey means that we have entered a state of awareness in which we are ready and willing to accept full responsibility for the quality (the emotional content) of our life experience. It means that we have elevated ourselves to living at the causal point of consciousness. Living at the causal point of consciousness is akin to continually sowing seeds in fertile ground, seeds that will automatically sprout and grow.

In addition to entering causal consciousness, "completion" according to The Presence Process also means that we are now saturated with the awareness of responsibility. Therefore, as the seeds that we plant with our conscious thoughts, words, and deeds break through the soil and come to light, we are willing and eager to water and to take care of them. We are intent on living each moment of our life consciously because we know that there is no other way to be.

We must endeavor to embrace each moment of our life experience in a manner that waters and nurtures our present moment awareness. We now know how to accomplish this: by choosing to be responsible instead of reactionary, by being a vehicle and not a victim or a victor. This final moment of *The Presence Process* takes a brief look at the road ahead. It offers us some valuable insight into the resonance of living as "a cause" and the responsibility of embracing such a profound intention.

<hr />

FREEDOM IS OUR RESPONSIBILITY

WE HAVE NOW SUCCESSFULLY completed our journey through The Presence Process, and there are just a few more insights to be shared before we close the final pages of this book. Before we go any further, we must acknowledge ourselves for reaching completion of this beautiful and profound journey. Only we can appreciate what we went through. Completion of an experience like this, whether we read it or entered experientially into it, is no small accomplishment. It is a gem that no one can take from our treasure chest of acquired insight into the nature of present moment awareness. We must be sure, therefore, to take a moment to *appreciate* what we have given to ourselves. We have accomplished something real for ourselves. We have activated real movement in the quality of all our life experiences. We may have gone through our own personal hell to get to this point, and so it is very important to stop, to gently connect our breathing, to smile inwardly, and to enjoy this moment.

Fortunately, this is not the end of anything: this moment marks a powerful continuation point of our profound journey into an ongoing experience of present moment awareness.

Essentially what we have accomplished by completing The Presence Process is turning the ship of our life around and pointing it in a direction that now serves us. We are now heading out of, as opposed to heading further into, time. We will be reaping the fruits and flowers of this journey forever because it is a journey that inevitably delivers our awareness into eternity. Our experience of the world will never be the same again. We are now gently awakening from a long unconscious dream by consciously grasping the gifts of an authentic life.

This is where living as a responsible human being really becomes important.

Just because we are now moving in the right direction does not mean we can take our hands off the steering wheel. Even though living responsibly empowers our life experience to begin flowing seemingly automatically and more effortlessly, the consciousness of responsibility does not come equipped with an automatic pilot button. There is nothing unconscious about responsibility. On the contrary, now more than ever, we must embrace a conscious hands-on approach to steering the quality of our life experience in the direction we choose to move. From this point onwards, it is beneficial to keep in mind the following metaphor:

A pilot flying a plane never stays on course. They are always correcting their course because the plane, buffeted by the winds of atmospheric turbulence, is constantly being pushed off the intended flight path. Consequently, the pilot is constantly adjusting the course of the plane to compensate. Compensation must be attended to consistently to ensure that the flight path will lead to the intended destination.

Remember that by completing this book, we have initiated real movement in all aspects of our life. We are now like a train that was once stationary but that is now moving along the rails at higher and higher speed. If we now choose not to take responsibility for the quality of each moment of our experience, we will inevitably crash. If we suddenly stop the locomotive of our intention to remain present and intensify our relationship with present moment awareness, we will feel the long line of carriages that represent all the aspects of our life experience piling onto and derailing us from our conscious journey into authenticity. This is not meant to appear threatening. This is the predicament that unfolds automatically because with increased awareness comes increased responsibility.

Crashing is the consequence of allowing ourselves to become unconscious again. Crashing is allowing ourselves to return to a deathly dance with our imaginary reflections of an unreal past. Crashing is allowing ourselves to continue unconsciously projecting our fear, anger, and grief upon the neutral screen of the outer world. Crashing is allowing ourselves to become physically distracted, mentally confused, and emotionally unbalanced. Crashing is choosing to become irresponsible about the quality of our thoughts, words, and deeds. If we choose to crash by not being responsible for maintaining and increasing our present moment awareness, this time we will not be able to plead ignorance about the mechanics of our experiences. This time, if we become unconscious, we will have made a conscious choice to become so. Crashing is not necessary. However, we may manifest the experience every now and then just to remind ourselves that being responsible is preferable.

It is our responsibility to remain clear about our intentions and to make adjustments when we lose focus. It is inevitable that we will have experiences in which our awareness appears to plummet, causing us to get confused and to seemingly unravel the fabric of our intentions. Why? Because the atmospheric turbulence of our life and of our experiences amidst the energetic cycles of the physical, mental, and emotional universe will constantly bump us off course. We must therefore remember how to respond.

Our intention is our flight path. How then, when we feel ourselves being tossed into unconsciousness by "'time" do we consciously respond? How do we compensate and make the required adjustments?

We stop whatever we are doing and connect our breathing until our present moment awareness is restored. It is that simple. It is that obvious. It is that easy.

Consciously connecting our breathing will always restore our present moment awareness and remind us of our intentions when the turbulence of life causes confusion. Consciously connecting our breathing will always rescue us from the wreckage of any crashes we may experience. By committing to making our 15-minute Breathing Exercise as much part of our daily routine as brushing our teeth, we will ensure ourselves against Presence decay. Our breathing routine *is* our responsibility because it will ensure that we have consciously established a route in to ourselves, where all our navigational adjustments are made. Our breathing routine will be our safety belt in times of excessive turbulence, our jaws of life in times of calamity, and our compass through all confusion.

We are and always will be the center of our own experience. Our experience is happening *because* we are in it. Therefore, it is our responsibility to constantly recommit to being as present as possible. It is our responsibility to keep the peace within ourselves. It is our responsibility to give ourselves what we seek to receive. It is our responsibility to be open to receive what we enjoy giving. It is our responsibility to steer the ship of our life experience gratefully into the heart of our authentic self. It is our responsibility to remember our innocence and to nurture our spontaneous joy and creativity. It is our responsibility to give ourselves unconditional love. And most of all, it is our responsibility to remember to stop every now and then to appreciate the eternal precious moment called THE NOW that we have been given in which to take another consciously connected breath. It is our responsibility to live.

When we review The Presence Process, starting from the beginning of the book, we will be astounded at how many Perceptual Tools we have been given to supplement our journey. We will realize that we are very well-equipped to consciously navigate this awesome journey we call life. By rereading this entire book, we will also discover that we have a greater understanding of all the information it contains. This in itself will be a barometer of how much and how quickly we have grown. It will inspire us to continue consciously awakening to the unlimited and breathtaking potential of our shared Inner Presence.

After a period of integration, we may, like many others have, choose to repeat this experience or reread this book to access deeper levels of present moment awareness. This Process can be repeated as often as we choose. It will always meet us where we are and lead us into greater depths of present moment awareness.

ROSES HAVE THORNS

ONE OF THE MOST PROFOUND and powerful teachings laid before us through The Presence Process is that life is a rose and that a rose has thorns. God deliberately created roses to be the symbol and scent of the Saints and of love itself. God also deliberately adorned these beautiful flowers with sharp thorns. This is to remind us about balance. This is to stimulate integration. This is to awaken us to gentleness and respect.

We have all felt pain. We have already each experienced so much physical, mental, and emotional discomfort in this life that our tendency is to consciously and unconsciously seek a state in which we are eternally joyful. Such a state of Being is possible here, but it does not come from choosing a path that has a "destination" or a path that practices exclusivity. If God is infinite, then the journey into God-realization must be an eternal one. If God created everything, then *everything* must be embraced to integrate what God is.

Therefore, the way to achieve authentic joy in this world is not through pushing certain experiences away from us and only desiring to pull certain circumstances towards us. Joy is not about reaching a point of endless happiness. This is not what life is about at all. Any preoccupation with wanting to feel good all the time, or to have our circumstances be easy all the time, or wanting to achieve complete and instant resolution in every aspect of our life experience, is delusional. Life is both sides and ongoing. Life is always and all ways.

The path into an authentically joyful life experience is only possible when we embrace every single experience that life has to offer. Joy stems from embracing the beauty, the fragrance, *and* the thorns of life. This may not make complete sense to us right now, because we may still be attempting to flee one state of Being in favor of another, but it will make sense to us in due course. By continuing to practice what we have learned in The Presence Process, without focusing on an endpoint or an outcome to our journey, we will inevitably enter a joyful frequency. Joy is the inevitable effect of all that The Presence Process causes. Within the frequency of patience, all our seeds will sprout, and all our blossoms will bear fruit.

It is important, especially when the going gets tough, to remind ourselves that everything in this life is an expression of God, no matter how we may interpret it in any given moment. To *embrace* instead of to *resist* is the key to experiencing integration. We cannot enter our inherent holiness, our wholeness, by excluding any expression that we see upon the material, mental, emotional, and vibrational face of God. This is what "growing up" really entails. There is a way to know when we are at peace with the path of growing up and embracing authenticity: we will metaphorically be able to

320

any walls that are created by fear, anger, and grief. It heals all the wounds inflicted by careless thoughts, words, and deeds. It instantly dissolves misunderstandings. Our calming present moment awareness is the balm that soothes all the experiences that have been infected by the perceptual virus we call "time". Our present moment awareness forgives anyone of anything and everyone of everything. It gives comfort to the lonely and rest to the weary. It is a home for the lost.

Our choice to show up and be present in all our life experiences empowers others to show up and be present in theirs. In turn, they are able to share their present moment awareness with others. Our present moment awareness therefore ignites a chain reaction that grows infinitely brighter. Our present moment awareness is an eternal flame of consciousness that once shared radiates infinitely. There is no power in all creation that can extinguish it when we consciously choose to awaken and share it.

Given unconditionally, our beautiful present moment awareness allows whatever God is for any of us to be present physically, mentally, and emotionally in our experience of this world. It enables unconditional love to be expressed despite all conditions. By sharing our present moment awareness, we *know* that God is Love. Then, and only then

ARE WE BEING RESPONSIBLE
WITH THE GIFT
OF LIFE.

ABOUT THE AUTHOR

Kevin Rudham

Until 1989, South African-born MICHAEL BROWN was living what he called a blissfully unconscious life as a music journalist. He then developed an acutely painful neurological condition for which conventional medicine had neither cure nor relief. This caused him to set out on what became a 9-year odyssey of self-healing. His exploration took him into numerous alternative healing modalities—then beyond. The outcome is an evolutionary new healing procedure called The Presence Process. Michael currently lives in South Africa where he has beensharing The Presence Process through personal facilitation.

n)

NAMASTE PUBLISHING

Our Publishing Mission:
To make available publications that acknowledge, celebrate, and encourage others to express their true essence and thereby come to remember Who They Really Are.

Namaste Publishing
P.O. Box 62084
Vancouver, British Columbia v6j 4a3
Canada
www.namastepublishing.com
Email: namaste@telus.net
Tel: 604-224-3179
Fax: 604-224-3354

To place an order, see www.namastepublishing.com
or E-mail: namasteproductions@shaw.ca

To schedule Michael Brown for a teaching or speaking event,
E-mail: namasteteachings@telus.net

B
Beaufort Books

Beaufort Books is dedicated to publishing the highest quality fiction and non-fiction books and making them available to the general public.

For more information about Beaufort or our books, contact:

Beaufort Books
27 West 20th Street
Suite 1102
New York, NY 10011

Phone: 212-727-0190
Fax: 212-727-0195

Email: service@beaufortbooks.com
www.beaufortbooks.com